Dylan Heath with
gratitude —

8/05/s

W9-CPK-351

GROWING MORE MATURE

Insights from the Lives of Highly Achieving Men and Women

Douglas H. Heath, Ph.D.

with the assistance of

Harriet E. Heath, Ph.D.

Conrow Publishing House

Growing More Mature
Insights from the Lives of Highly Achieving Men and Women
By Douglas H. Heath with the assistance of Harriet E. Heath

Copyright 2005 by Douglas H. Heath

Copyright under International, Pan American, and Universal Copyright Conventions. All rights reserved. No part of this book may be reproduced in any form—except for brief quotations (not to exceed 1,000 words) in a review or professional work—without permission in writing from the publisher.

Published by Conrow Publishing House,
223 Buck Lane, Haverford, PA 19041-1106

Printed in the United States of America
by Thomson-Shore, Inc., Dexter, Michigan

Book Design and Cover: Mary Helgesen Gabel

Library of Congress Catalog Card Number: 2005051000

ISBN 0-9769673-0-8

To my extended family
with affection and gratitude

CONTENTS

APPENDIX

Preface

On October 2, 2003 CNN's Larry King interviewed Stedman Graham, the life partner for seventeen years of Oprah Winfrey, about his new book. Its mantra was "growing," actualizing our potential talents. His prescription? Begin by making a list of our passions. Then plan how to organize our lives to fulfill them. My mind wandered to two questions: What does "growing" mean? Growth is an ambiguous term. There are many kinds of growth, even bad kinds like cancers, or psychic ones that get in the way of other growths and so unbalance, or worse, distort healthy growth. We can even grow "backwards," so to speak, when we deliberately retreat or regress to seemingly earlier levels of maturity. Or playfully let our restraints go to recover our more childish, less conscious, and even creative selves.

My second question was: What might Graham mean by what I assumed to be healthy growth—the first question that Erik Erikson asked of how adults developed? (Hoare 2002) I have studied in great detail men and women who had grown, matured, become more psychologically healthy, optimally functioning, and fulfilled during their adult years. I also have studied men and women whose growth was blocked, whose marriages and jobs were becoming stale and boring. Must we resign ourselves to being stuck the rest of our lives? Is it true, as Graham believed, when he answered "Yes" to a 50-year-old woman's call-in question, "Can everyone continue to grow?"

However, those who study aging are not of one mind about how to answer her question. Can anyone who has the talent and passion become the Grandma Moses of painters or graduate from the University of Maine in their eighties? In his September 1955 inaugural address as President of the American Psychological Association, E. Lowell Kelly summarized his findings about growing from his 20-year study of married couples.

> Our findings indicate that significant changes in the human personality may continue to occur during the years of adulthood. Such changes, while neither so large nor sudden as to threaten the continuity of the self-percept or impair one's day-to-day interpersonal relations are potentially of sufficient magnitude to offer a basis of fact for those who dare to hope for continued psychological growth during the adult years. (Kelly, 1955, p. 681)

In 1990, a controversial summary of research on growth through the adult years concluded that most adults' principal growths cease by their thirties. (McCrae & Costa) Others disagree. (Helson & Kwan, 2000; Willis & Reid, 1999)

That same September 1955, I began teaching a course on child and adolescent psychology at a small men's college, Haverford, in Pennsylvania. Only Erikson and a few others had written about adults' middle years. I also began to explore how young men grow healthily in their ideas about themselves and their relationships. The men included those selected by their peers, faculty, coaches, and deans as the college's most and least effective, all-around persons. A larger number of randomly selected men completed the group of 80. Though I had not planned to follow their growth (and then their partners' from their thirties on) through their adult years, I have. I collected extensive information about the men from interviews, numerous psychological tests when they were 17-year-old college freshmen and 21-year-old upperclassmen, and then even more information about them when they were in their 30s, 40s, 50s, and finally their 60s as they began to retire. I also tracked down the causes of their changes and evaluated how mature or healthy those changes were.

The book has three sections. The **first** describes the men and women *who changed the most during their adult years,* either maturing or regressing to an earlier level of maturity. I had not anticipated that almost all of the entire group would turn out to be so productive. So I have subtitled the book *Insights from the Lives of Highly Achieving Men and Women.* Who are these men and women? The book's first nine chapters describe *those who changed the most;* Appendix B includes examples of the variety of the entire group's achievements.

The **second** section shifts the book's focus from understanding the course of an individual's growth to examining the entire group's lives. I describe a scientific model of healthy growth that is firmly grounded empirically, is comprehensive, testable, valid, replicable, and generalizable. Probing deeply into how the same men and women change over 30 to 45 years offers insights about the modifiability of our adult personalities, current myths about adult growth, alternatives to stage models of adult development, predictors of adult success and fulfillment, and provisional answers to critical contemporary questions such as:

Can highly achieving partners really be happily married and fulfilled parents?

Why may highly intelligent young men be at risk of failing their adult responsibilities?

Why may many American men need their children more than their children need them?

Are sexual compatibility and fulfillment necessary to be happily married?

Do modern women really differ from men?

Do middle-aged men become softer and women tougher?

Must one have a mid-life crisis? If so, is it necessarily caused by reaching one's fortieth birthday?

Why do psychological maturity, virtue, and androgyny (an optimal balance between stereotypical masculine and feminine traits) turn out to be the best youthful predictors of an adult's success?

Of the numerous other questions the book provokes, two may be of most interest to you:

How psychologically mature, vocationally and parentally fulfilled, interpersonally intimate, and sexually compatible with your partner are you?

Would you like to discover how you compare to the book's men and women by completing the surveys given in Appendix D?

I have been challenged to make the study accessible to both professionals and educated non-professionals. Appendix A includes a glossary to help you keep track of the study's methods. Appendices B to F provide supplementary information that may be of more interest to those who wish to know more about the study itself. Some readers wanted to know more about my own growth as an adolescent and whether I continued to grow after retirement. www.Conrowpub.com includes an autobiographical history, titled *Doug: Growing from 16 to 80: How?*

The book's **third** section illustrates how 20 strategies can be used to assist a child or anyone become more mature. It concludes with some summarizing reflections about the course of healthy growth from adolescence to retirement.

Acknowledgements

A longitudinal study rooted in the mid 1950s and continuing for 50 years inevitably is influenced and assisted by innumerable others to whom I am most grateful. Of those who have assisted with the creation of this book, I am grateful to Robert Holt for his thoughtful and superb editorial guidance and decades of support and to Mary Gabel for her meticulous care in designing this book. Richard Lederer, Michael Levin, Russell Heath, Suzanne Stronghart, Richard Wagner, Connie Mardis, Sandy Heath, David Mallery, Holley Webster, and William Oswald also assisted me along the way. In addition to his continuing advice, George Vaillant made some of his materials available. All mistakes are, of course, mine.

I am most indebted to the book's featured exemplars who permitted me to draw upon and share their lives with you. They reviewed and approved publishing the chapters about them, though a few took issue with how I described them. It takes maturity and courage to be so publicly open about some of the most sensitive private issues humans confront. With the exception of Barbara, Jim, Richard, and Charlie, I have disguised the names and most other information about the exemplars that might identify them.

I regret I cannot acknowledge my gratitude to the numerous researchers who have influenced me. Making five decades of one's research accessible means slighting researchers who don't deserve to be ignored. Fifty years ago few persons had comprehensively studied optimally functioning, mentally healthy, and successful adults as they grew from adolescence to retirement. In the recent past, so much research has now been done to merit a new field called "positive psychology."[1]

Clarifying descriptions and summaries by others of their and others' longitudinal research can be found in the appendices and references listed in my earlier articles and books. *Lives of Hope,* which reports the *attributes* of the study's successful and fulfilled men and women, is a close companion to *Growing More Mature,* which focuses on the *process and causes* of maturing.

The research would never have been completed without my wife's faithful collaboration. See www.Conrowpub.com for more information about us, the book, and our other work.

The men and women I have studied have given me the greatest gift it is possible to give another: their trust and openness, in effect, themselves. They have been at the heart of my calling for almost half a century. So I dedicate this book to those whom I affectionately call my extended family. It is with poignant nostalgia that this book closes our lives together.

Douglas H. Heath
Haverford, Pennsylvania
June, 2005

Chapter 1

———————

BARBARA AND JIM:

BECOMING A HAPPILY MARRIED
AND ACHIEVING COUPLE

*"This job is a dead end one. A lot of people have done
a lot more. I'm not satisfied with myself," Barbara*

*"Parenting is the most demanding, challenging,
frustrating job one can do," Jim*

Barbara and Jim's stories tell us how two highly achieving people worked
hard to create a mutually supportive, happy, and enduring marriage. How
Barbara overcame her career dissatisfaction introduces you to some of the
study's methods and guiding ideas for understanding a person's healthy
growth and its causes. How Jim reacted to parenthood's frustrating effects
on his relation with Barbara shows how the potential perils of two high-
powered career marriages can be moderated.

———————

Barbara's Vocational Uncertainties

During the winter of 1971, I first met and interviewed Barbara for several
hours about her marriage to Jim, whom I had been following since he had
entered Haverford College in 1956. My most vivid memory of that interview
was her guilty lament that she was not fulfilling her intellectual promise
and Bryn Mawr College's expectation that its women graduates would

1

distinguish themselves in their careers. Like Haverford, a men's college at the time, neighboring Bryn Mawr was a small highly selective college for women. Though proud of its academic reputation, it is ironically also very proud of its most widely known graduate—Katharine Hepburn.

In 1983, 1995, and again in 2002 Barbara eagerly accepted my invitations to participate in each of the twelve to fifteen hours of interviews and surveys about her adult growth.

Barbara is dark haired, of medium height, though her thinness accentuates it. Aging made her look smaller, even more petite, however. More prominent continues to be her predictable manner: informally casual though intense, objective, matter-of-fact, direct, conscientious, dependable, and introspective. She has always impressed me as a no-nonsense, focused, efficient, and task-oriented person.

She turned out to be an ideal participant for our one- to two-day visits. I had to tightly plan such intense meetings, squeezing them in between the available time of 68 men (I had lost track of 12 of the original 80 men) and 40 women, unforgiving plane schedules, academic classes which I never missed, college responsibilities which I never slighted, and speaking engagements whose fees helped pay my expenses. Most visits took place over the weekends and evenings which my patient, accepting wife, Harriet, silently tolerated.

Barbara completed the extensive survey questionnaires and test materials, promptly returned them, and planned her time, also Jim's, to be free, with minimal interruptions. "Compulsive," said Jim. "Exceptionally well-organized," she and I, gratefully, would say.

Defying (or ignoring) the Bryn Mawr College's unwritten mantra that only its failures marry, she and Jim married in 1962 while she was a junior. In 1983, when in her early 40s, she reflected about the effects of her early marriage on her career development. "The mores were different then. We might not have married so young. We got married because we didn't think it was right to hop into bed." She has scarcely been a failure by any standard of success. Her early marriage had not hindered her academically. She majored in biology, graduating magna cum laude in 1963. Torn between wanting to go to graduate school or beginning her family, she chose graduate school where only five years later she earned her Ph.D. in microbiology and had her first of three children spaced two years apart.

But by 1983 she believed her marriage and family responsibilities had retarded her career and that she had reached what she called a "dead end."

Deferring her own career aspirations, she had followed Jim's àdvancing administrative medical career to Washington, D.C.'s Walter Reed Hospital's endocrinology clinic, then back to Philadelphia where he headed and reformed the medical service of the city's General Hospital. Assuming the full-time responsibility for raising their children, Barbara had kept her career hopes alive by teaching and doing research part-time and subsequently full-time when in Washington at George Washington University, and then in Philadelphia at the University of Pennsylvania's medical college and bio-chemistry departments. She continued an active grant-supported research program on lipoprotein metabolism in cultured cells, published numerous research papers, and edited a book that brought her national and increasingly international recognition. She received the inevitable invitations to speak at professional conferences as well as serve on national review committees in her specialty areas.

When Philadelphia's local city council decided to no longer support its General Hospital, Jim accepted a position in medical education in Phoenix, partially because of its climate, his interest in horses, and its remaining "wild west" character. His decision precipitated Barbara's lingering resentments. She had to abandon her long-held goal of achieving academic tenure in a medical school that she was eligible for. (Besides she was a dyed-in-wool easterner and didn't care for the southwest.) At Phoenix, she became the associate chief of a National Institutes of Health (NIH) research unit, responsible for supervising three Ph.D.s, one medical doctor, and ten technicians. She continued her own research, now focused on lipoproteins and diabetes in American Indians. Since the National Institutes of Health required chiefs of NIH-funded clinical units be physicians, she felt she was now caught in a dead-end position with no opportunity for advancement. Though distinguished in her field, as the only female and as a Ph.D. researcher in a male-dominated profession, she felt acutely isolated at medicine's periphery, with no power to make decisions. Thoughts of becoming a physician able to work with patients entered her mind and aggravated her growing discontent.

I asked her, "How are you dealing with this problem?"—one of the standard questions in an interview seeking to understand how people cope with their most troubling disappointments.

> I've become irritable. Still am at home. And I complain.
> Then I become more rational and talk about it with Jim

and my friends at work and now the children. Just trying to accept it for what it is and finding what I can let go to make life more pleasant. I'm not sure I want to stay in this job.

I asked,"Why?" Then an unexpected kicker. She replied,

I was ambivalent about going to graduate school. I've never liked laboratory research, but I've learned to do it quite well. I'm not bad at it, but I don't think I have any talent for it. What I do best in this job is organizing and relating to people. I'd like to switch careers to do something that I'd like better.

"But you've been so productive," I said.

When I have a job to do, I do it. I work hard; I'm smart and quick to learn, but I'm not particularly creative. Research is getting done what has to be done and learning how to do it. I'm not as successful as a lot of men at my level who started when I did. A lot of people have done more. I had to give up time for the children, so have not been as effective as I could have been. That's why I'm not satisfied with myself.

Severity of Barbara's Vocational Discontent

I had sensed but not clearly understood the severity of Barbara's discontent from a questionnaire I sent to participants prior to each visit. They rated on five-point scales the degree of their satisfaction with each of 28 attributes of their vocation. (Vocation Adaptation Scale —VAS [see glossary, p. 259]. The VAS can be found in Appendix D-2 if you wish to assess your own career satisfaction.) Barbara was not very satisfied with any aspect of her work. She was quite satisfied only with her involvement in and quality of her work, the opportunity it provided to be creative, and the amount of growth she had experienced. The telltale sign of the depth of her unhappiness was that her work did not provide her the chance to continue her personal growth in the rest of her professional life. She was somewhat dissatisfied with fourteen attributes of her work including the attributes of her work as a calling, not just a job: work utilizes her best potentials, provides opportunities to achieve at her potential capability, and meets most of her strongest needs. Though one of the study's most productive persons, she paradoxically was the second most dissatisfied woman with her job.

I never escaped feeling uneasy asking extraordinarily busy, productive people, like Barbara and Jim, for hours and hours of their time to help me with our study. To assuage my guilt, I gave each at the end of my visit, a full analysis of all of their test results. I told Barbara that my analysis was probably unreliable because I could not make coherent sense of her test results. They did not agree with her vocation. The most widely used vocational test at the time (Strong Vocational Interest Test—SVIT [see glossary, p. 258]) matched her interests and temperament with persons who succeeded in a variety of occupations, including twenty-two different professional ones. Barbara was only moderately similar to physicians, biologists, and professors, but more similar to administrators, personnel managers, and other people-centered occupations—as well as to dieticians! She was only average in being comfortable with academic people. She spontaneously broke in to say, "The analysis is correct; I hate getting up in the morning to go to the lab."

"What other work would you like?"

> For my own peace of mind, I have to make room for other things. I really miss not having more time for exercise, for joining community activities, reading, and learning things on my own. I'd like a 40-hour-a-week job and be able to feel I had everything done so I could go onto other things. I realize no job is like this, so I have to learn how to set limits. I probably could restrict my work very easily if I were content with being average. But I've always been best in everything. The Bryn Mawr syndrome expected everything to be perfect.

For a Bryn Mawrter to be average is to fail. Barb was not about to settle for failure.

When she next said, "There has to be some happy medium" and "I need a better balance to my life" she, like so many other high achievers in the study, intuitively identified a basic principle about healthy growth. In more technical jargon, she had been violating the equilibrating principle: too extended development in one sector of one's personality, as in her mind, begins to create resistance to its further growth until one develops in the neglected areas of one's personality. Like a rubber band, if stretched too far it snaps back too far and zips off into some other direction—into alcohol, drugs, dropping out, apathy, sex.

In the 1995 visit, Barbara claimed her test results "made a huge impression," helped to solve her vocational uncertainties, supported and clarified her future direction as a "people person." She became aware that she wanted to work in organizations with people and would like to do it in some other setting.

Finding Her Vocational Niche

In 1988 Jim and Barbara were recruited as a team to join a medical research group in Washington, D.C. In 1990 she became the research institute's president. She clarified its mission, strengthened its relation with the two sponsoring hospitals whose physicians wanted stronger research support, expanded its staff to 430, and "tightened the review process" to improve the quality of projects that helped generate forty million dollars in grant funds. Barbara also secured money from the two hospitals to support an animal facility. In her presidential role, she became involved in policy issues about regulating research and has tried to tailor research to meet society's future needs. She continued to publish research on obesity, diabetes, and cholesterol and had published by 1995 a "fair amount"—more than 200 papers. Barbara has stressed research with minority populations and chairs a steering committee studying diabetes and cardiovascular diseases in American Indians. She was also a principal investigator for NIH's Women's Health Initiative studying post-menopausal women, evaluating cardiovascular disease, cancer, and osteoporosis. Her center recruited 3600 local women as part of a much larger, national, ten-year longitudinal study of 163,000 women, funded for $600 million dollars. She has, in her words "wound up" a two-year term as the chairman of the study's governing board.

Barbara is now very highly satisfied with her career. She scores among the study's top seven most satisfied women; understandably, she is least satisfied with the amount of time her work now demands of her. Several objective standards measure her success. She wrote me she had been offered a sabbatical at a European university and added a postscript that she hoped her children would find themselves much earlier than she had. The Franklin Institute has awarded her the Corson medal for her research on human nutrition, the Slovak Academy of Sciences one for her research, and the American Heart Association for a Distinguished Investigator award.

Scarcely a Bryn Mawr College failure, not in spite of her marriage, but in part because of it, as I will describe shortly.

A major contributing cause of Barbara's discontent in 1983 had been Jim and her teenage children. I have described Jim in *Lives of Hope* (Heath, 1994b), disguised as Harry Barnett, as an exemplar of a concerned, contributing citizen, and caring father. If Barbara had been more content with herself at the time I would have included them as one of the study's most all-around successful couples.

Jim's Vocational Commitment

Jim is a stocky, slightly overweight, energetic dynamo who walks with a limp. When nine, he developed a condition that caused a deterioration of his left hip. On crutches for four years, he was determined to live his life regardless of his shorter leg. He told me how proficient he became on his crutches. He climbed stairs on his crutches as quickly as his non-handicapped peers could. Jim does not withdraw from adversity. When I asked him what he planned for retirement, he replied,

> I don't plan to be one of those martyr physicians who work until they drop. I have too many interests outside of medicine. I enjoy traveling, riding horses, fishing, hunting, teaching. I enjoy flying. I have a private pilot license which I got while at Haverford.

Jim had never doubted that he would be a physician. He had a continuing desire to have contact with patients, even as a medical administrator. I had re-asked the standard question when he was in his fifties: "Regardless of how satisfied and successful you are in your work, is there any other kind of work you'd rather be doing?" His answer revealed the depth of his concern for patients.

> I would enjoy medical missionary work: not from the perspective of the religious part but from the aspect of minimal health care, and having a chance to provide that. It would be extremely rewarding to provide a fundamental right and fulfill a need that hadn't been there before.

> There is great pleasure and satisfaction in being able to
> reduce or end suffering or make a difficult diagnosis and
> embark on a cure to relieve disease.

Predictably, as an administrator responsible for the continued growth of his hospital's staff, he had little patience for physicians whose primary motive was to make a lot of money, not the care of patients.

Jim's temperament and talents had early provoked ambivalence about what specific medical role he was going to play. Just as Barbara's SVIT pointed to her future direction, so it prefigured how Jim resolved his ambivalence. The SVIT suggested that day-to-day patient care in his office would not be fulfilling, nor would academic medicine and research, though he had the talent to do either capably. Temperamentally, he was most similar to professionals like psychiatrists, ministers, and others directly involved in individuals' personal welfare. But he was also most similar to professionals in managerial, administrative positions which offered the opportunity to be politically persuasive—like medical administration focused on the welfare of his staff, patient care, and policy, not on detailed financial issues. His ultimate goal was to head a health care delivery organization.

Intriguingly, Jim was one of the study's three men whose vocational satisfaction consistently improved more than that of any other man from their 30s to their 60s. The improvement mirrored the course of each of Jim's positions from academic medicine, to Philadelphia General Hospital and its financial issues, to his job in Phoenix in charge of patient welfare, and finally to his Washington's administrative and national policy responsibilities.

I was also intrigued that Jim was one of the study's four most overall vocationally satisfied and fulfilled exemplars. (I later describe two others' changes, Rich's and Charlie's; I've have already described the third, Chen, in *Lives of Hope.* He was a productive university professor and chair of his department.)

At varying times in his career, Jim has been on and a chair of numerous medical and educational boards. He has been president of a chamber of commerce. In Washington, D.C. he was responsible for the practice of medicine in a 905-bed hospital and for the medical education of 250 residents. As a senior administrator of the governing executive group, 200 physicians report to him; he also has liaison responsibility for 1600 private physicians who practice at the hospital.

Both Barbara and Jim have grown to be distinguished people in their fields. How has their family life been affected by their professional success? In a time when many couples are juggling marital and vocational fulfillment not very successfully, Barbara and Jim show us how each partner can be vocationally successful and yet have a mutually fulfilling marital relationship.

Marital Fulfillment—and Frustrations

Barbara has consistently rated herself to be very happily married and to bemoan Jim's one negative idiosyncrasy and one troublesome universally shared masculine trait—both of which she has tried to change since 1962 with only limited success to date. In 1983 she was really peeved because she finally accepted that she was not going to change him and had to find ways "to work around him." She gave me a delightful example of his special irritating trait:

> He just doesn't care much about getting things done around the house. I sit down with him ahead of time and outline what he is going to do and make a list of the things I know I'm not going to get done and then not get bothered by them. That is very hard to do because I do get bothered by a lot of things so I then go ahead to do them myself. For example, I take care of my own car's maintenance. He doesn't, as he should. He has two cars to take care of. He insisted we keep the old Porsche. If they need repairs I just try to ignore them. He'll often leave them to the last minute. Once his car was being repaired and the Porsche's battery was down. I refused to allow him to use my car. I told him that I took care of my responsibility and he didn't of his. So I'm not going out of my way to help him about what we had agreed to do.

I asked Barbara if Jim showed the same traits at work. "No. He's very effective, efficient, and organized. He is just not so at home which he leaves me to take care of."

As every other fully engaged man and woman reported, the demands of their careers upon their time and energy were unremitting; clean homes, washed windows, and immaculate yards as well as recreational and social activities paid the price. But not the children, usually. Barbara had no complaint about Jim's devotion to the children. Their children's expanding geographic universe in their early teenage years in rural Phoenix meant drives of hundreds of miles to music and other activities during the week. Her home management organizational skills made her the grudging "natural" coordinator and chauffeur. She later traced her ability to juggle five to six different activities simultaneously to her home management training experience.

Barbara's second complaint echoed that of every woman of the study. "He doesn't really like to hash things over and talk about things: his feelings, decisions to be made, reactions to things that happen, worries. He has never told me he is worried about anything—ever."

Intimacy or openness in communicating personal feelings is a key to marital mutuality and companionship. Lack of intimacy is one of the most frequently cited reasons by women initiating divorce.

To measure intimacy, I asked each participant to rate on five-point scales how comfortable he or she was discussing each of twenty potentially sensitive topics like death, greatest insecurities, and dreams with his/her partner. They then rated the topics with their closest same sex friend and then with the child they felt closest to (Interpersonal Communication—IC which can be found in Appendix D-4 in case you wish to take and score it before reading further.) Marital partners agree quite well about the topics that they are most comfortable discussing with each other: their successes, joyful times, and problems with their children. They also agree about which topics are seldom discussed because they make them uncomfortable: socially unacceptable wishes and acts, greatest insecurities, and sexual desires and activities. Males are very comfortable talking about the accomplishments of their partners and children; wives are less so. Men are more uncomfortable talking about their failures; their wives are more comfortable sharing theirs.

Since middle age, Barbara and Jim had become marginally more comfortable talking about sensitive issues like their finances and insecurities. Given Barbara's persistent complaint about Jim's reticence, I was surprised that she did not differ noticeably from him in her overall comfort level. Jim felt more comfortable talking about sex, dreams, and their marriage than she; she felt more comfortable sharing feelings about her bodily dysfunctions and her discouragements. She actually was somewhat more uncomfortable talking about her socially unacceptable wishes and dreams.

Perhaps because we live in a time of cultural permissiveness, Jerry Springer, the *National Inquirer*, and presidential sexual peccadilloes, most participants felt quite comfortable talking about most issues with their partners as well as with me. Jim was quite gleeful when he heard their results, exclaiming, "See, I'm not so bad after all!"

Jim also rated his marriage to have been very happy in his forties and extremely so since. For more than thirty years, both have agreed about the strengths of their marriage: affection, companionship, shared work and interests, and persistent efforts to mature together. Jim answered a standard question about the best things about their marriage this way:

> It has been a changing relationship in the sense that we have tried to mature with each other. We started with very different expectations than we have now. I had never thought of my wife having a career when we first got married. We went through the whole period of women's consciousness-raising and survived it. Even when communication has not been easy, we have worked at it, tried to make it happen with mutual respect and admiration for each other.

When I asked what was not as good about his marriage as he would like, he had only one complaint:

> I'm fairly easy-going in emotion. Wife is a little more volatile, a hot blooded Latin. She goes to excesses. She is more cyclothymic, tending to become more upset and depressed more readily. I'm just as hard on her as she is on me. I am probably more physically passionate than she is.

I asked each what were the principal ways the other was a good partner. Barbara said that despite her two complaints:

> Jim is easy to get along with; he's loving, a very good father, loyal, and cooperative in most ways. Though he doesn't like to talk, he is always there if there is a big problem, so I know I can always turn to him. He has a positive outlook on life from which I've learned a lot. He is very helpful to me.

Jim answered,

> Very supportive. Very able. Extremely dependable. I
> don't have to worry about finances; she is a much better
> financial manager than I am. Extremely organized and
> bright. Hard worker. Does at least her share of things.
> Again, warm and loving and very supportive.

Parental Fulfillment—and Frustrations

Most adults, nowadays even women, confront three responsibilities:
working to support their family, creating a marriage, and raising children.
The responsibilities can affect each other. For the most part, Barbara and
Jim's vocational achievements and marriage supported each other. What
about their parenting? More than any other person in the study, Jim valued
most highly his role as a parent, one reason he found being a parent "was
the most demanding, challenging, and frustrating job that he had." I had
asked each person to list the ten "most important specific personal wishes,
daydreams, hopes that you would like to fulfill before you die" No other
person, including Barbara, hoped their children would be successful and
happy as consistently as Jim had been in his 40s, 50s, and 60s.

I asked,"Why is it so important that the children succeed and marry
happily?" (his greatest hope).

> I suppose because of a deep feeling that I have about
> the kids. The sense of their worth. And ability and the
> tremendous obligation I feel to provide what it takes for
> them to use their abilities. We both feel very lucky to have
> three very bright and able kids. What would probably
> blow my computer most would be for them not to be
> successful and happy. That would be one of the hardest
> things for me to be able to cope with. Gets back to those
> feelings of their potential worth, how much that means
> to me. I'd feel a certain personal loss and responsibility.
> Clearly the kids are the center of our lives.

Harriet, a national expert in parenting, had used the 28 criteria that define
vocational adaptation or fulfillment to create a similar measure of parental
satisfaction (PAS). If you wish to measure your own parental fulfillment,

complete the survey in Appendix D-3 now before continuing.) Both Barbara and Jim scored only average in parental satisfaction at Time 4. But both had changed in their satisfaction more than most others by Time 5. Jim now ranked second among the fathers, Barbara seventh among the mothers in their parental satisfaction. Why had they been only average at Time 4 when they had Helen, their 16-year-old first child? Jim explained for them both,

> She's a real problem. She's been very challenging Very strong, decisive, but somewhat insecure. Being the first child, her unpleasantness here in the home reverberates to the other two kids. She is caught between her insecurity and push to be independent and rebel against us. And she's so outspoken and aggressive. She really rakes Barbara over the coals. It has been a hard time for Helen because she "matured" early and when thirteen wanted to try her wings. We didn't think it was time yet. Well! We got into these huge spiraling conflicts. Nothing got accomplished. All of our ideas went up in smoke. We have sought counseling about her and learned that in our attempt to have an open communicative relation with her we may have blurred the generational boundaries.

Barbara picked up the story at this point:

> I made the mistake of assuming they are adults and expecting them to be rational. They think they can tell me what to do, think they can tell me what they think about me. I just figured this out about six months ago. We don't have a physical discipline problem. When they are supposed to do something, we make them do it. But we have a verbal discipline problem. They say too much; it is hard dealing with that.

I then asked how they had dealt with Helen. Jim began by saying,

> We both persevered. We are both strong. We both are determined. We both did our best to intellectualize as much as we could to try to understand what she was going through. We sought professional help, which was

partially helpful. It reassured us there were no deep and dire problems we were facing. We supported each other. We never allowed Helen to split the two of us. The kids make fun of us for being a team. "Of course you will support mom." They tried. They did their damnedest to divide and conquer. It wasn't as much a forced effort as a kind of natural way. Parenthood is most demanding. You become an expert only when it is over. Very difficult to be an expert while going through it. First product off the assembly line. But you can't recall it to make it right.

Ten years later Helen trekked in Nepal's Himalayan Mountains. [Having trekked ten times in Nepal and encountered single girls and pairs, typically Australian, on the trails, I valued their daughter's intrepid spirit.] She is now a highly successful investment banker at a level that few women have achieved.

Later I asked Jim what period of life would he not want to relive. He said, "Early middle age. The conflict with the children in Phoenix. Very hard on Barbara and on the family. I don't think as a professional I was as productive then as later."

Identifying the Causes of Barbara and Jim's Growth

To identify how people change during their adult years and the determinants of or contributors to such change, the participants completed the same standard judging procedure. They described how they had changed in the past ten to fifteen years in each of four personality sectors: their minds, interpersonal relationships, values, and self-attitudes. Fifty critical events that might cause change had been identified by judges, e.g., partner's personality, first child, type of vocation. Each was listed on a 3 x 5 index card. Each person sorted the fifty cards into five piles representing increasing degrees of influence in producing the changes described in each of the four personality sectors. The participants then ranked the selected most influential determinants, after which they were interviewed about how each of the four most influential determinants had affected them. For example, in her 40s, Barbara judged the four principal determinants of her growth in attitudes about her self to be: her husband as a partner, parental role, occupational associates, and major change in her work. In his 50s, Jim selected Barbara's personality, their children, major change in his work, and demands of his role as a partner. (Interview Determinants—INTD)

Barbara's descriptions of Jim's and parenthood's effects illustrate the type of responses I later scored for signs of maturing.

Jim's Contribution to Barbara's Growth

She said of Jim's effects:

> I've learned a lot from things he does differently, learned to be more relaxed; am much calmer. I don't overreact as much. I have learned to let things go and be less compulsive. I've learned from him the way he handles his associates and ways to deal with people. One of his real strengths is he relates to people so well. Learned some of those things from him. I don't do it anywhere near as well as he does.

Barbara and Jim had created one of the most mutually supportive marriages of the study. She was quite sensitive to and articulate about how she and Jim differed, e.g., he was more laid-back, worried less, less compulsive about being ready on time, more impulsive, like buying a VCR or new puppy on the spur of the moment.

Both agreed that their shared, though not identical, research interests and managerial experience reinforced their mutual growth; their interests provided the content for discussions and, recently, collaboration in writing an article. Such overlap in compatible interests strengthened their close friendship, joint decision-making, and reliance on each other as resources in their careers. Both independently agreed that their late 30s and early 40s had been their least productive and happy years.

But I thought their less obvious similarities in their personalities and qualities of mind contributed far more to Barbara's changes. I relied on other types of measures to assess their compatibility. I gave each person in the study the ten Rorschach ink blots (ROR) and asked them to tell me what they saw in each. [How individuals perceive and organize the test's colored and black-gray blots reveal to trained clinicians their less conscious personality needs, relationships, and mental processes.] The men were given the Rorschach when in college, as well as in their 30s and again in their 40s; the women took the Rorschach in their late 30s and early 40s when they joined the study full-time. Some requested they receive it again in their 50s, among whom were Barbara and Jim. When analyzed to identify their managerial skills, their tests suggested that personal agendas did not get in the way of their relationships with others. Others would view them to be fair, objective, certainly not personally vindictive or seductive. Both Jim and Barbara made realistic judgments but were not highly imaginative or creative in expression. Both were sensitive to interpersonal nuances. As managers I felt others would trust their judgments, and each would trust their partner's judgments.

Another clue to Jim and Barbara's basic personality similarity came from a Personality Trait Survey (PTS) consisting of seventy different traits which each participant rated about himself/herself and about each other. Also two persons who knew them most intimately, like a colleague or their closest friend, described them on the same traits. Barbara and Jim are ethical persons of high integrity and honesty. Neither thinks of him- or herself as moody, emotional, or feminine nor believes that their feelings are easily hurt. Both are understanding, sympathetic, and sensitive to others' feelings; they are cooperative and, as I noticed when living with them, they did not defensively compete with each other. Each also valued creating similar staff relationships and apparently succeeded, perhaps due to modeling such interpersonal strengths in their personal lives.

Barbara subsequently said she had not realized how similar they were and planned as her next "project" to reflect about their similarities!

In the interviews, both spontaneously spoke of their pride in each other's achievements—a pride that can provide immeasurable support to the other. Jim said, "I take great pride in what she has done. She has an international reputation. Has she shown you her medals for her research?"

"No." And she modestly never did.

"She has been a terrific role model for my children. We have worked very hard to sustain a meaningful relationship and we have and we take great pleasure in being together."

"What is your greatest reservation about her?"

"This issue of male-female communication. She wants to talk."

She said, "He is the most optimistic person I know and is a wonderful manager who has a 'big' picture view of medical needs."

Parenthood's Contribution to Barbara's Growth

In discussing the effects of children on her own growth, Barbara said:

> Parenthood makes you patient and understanding and tests your limits of everything. You learn to do better when there is stress between you and your children over an issue and you learn to resolve it, to deal with it. You learn skills that are applicable to other situations.

"Could you give me an example?"

> This business of setting limits with my daughter applies very often to some of the people who work for me, like secretaries who are only a few years older than my daughter was at the time. Being a parent has taught me to reanalyze some of the things I had thought about myself. I hadn't agreed much with my parents when in high school, I thought it was they. Now I have some insight into what I may have been like at that age.

Twelve years later Barbara expanded on some of these changes. "They have sharpened my mind. Broadened it with new ideas."
"Like what?" I asked.

> From Helen I have learned a lot about business; she consults around the world. I use lots of skills I learned from managing kids. I understand how young people are, what their limitations are, and where they are at. I try very hard to be understanding of working mothers.

How typical are these selected causes among the study's participants? Are some of their reported causes so rare as to preclude any generalizations about why people change? To provide you with the comparative information to evaluate the usefulness of Barbara's and Jim's lives for understanding change, the chapter ends by listing the principal causes reported by all of the participants. After each chapter I will provide a commentary on the entire group's results about an important contribution or the insight each exemplar's life gives us about growing more maturely.

What Does Barbara and Jim's Story
Tell Us about Healthy Growth?

If growth has stalled, making a major change requiring a new adaptation may restart it.

Marital mutuality means similarity in personality traits, interests, and openness in communicating about potentially threatening topics.

Growth may be inhibited by choices that are not compatible with one's temperament.

Marital mutuality and vocational satisfaction are possible, but it takes self-conscious work to prevent a career from adversely affecting a marriage and for marital partners to support each other's vocations.

Too great ambition may limit growth.

Becoming a parent is very risky. Children provide the opportunity to discover how one needs to become more mature.

Commentary

This first two-part commentary summarizes what the study tells us about the attributes that a couple needs for both to feel happy about their marriage and to be successful in their careers—an issue troubling millions of today's two-career marriages.

I then list the principal events in adults' lives that the study discovered contribute most to their healthy growth overall.

Marital Success

However we measure an ideal marital relationship or identify the traits of the partner who is happily married, the results are very consistent.

Attributes of an Ideal Marital Relationship

- Love and trust
- Interpersonal communication skills such as empathy to understand how a partner feels
- Shared interests and sexual compatibility
- Loyalty and commitment to the relationship

- Personal strengths such as sense of humor, cheerfulness, self-confidence, and optimism
- Commitment to honesty and fairness

Barbara and Jim had self-consciously worked hard to develop these qualities; their mutuality and companionship were exceptional—and rare.

Attributes of Marriages Whose Partners Are Happily Married

Men tend to rate their marriages as happier than women rate theirs; women expect more of their marriages than men do.

Happily married couples are

- competent sexual partners and parents. Competence in one role generally goes along with competence in other roles that depend upon interpersonal skills and attitudes like those of the ideal marriage.
- mature. Other studies of happily married persons agree. They are self-confident, cheerful, loving, and emotionally healthy.
- androgynous. Each shares enough strengths of the opposite sex to enjoy, understand, and participate in some of each other's interests and activities.
- happy throughout their early lives, especially during adolescence. Happy people are mentally healthy, optimistic, feel in control of themselves, and so are willing to risk learning new things. Happiness is anchored deep in our character. Pursuit of pleasure may bring pleasure but does not guarantee happiness.

Career Success and Fulfillment

Success in a career has different meanings. It can mean fulfilling one's calling, as it meant for Barbara and Jim. Their administrative work was their identity and is most clearly seen in their high career satisfaction. Others define their success by their income, prestige, or recognition of their creativity. Generalizations about vocational success and fulfillment are hazardous; I must limit them to highly achieving men. The study's women, first seen during the heyday of the feminist movement, had more diverse reasons for working; they were more conflicted about their familial and job roles and so shared few attributes. However, the men shared many attributes to warrant some firm conclusions.

Vocationally Successful and Fulfilled Men

- share a rich variety of strengths, beginning with intellectual skills, motivational commitment to work hard, ability to understand and manage interpersonal relationships, communication skills, especially empathy.
- share numerous stereotypical masculine attributes: self-sufficiency, self-confidence, energy, independence, and aggressiveness among others. Typical core "macho" strengths such as dominance, forceful-ness, and competitiveness are not commonly found among men fulfilled by their work.
- are androgynous. Masculine attributes are mellowed by stereotypic feminine ones like understanding, gentleness, eagerness to soothe hurt feelings.
- are mature and have high self-esteem. Psychological maturity is the single best predictor of vocational fulfillment.
- are more competent in their other adult roles, especially their marital and parental ones.

Income is not a reliable measure of vocational fulfillment. If it were, teachers, service workers, and others not paid commensurate with their talents and education would be miserable.

Marital happiness and career satisfaction and fulfillment share similar core character strengths, most notably maturity and androgyny. These are the psychological links that the study discovered that contribute most to the partners' healthy growth and the likelihood that those who succeed in their dual careers can successfully create a happy marital relationship.

Causes of Healthy Growth

What are the principal events in adults' lives that contribute most to their healthy growth? The causes of healthy growth or maturing are multiple, differ in their potencies to effect change from one individual to the next at different periods of their lives, as well as between males and females. Recall the participants rated the degree of influence of fifty determinants that changed them. Of the ten most frequently cited causes, the following lists the most to the least frequently cited ones.

Top Ten Causes of Change from the Men's 20s to Early 30s

Personality of wife/partner
Type of occupation
Demands of the husband role
Graduate/professional school
Occupational way of life
Atmosphere of home
Children
Close male friend
Occupational associates
Demands of father role

Top Ten Causes of Change from the Early 30s to Mid 40s

For the Men	For the Women
Type of occupation	Personality of husband/partner
Personality of wife/partner	Demands of mother role
Partner as spouse/partner	Partner as spouse/partner
Major change in work	Physical/emotional health
Demands of father role	Demands of partner role
Demands of partner role	Type of occupation
Counseling	Women's liberation
Physical/emotional health	Children
Approaching middle age	Closest friends
Closest friends	Counseling

Top Ten Causes of Change from the
Mid 40s to the Early 60s

For the Men

Personality of wife/partner
Physical/emotional health
Demands of partner role
Type of occupation
Children
Major change in work
Approaching retirement age
Biological aging
Non-career activities
Death of loved one

For the Women

Personality of husband/partner
Children
Physical/emotional health
Biological aging
Major change in work
Demands of partner role
Counseling
Type of occupation
Demands of mother role
Non-career activities

You may wish to refer to these ordered lists when I tell you about the causes of the healthy growth of other persons who changed most over the years. Though the order of the causes varies, of interest is the similarity of the determinants of growth over forty years. The lists also reflect the changing life tasks of men and women over time. They map the psychological world that any "theory" about development of adults must deal with.

Chapter 2

THE MODEL OF MATURING:
UNDERSTANDING BARBARA
AND JIM'S MATURITY

Without some model of healthy growth, I would have no way to organize, compare, and measure the reported changes of the men and women. Absent such a model or framework, the book would be a chaotic anecdotal collection of fascinating people about which few generalizations of psychological significance could be made.

What does *healthy* growth mean? It does not mean just any kind of growth. There are pathological types of physical growths like cancers. More subtly, there are distorting psychic growths, like Barbara's ambitious research-driven life, that *seem* at one point to be healthy. But when viewed over time from the perspective of a person as an integrated system, such ambition may bode strain, like her increased job dissatisfaction.

"Healthy growth" means the maturing of the whole person, not just of a specific sector like the mind. The fifth-century Greeks understood this fundamental meaning of healthy growth. Kitto describes the "generous Homeric conception of *arete* as an all-around excellence and an all-around activity implies a respect for the wholeness or the oneness of life, and a consequent dislike of specialization." (1951, p. 16) Twentieth century philosophers, like Alfred Whitehead, agree. He insisted that educators should educate for the "complete development of ideal human beings" (1917, p.

23

60)—the maturation of mind, character (interpersonal skills and values), and self. Teachers, society's custodians of children's healthy growth or maturation, know meaningful growth leads to wholeness. I have asked numerous experienced teachers, "What is the most important enduring gift you yourself received from your most valued teacher?" Invariably they reply with attributes of a *mind*, e.g., "a new way of thinking;" "lifelong interest in philosophy;" of character's *interpersonal attributes*, e.g., "an understanding of what compassion was all about" and of *motives or values*, e.g., "the will to follow my dreams;" and finally of self, e.g., "belief that I was special;" "knowing that I was responsible for my own decisions and acts."

When I began my studies of healthy growth fifty years ago, neither psychologists nor educators had provided a practical, verifiable model of psychological health that helped me. I made some powerful, controversial assumptions which I tested in the following years.

First, the criterion of healthy growth had to be the health of the whole person or system, not just of a sector or part of a person. The goal of a school had to be more than just the maturation of mind. (Heath, 1994a) Research on maturity had to be comprehensive. I had to include mind or cognitive competencies, character, including interpersonal and value attributes, and self-attitudes.

Second, a systemic understanding of humans assumes both developmental dependencies and interdependencies. Mind or cognitive growth is a baby's leading growing edge; it prepares for the emergence of interpersonal growth at the forefront; interpersonal skills in turn provide the crucible for enduring values and interests which eventuate in the ultimate emergence of an over-arching integrative self-identity. Of course growth in all personality sectors, as Erik Erickson (1950) taught us, occurs concurrently with different sectors becoming sequentially predominant at different phases. Japanese preschool and elementary teachers believe, for example, that interpersonal cooperative and communicative skills facilitate a child's later cognitive growth; so they focus first on educating for such skills before emphasizing reading.

Third, maturation of personality sectors such as mind and values follows a developmental ground plan that progressively increases a person's adaptive competence. I believe that this intrinsic psychic ground plan involves five interrelated dimensions: increasing awareness (or more technically, symbolization) enabling reflection, movement out of egocentrism into what I will call other-centeredness, increasing integration, stabilization, and autonomy. Table 2.1 pictures the core adaptive competencies that dimensional growth in the personality sectors enhance. Maturation of mind increases competence, mastery, and power. Maturation of character increases the ability to create intimate relationships and frees energy from self-entanglements to develop new interests and humane values. Maturation of self leads to its transcendence, objectivity, and perspective that contribute to a sense of humor and joy.

Fourth, humans growing healthily mature in similar ways, regardless of their age, sex, ethnicity, and social class. I believed that any model of maturity should be transculturally general or universal as well. Yes, people differ in observable ways; but they are similar in their generic or underlying ways of growing healthily. As I discovered, American Protestants and Jews, northern Italian and southern Sicilian Catholics, and eastern and western Turkish Muslim males matured similarly, though differing in their religious beliefs and interpersonal relationships. (Heath, 1977a) Chapter 13 explores how males and females grow similarly and differently, and traces the principal types of growth from adolescence through late middle age. For example, as persons mature, their minds become more reflective, empathically capable, synthetically organized and relational; they function more predictably, adapt more resiliently to disruptions of stress; and they become freed from immediate situational demands to create novel responses. If you keep this schematic model in mind as I sketch how different men and women have changed during their adult years, you could become more sensitive to the signs of maturity in others and your self.

The Model of Maturing and its Measurement

All measurement must begin with a clear definition of what the to-be-measured trait is. This obvious first step is more difficult to make than it seems. To assist one school's teachers to clarify and then measure their goal to increase students' curiosity or desire to learn, I asked them to identify the most curious students in their own classes. I then asked them to identify the students' specific observable behaviors that led them to their selection. If I, a stranger, visited their classrooms would I be able to identify their most curious students from their list of behaviors? We then translated each cited behavior into a statement, e.g., student asks questions in class, that could be rated for its frequency or strength. Even seventh graders can collectively create their own measure of curiosity when guided through the steps of how to clarify and then measure their own curiosity. (1999a)

To make the model's dimensional categories more concrete, I first quote the wise words of some persons who have reflected deeply about humans' potentials for growth. To further define the dimension, I next quote from reflective adolescents about how they had grown in school. Though they knew nothing about the model of maturity, their manifest examples illustrate the dimension. Their words not only help to clarify the underlying dimension but also demonstrate the applicability of the model to adolescents as well as to adults. After a brief explanation of the first dimension of maturity—Awareness—I immediately show you how I measured Barbara's growth over time in it and identified some of the causes of her growth from her interview. [I focus on Barbara because she changed more than Jim from her 40s to her 50s.] I then return to describe the remaining four dimensions of the model of maturing or healthy growth.

Increasing Awareness—Its Measurement and Causes

The first dimension of healthy growth is increased symbolization or awareness. Jerome Bruner, noted psychologist, says the "very essence of being human lies in the use of symbols." (1966, p. 89) Symbols can be words, images, numbers—anything that represents, stands for something else. The use of symbols brings great power and freedom from the chains of time and space. They enable us to accurately represent the real world and our own desires and values, to think about alternatives and their consequences, and so facilitate effective adaptation. More colloquially, Erich Fromm, influenced by Buddhist views of growth, told me his therapeutic goal was to wake people up more and more—to become more aware and so more alive.

Students' Description of Their Awareness.   Michigan's Bloomfield Hills Model High School (MHS) asked me to assess how its students had changed by the end of a school year. I asked them to write how they had changed, how they were now different from when they had entered the school. Like hundreds of other students of more traditional schools, none mentioned the specific skills for which their teachers test, like having learned French or how to solve a calculus problem. They unanimously and perceptively wrote using words describing the model's generic dimensions, like symbolization, though none had ever heard of them. (1999a) Table 2.1

Table 2.1 Model of Maturing: Strengths that Contribute to Healthy Growth

The Person's Strengths	Developmental Dimensions of Maturing					Visible Signs of Maturity
	Symbolization (Awareness)	Other-Centeredness	Integration	Stabilization	Autonomy	
Mind	Aware of how mind works; articulate, imagines solution	Empathically grasps others' views	Thinks relationally and sees the whole picture	Functions well and resiliently under stress	Educates self and can create novel solutions for varied situations	Increased mastery and competence
Character *Relationships*	Sensitively aware of and reflective about others	Cares for and loves others	Creates mutually cooperative relationships	Friendships persist	Self-reliantly forms selective friendships	Increased ability to create intimate and loving relationships
Values	Honesty	Compassion	Integrity	Commitment	Courage	Lives by ideals which defends with enthusiasm
Self	Accurately understands self	Accepts self as fully human and understands how others view self	Self so together acts naturally and spontaneously	Strong sense of self and confidence	Affirms own worth and directs and controls own growth	Heightened capability for self-transcendence, objectivity, and sense of humor

lists some of the skills, like thinking and reflecting, which require the use of symbols. They wrote of the maturation:

Of mind   12th grade girl: "My thinking skills have improved tremendously. I challenge myself to find out why things are the way they are and to find answers to my questions."

Of interpersonal relationships   9th grade boy: "MHS made me more aware of situations in high school with students and faculty—their feelings, their problems, and how they cope with them."

Of values   9th grade girl: "I realized school work is not the most important aspect of school, but that I enjoy myself while learning."

Of self   10th grade girl: "MHS helped me discover parts of myself I never thought were there."

Measurement of Awareness: The Perceived Self Questionnaire. The model provided the rationale for the creation of the Perceived Self Questionnaire (PSQ) to measure the maturity of the five personality sectors (for the adult form interpersonal relationships were divided into male and female items) on each of the five generic dimensions. So a person's maturity could be mapped into 25 categories (five sectors by five dimensions). (The PSQ can be found in Appendix D-1. You may better understand the rest of this chapter if you now complete and score your own PSQ before reading further.) The PSQ consists of 50 scales (40 for the adolescent form), two scales each describing one of the 25 categories. A person checks one of eight boxes indicating increasing agreement with the item. The more mature end is given a score of eight; the least a score of one. Barbara's responses to two PSQ scales measuring mind's awareness and two of self's illustrate how the 25 categories were measured.

Increased mind's awareness was measured by two PSQ items: "I can readily recall the facts necessary for analyzing an intellectual problem." In her 40s, Barbara checked the box closest to the most mature end; I therefore gave her a score of seven. In her 50s, she checked the most extreme box to receive a score of eight, for an increase of one.

"I could accurately recall the thoughts I had several years ago about various intellectual issues." She was scored six in her 40s and also six in her 50s, for no change in her mind's awareness.

Now note her maturing in her self-concept.

Increased self-awareness was measured by two PSQ items: "I know my self reasonably well and could describe myself quite accurately if asked to do so." Barbara scored five in her early 40s and seven in her 50s.

"I am able to recall in detail the way I was and the feelings I had when I was much younger." She scored four in her 40s but five in her 50s.

Predictably, Barbara in her early 40s scored highest in maturity on the PSQ's ten items about the growth of her mind, i.e., for its symbolization, other-centeredness, integration, stability, and autonomy, for a total score of 68 out of a possible score of 80. She scored only 45 in the maturity of her self-concept, a large enough discrepancy of 23 (68 minus 45 = 23) to alert me where maturing was most likely in the future. As did occur in her 50s: she scored 71 in the maturity of her mind for an increase of 3 (71 minus 68 = 3) but 56 in the maturity of her self, an 11 point growth in her view of self (56 minus 45 = 11).

A similar adolescent form has been used to assess the maturity of high school students. For example, self-awareness was also measured by degree of agreement with two items: "I have a good idea of what my good and bad qualities are," and "I have no trouble describing what kind of person I am."

Causes of Barbara's Growth in Awareness: We don't yet know how such scores reveal themselves in Barbara's actual behavior. One way to find out would be to score her interview about the maturing effects of the causes of her growth and discover if the pattern of growths for maturity's dimensions and sectors was similar to the PSQ pattern. We can review her interview about the determinants to identify which ones produced increased awareness. When we do that we discover that

- her children's questioning of her values "helps you in thinking and recasting totally your own."
- parenthood has "taught me to re-analyze some things I had thought about myself. Now I have some insight into what I might have been like to my own parents when a child."
- occupational associates have "taught me that my limitation is to take things personally."

I return now to similarly define the remaining four dimensions. You can identify the items measuring them in Appendix D-1.

Increasing Other-Centeredness

The second generic dimension of healthy growth is other-centeredness. John Dewey said, "the individual is always a social individual. He has no existence by himself. He lives in, for, and by society." (1897, p. 109) As one parent said of his adolescent son, "He is actually beginning to think of others." Such growth frees us from viewing our world only from our self-centered view; we can become more empathic, objective, and realistic as we gain multiple perspectives about others. We learn we are not so different from others and begin to feel more positively about ourselves; we learn to care for others.

Adolescents readily recognize their growing other-centeredness, as the MHS students report.

Of mind   12th grade boy: I am "more objective now because I have been forced to look at many facets of particular problems here."

Of interpersonal relationships   10th grade boy: "I learned to be more tolerant of other people's problems."

Of values   11th grade boy: "MHS showed me you can still be powerful, yet loving and having open arms toward people."

Of self   9th grade girl: "I learned how to do better and accept myself."

Barbara changed little on this dimension. I am not sure why. She was very maturely other-centered in her intellectual growth: realistic, practical, anticipating other's views about problems. But she thought she was very different from other persons, which she was of course. She was a Bryn Mawrter—a highly independent masculine one at that, working in a very masculine career and environment.

Progressive Integration

The third dimension of healthy growth is progressive personality integration. Mark Van Doren, a philosopher and educator, has said of the maturing person, "Man is in the same breath metaphysician, philosopher, scientist, and poet." (1943, p. 109) Healthy growth leads to increasing differentiation and relational connectedness, internal coherence, and external harmony. To create a way of life that integrates the inner scientist and poet, the feminine and masculine, the demonic and godlike is to act out of wholeness with integrity.

Again, note what reflective adolescents write about getting themselves together at one level of maturity.

Of mind   9th grade boy: "I relate many things without knowing much about them."

Of interpersonal relationships   9th grade girl: I "talked to my teachers as if they are my friends only because they are; I never had such great relationships with teachers before."

Of values   12th grade girl: "I found passion and stimulation in learning; it made me increase the positivity [sic] in the person I am today [also Other-centered self]; consequently carried over to my relationships."

Of self   11th grade boy: "I felt a sense of understanding and fulfillment; found freedom to express myself and be myself."

Barbara was least mature on this dimension in her 40s when she was so torn and divided about her career and family. She disagreed with items like, "I seldom feel I am a divided, inconsistent, and contradictory person;" "I am reasonably sure of what I am and what my direction is." In her 50s she agreed with those statements. Her lowest-rated score for integration was her disagreement with "I develop new interests and become more sensitive to new feelings and thoughts as a result of a close male friendship." Despite her close collaborative friendship with Jim, she was one of the few women who, in her 50s, had not selected her partner, Jim, to have influenced her growth. Why? Perhaps because they are one of the oldest married couples in the study who knew each other very well, and were similar in their values, qualities of mind, and vocations. Maximal impact on another is more likely to occur when there are uncertainties and differences to which one must learn how to adapt—one reason why parental conflicts with their teenagers can so shake either to discover more mature ways to grow.

Increasing Stabilization

The fourth generic dimension of healthy growth is stabilization. Earl J. McGrath, an educator, says the direction of growth is "toward a provisionally firm set of convictions, an examined philosophy of life . . . [that] structures the purposes and directs the activities of his existence . . . [that] give stability to his being." (1959, p. 6) Every healthy living system must learn how to preserve its essential self while adjusting to life's continuous stresses, like divorce and ill health. Habits can facilitate efficiency and free awareness and energy for new knowledge and skills as well as provide for resiliency to recover from temporary disorganization. A more stable identity, predictable purposes, and enduring relationships describe a mature person.

Model High School's students wrote about this growth this way:

Of mind   11th grade girl: My "mind has matured; I don't get so frustrated as easily when I'm faced with a problem."

Of interpersonal relationships   11th grade girl: "I have met lots of other people and have very strong and special bonds with them."

Of values   9th grade boy: "I am more motivated to learn as opposed to just finishing and turning in work."

Of self   11th grade girl: I "feel special, supported, and celebrated; feel confident about myself and my actions."

Barbara has consistently scored high on cognitive stability. She is an extraordinarily well-organized person able to function at a high level of efficiency in potentially very disruptive situations—even though she was going through an "identity crisis" in her early 40s. Her lowest PSQ score at that time was her disagreement with the item, "My ideas about myself are reasonably stable and don't differ too much from what they were several months ago." Resolution of her vocational conflict and learning from Jim "to relax, take living more calmly, letting things go, and being less compulsive" led to greater self-confidence and certainty about her direction.

Two of Jim's foremost dimensional strengths were his awareness and stability. Like Barbara, he functioned very effectively and predictably in very stressful situations.

Increasing Autonomy

The fifth generic dimension of healthy growth is increasing autonomy. Alfred Whitehead, the philosopher, says the "creative impulse comes from within. The discovery is made by our selves, the discipline is self-discipline, and the fruition is the outcome of our own initiative." (1923, pp.50-51) When we become more stably grounded, we don't hesitate to take bigger, more adventurous steps. We have the confidence to try new things, for we know our strengths and have the resilience to recover from our mistakes. Self-discipline and self-command of one's drives and talents empower mature persons to be agents of their own growth.

Most parents of teenagers in the study wearily acknowledged their children's striving to become more autonomous of their control. The striving for independence showed up in MHS's students' growth these ways:

Of mind   9th grade boy: "Using my mind as tool to do what I want to do; using it to see viewpoints other than my own" [Also Other-centered cognitive growth].

Of interpersonal relationships   11th grade girl: I am "no longer influenced by people who don't care for me."

Of values   11th grade girl: I am "learning more than I have in my entire life. I seem to learn better when working for myself; am more motivated and generally self-directed. Friends and family find me to be a happier person."

Of self   11th grade girl: "I am an individual and my feelings and actions are mine; I know I am special."

Barbara scored highest on autonomy generally and again predictably in her cognitive skills in her 40s, the maturity of which changed only marginally by her 50s. Of her three highest scores on the PSQ, two were about controlling her impulses in her relation with men and women. In the jargon of the psychoanalyst, she is not an id-dominated but an ego-controlled person. Words like "playful, passionate, emotional, and child-like" do not describe her; words like "organized, independent, conscientious, self-commanding, decisive, self-sufficient" do.

Whitehead identifies creativity as a sign of autonomy. [Japanese educators concerned why their students seldom became very creative adults identified their culture's value on conformity to be the principal culprit.] In her 40s, Barbara rated her creativity as less than average, in her 50s as average, and in her 60s, again as less than average. I don't know how to interpret her creativity but surely her colleagues can. She has been a productive researcher for decades and awarded medals for her work. Her colleague rates her above average in creativity. Regardless, Barbara has been on top of her talents and been able to effectively make them work for her for decades—whether creatively or not but certainly productively.

Her children and associates were the principal causes of her increased autonomy. Of her children's effects she said "because they are so strong-willed and are trying to assert their independence. I have to learn how to do that within the confines of our own rules and family goals; I have become much stronger, much more resilient."

"What do you mean by 'stronger'?"

"It takes a lot of self-control and will-power to deal with an adolescent like my oldest daughter when she is upset."

And as a result of managing her associates, she said, "I am learning to be very direct with them in telling them what I expect, what I think, and what my impressions are, and I am learning ways to help them to reach their own potential."

Working for a demanding boss taught her how "to take criticism and stand up for what I think is right, to be assertive."

Barbara's Future Growth

A total self-reported score for maturity combines all of the dimensional or sector maturity scores. Comparing Barbara's total score during her adult years provides a capsule summary of the pattern of her growth. In her 40s, Barbara initially scored slightly below the average of the study's women in maturity, i.e., 284. In her 50s she scored 322, an improvement of 38 points. However, in her 60s, she scored 306, a decline of 16 points, due primarily to reporting her relationships with other women to have become less mature. She believed she seldom had acquired the interests of a close female friend nor done things for a close friend at the expense of her own interests. She did not feel she could be her real self with her friend. How much this change was due to her leadership position or to her own perceived masculinity that might isolate her from more feminine female friends is debatable. But clearly, Barbara lagged in developing as mature relations with women as she had with men. She was selected as an exemplar of growth because her change in maturity from her 40s to her 50s was one of the largest of the group.

Jim reported considerable maturing from his senior year at Haverford to his mid 30s (from 318 to 337 for an improvement of 19 points) but he then stabilized at the same level of maturity to his 60s. Because he scored so high in awareness as a senior, the PSQ provided him little room to score higher.

My summary report to participants about their personalities focused on the strengths that contributed to their productivity. I mentioned results that I felt suggested vulnerabilities that might limit their future healthy growth. We then worked together to explore some of their implications. Barbara's clues suggested she had more growth to work on. Do the following results suggest any clues to where her future growth might lead her?

- She scored at the eighty-second percentile on MMPI's score for dominance—one of the highest scores I have seen for either females or males.
- She rated herself on the Personality Trait Survey (PTS) as very self-reliant, independent, analytical, decisive, self-sufficient and quite assertive, able to defend her beliefs, strong personality, forceful, dominant, aggressive, competitive, and acts as a leader. She did not believe she was soft-spoken, playful, emotional, gentle, feminine, child-like, humorous, or sentimental. She scored 21 points higher on stereotypic masculine than she did on feminine traits. However,

the three persons who knew her most intimately rated her to be more androgynous; her masculinity score was greater than her femininity one by only three points.

- She rated her strongest needs to be widely recognized, to be in the "limelight," to have and exercise power and influence, to be in control as one's own boss, and achieve and succeed in the world. Her weakest needs were to depend emotionally on women and men, have sensual bodily pleasures, to cry when depressed, and be sexually attracted to or demonstratively affectionate with males and females.

- To the Incomplete Sentence (ICS) test she completed the stem, *My mother and I* . . . "did not have enough chance to be together" and *When she thought of her mother* . . . "she missed her."

- To the interview question of whether she had any unfinished business with either parent, she said, "I wish I could have talked to my mother" and she started crying. She then explained,

> Both Jim and I are only children. I was raised in a large, extended Italian family. My mother didn't marry until she was 35; she was proud of her job; a very independent feminist. She was fearful and stifling; I was not allowed to do the normal things that kids could do. I couldn't go to social activities."

- In two of the Rorschach (ROR) cards she could not see the women most people see but saw instead a parfait glass of ice cream and a piece of fried chicken in the same areas.

I have one grand hypothesis with three interrelated sub-hypotheses about Barbara's future growth. Assuming her three judges to be correct, she will begin to fashion a more androgynous self-concept. Her image of herself as stereotypically masculine may be too severe. Though she thinks of herself as compassionate and concerned to nurture the well-being of those who work for her, her strong atypical wish to have another baby suggests to me her suppressed femininity may be speaking more loudly.

She will continue to grow beyond the psychic legacy her independent, achieving, feminist mother left her. Recall that her mother enjoyed her career, married when 35, and had only one child. Barbara began letting her mother go when she married Jim while still in college, had three children, and wanted another. But her Rorschach tells me she is still conflicted about her mother towards whom she may have lingering needs for love, which when frustrated can lead to considerable resentment. Why? You may believe this fanciful, but replacing commonly seen maternal images with food images suggests her oral dependency needs are still festering, that she unconsciously needs to be given love from possibly older maternal persons.

Next, Barbara may begin to reclaim some of her Italian emotional, passionate, sentimental, playful, child-like, and *coloroso* heritage. Has she been too constrained by her rational, disciplined, organized way of life and so needs some freedom to be spontaneous, sensual, impulsive, and sexy?

To continue to grow healthily, she needs to bring into awareness her unconscious wishes and fantasies, experience their passions, and integrate their more primitive, child-like disorganizing emotions with her more rational, controlled, organized self. I have no apprehension she won't be able to control this regression and convert what she experiences from productivity into creativity.

Commentary

What Does the PSQ Predict?

The PSQ had been used in a variety of studies to test if its results are replicable and generalizable across groups that vary in age, culture, social class, and gender. The model of maturing identified the effects of becoming liberally educated at Haverford College from freshman to senior year with three different samples. (1968) Precise replication of and test of the generality of its validity for distinguishing judge-selected well- and poorly-organized young male adults was confirmed with five religious-cultural-class groups, i.e., Protestant and Jewish upper-middle-class Haverfordian students; Catholic urban Italian and lower-social-class rural Sicilian university students; Muslim poor rural eastern Turkish and wealthy western Turkish university students. (1977a) The PSQ predicts similar results for male and female adults as well as for upper class boys and girls. (1995)

The PSQ predicts self- and judge-ratings of both physical and psychological health. Mature men and women have reliably greater self-esteem, are happier and more satisfied with their lives, have greater self-insight, are more able to predict accurately what others think of them, and are more well-integrated.[1] Judges, especially their partners who know them most intimately, describe them as more mature on the Self-Image Questionnaire

(SIQ), whose scales were drawn from the research literature of the time. As chapter 10 will demonstrate, the course of mental health during adulthood, when defined by traditional MMPI and Holt's Rorschach scores, and of maturity, when measured by the PSQ, is remarkably similar. An adult's mental health or maturity is quite stable for thirty years. PSQ scores of men in their 30s predict very reliably their scores when in their 40s and 50s. Women in their 40s will also be similarly mature when they are in their 50s. Though tracking the course of mental health-maturity similarly, the MMPI (including its special scale presumably measuring ego strength) and Robert Holt's Rorschach scores do not predict numerous measures of adult competence, e.g., vocational, marital, sexual, interpersonal competence, as consistently as the PSQ.

The adolescent form of the PSQ was used in an intensive statistical study of the effects of the very wealthy Bloomfield Hills Model High School on the maturing of its students. The results paralleled those of the adult PSQ. Adolescent self-ratings of dimensional maturity reliably predicted a host of other independent types of measures: maturity of values, extra-curricular participation, comfort with close relationships with diverse types of persons, faculty ratings of students' maturity, and self-ratings of independence, adventurousness, and self-acceptance, among numerous other traits. (Heath, 1995)

Why might this substantial pattern of consistent results be the case? Because the model of maturity identifies the principal modes of coping that define the psychoanalytic idea of ego strength. Its dimensions of healthy growth map how the ego develops and the attributes necessary to adapt healthily to our life's tasks. Table 2.1 summarized some of the core coping skills that define ego strength.

Selection of Exemplars of Change

Because the PSQ was given at four different times in the men's adult lives, it is possible to chart different patterns of change from different levels of maturity for the men which the following chapters describe. Reliable PSQ scores for the women were available only for their 40s and 50s. As noted for Barbara and Jim, exemplars of greatest personality change were objectively identified by differences in their PSQ scores between different test administrations. [I again invite you to complete the PSQ in Appendix D-1, if you have not already done so, before reading further.]

Chapter 3

RICH:

BECOMING A HIGHLY ACHIEVING AND RESILIENT WORDSMITH

"I was put on this planet to share my love of language."

Barbara and Jim's marriage and vocational achievements reciprocally supported each other's growth. Rich's did not. His singular achievement of becoming one of the world's foremost wordsmiths occurred in spite of a deteriorating marriage and divorce. He had continued his growth since graduation from college and was about average in his maturity by his 30s. He slipped back in his 40s before bouncing back to exceed his former level of maturity. This chapter seeks to answer the question of why.

Rich stayed with us September 2001 while giving some lectures at Haverford College. Over six feet three inches tall, weighing 240 pounds, he gave me the impression of having grown another half inch since I had interviewed him February 27, 1995 at his wintry New Hampshire home. Though I had shrunk another half inch since that day, he does seem like a really big man, a sturdy, well-coordinated athlete, which he is.

Athletics was one of Rich's important playing fields on which to achieve for much of his adult life. He calls himself "a late bloomer," since he made the college's tennis team when, in the championship tennis world, an aging college junior. He won city and state singles and doubles championships for years. He coached winning tennis, basketball, and debating teams at St. Paul's, an Episcopalian boarding school, where he taught English for twenty-seven years.

But he is much more than an athlete; his life is much bigger than most people's. He has won awards for "best teacher of the year" and articles he has written. He has written hundreds of weekly syndicated columns on language usage which reach a million people every year. He publishes a new book about every year; they add up to more than twenty now and sell hundreds of thousand of copies. His *Anguished English* has sold more than a million copies. One of his favorite student bloopers is a classic:

> Then came the Renaissance when people really felt the value of their human being. It was a time of many great inventions and discoveries. Gutenberg invented the Bible and removable type. Sir Walter Raleigh discovered cigarettes and started smoking. And Sir Francis Drake circumcized [sic] the world with a one hundred foot clipper. (Lederer, 1987, pp. 14–15)

His most recent book, *A Man of My Words* (2003), was selected by three different clubs as their book of the month.

No other person has explored as broad a range of English expressions: puns, paradoxes, letter play, and personal essays, among others. English teachers over whom he towers as one of the most influential in the country use his books. He may be the world's most renowned expert on word usage, one reason he has been usage editor for Random House's unabridged dictionary.

Imagine my surprise when he turned out to be one of the four men who had matured the most from his 40s (fifteenth percentile) to his 50s (seventy-fifth percentile) after having regressed in the level of his maturity from his mid 30s (forty-second percentile) to his 40s. Like Barbara, he has not been selected to feature because of his successes, of which he is rightly proud, but because of what happened to him along the road to their achievement.

Also like Barbara and Jim, he is extraordinarily well-organized and hard-working, even compulsively so. Unlike Barbara, he found his vocational calling during his first years of teaching and has never looked elsewhere. He was easy to work with but I was frustrated by his talking faster than I could type. His departmental chairman and Roy Schafer, a recognized Rorschach diagnostic expert, rated him to be emotionally stable. On the basis of only Rich's first three cards, Schafer presciently wrote, "Tense but controlled adequately, with flexibility—playfulness, enthusiasm, spontaneity. Tenseness not directly connected with aggressive fantasies. He has lots of energy."

Rich has never doubted his vocational identity; he is in charge of his mind which he makes work for him; his energy reserves seem, to his wife, to be inexhaustible . He is outgoing and engaged actively with life, sociable, and a team player. He loves his children, even to having his "lie-ins" at bedtimes when they snuggled into his arms to tell him about their day.

Jewish Heritage

So who is Rich? He was born into a benign and accepting family and did not feel rejected by his parents. He is the last of five children but the first of two divorced parents: an orphaned Jewish father and an immigrant mother whose first language was Yiddish. The father never completed sixth grade. He eventually became a mill agent in a Philadelphia working class neighborhood. He took great pride in his kids' achievements, had a "tremendous temper," was a "real screamer, unfortunately worked too hard, and died with his boots on" when Rich was fourteen. Surprisingly, Rich had less to say about his mother, who never got beyond tenth-grade. She was "helpful and a damn good person," whom he enjoyed, cared for, and felt like a parent to in her old age, though he seldom visited her. Why surprising? Because Rich called himself a "Jewish mother," an identity he, an expert wordsmith, had difficulty putting into words. "I kiss my children a lot and hug them; my wife thinks I baby them." Would another example be his nightly "lie-ins"?

Twenty years later he called himself a "Jewish father," an ethnic Jew who spoke some Yiddish and valued the "Jewish mystique"—but again he had difficulty explaining what he meant. He did say he was not a Jew who follows Jewish rituals. Though he labels himself a non-theistic Unitarian, his humanism draws him to secular Judaism's values, which he again cannot define very clearly—at least to me. I think he finds them resonant with Haverford College's Quaker values to which he has been emotionally committed for decades. The closest he has come to a statement of faith is his belief

> that we basically are protoplasmic machines that wink on and· wink out and I don't think there is anything before and after—but the wink is fantastic because the world and people are very beautiful. All I know is those beautiful things have happened and have been built into my Jewish heritage.

To pin Rich down more concretely, I asked my standard interview question, "What are your strongest convictions that provide you with energy and hope?"

"You make the most that you can out of yourself, especially if it enriches the lives of others," a succinct statement of what he calls his "mission" in life.

Twelve years later I asked the same question. Without hesitation, he replied, "An absolute oneness with what I do in life—creative language play."

His Intellectual History

When I think of the Jewish heritage and mystique, I think of its high value on the cultivation of mind, its scholarly traditions, its two of the most influential minds of the last century: its Einsteins and Freuds. So I was not taken aback when one of Rich's first questions when visiting the college years after graduation was, "What were my SAT scores?"

"A little above average. About 60%." Very low for Haverford students, who typically scored about 90% in Rich's time.

"I thought so. I wrote only three short papers in high school." He was very apprehensive when he first came to Haverford. He had not read the books other students had and talked about in bull sessions in the dorms. His academic preparation at his city high school had not challenged him. At Haverford, he worked very hard to eventually attain a B+ grade average and achieve Phi Beta Kappa. His departmental chairman had rated his determination and emotional stability to be excellent, his intelligence and personality good, and his originality only fair. He wrote,

> He has all his wits about him, a firm mastery of his own abilities and his own time, able to get his clear-headed best into evidence all the way; thorough, conscientious, and lucid. I have never seen him do a bad job, no matter what the pressures of other studies or obligations might be. Lack of any special imaginative flair or distinctive original character in his work.

Functioning at one's best "no matter what the pressures of other studies or obligations might be" is a pithy statement of what I have found transculturally: that one of the best indicators of a person's maturity is cognitive stability and resilience. What does that mean? It means maintaining intellectual efficiency when working with disruptive ideas and recovering it if upset and disorganized by them. We shall see shortly how Rich depended upon this strength when he verged on what he felt was a threatening nervous breakdown.

Rich's intellect has puzzled him for decades. Given parents not formally well-educated, a home not culturally stimulating, a mediocre high school preparation, SAT scores more appropriate for entrance to a good but not outstanding college, how to explain Rich to himself, me, and others? Does his "Jewish mystique" also mean wanting high status as an intellectual? His MMPI score for status was higher than for most of his peers. How does Rich explain his adult achievements: successful college career, acceptance by Harvard into its graduate department in education, popular and international reputation as a linguistic expert, prolific publication activities? He decided in his 30s to put his mind to the most rigorous test of which he was aware to settle his lingering doubts about his intelligence. Could he be admitted to Mensa, the society for intellectually gifted persons? He took its test, scored above 99% on the verbal (of course) and slightly lower on its quantitative test. He is now a member of and columnist for Mensa's national magazine, though he still wanted to know his SAT scores twelve years later.

So how does Rich now explain his achievements?

> First of all they are genetically led. I have an incredible mind for language. I have an absolutely airtight memory for words and jokes. I am an incredible classifier which aids my memory. Once that happens, I have the parallel skill to put them together in ways no one else has. Second, I can relate what is rather abstract, abstruse linguistic material to human beings. All of this would not have given me my career without determination and dedication and a very strong belief in myself.

I would add his high energy, not dampened down or blocked by insurmountable conflicts, unexcelled organizational and self-management skills, much like those of Barbara, and a consuming and driven competitiveness, not tainted by aggressive hostility. They are the fuels for the exploitation of his native linguistic gifts.

Growing Through the 20s into His 30s

The themes of Rich's life emerged very early after graduating from college. In 1962, he met and married his wife, the "most brilliant woman," so he told me several times, he had ever met. Rich also began his teaching career in English at St. Paul's school in New Hampshire. An innovative teacher, who used film and video and later the computer in his classes, and an active school community member, he kept adding and adding more activities to juggle. His wife said, "He really has to be busy all the time." He began riding two horses: His teaching, which also provided the opportunity to collect his students' "bloopers" about which he began writing; and his coaching and personal athletic involvement. Rich published his first article the year he began at St. Paul's. His publishing horse was now out of the gate and has been racing ahead ever since. Age has slowed down his other horse only slightly; he still exercises him, by playing in USTA tennis tournaments.

When asked what were his principal traits during his 20s and 30s that contributed to his success, he replied,

> I'm pretty firm about achieving goals. I'm awfully conscious about how other people react. I'm terribly aware of the impression I'm making. I'm so achievement-oriented and achievement is such an evanescent thing to hold on to. In the instance that I achieve, I'm already thinking of the next thing and this keeps me running. This is a problem that really bothers me. I seem to need challenges almost like a drug. I'm running harder than I like to run.

His wife confirmed this self-diagnosis.

To my question about what period of life was the happiest, he instantly said, "Now." To "Why?" he talked about how he changed into his mid 30s:

> First, a little bit more aware of what's important and what isn't. Perspective. All the cliches. Second, increasing competence that is very important to me. Third, I just feel people respond to me more positively now. I can feel it.

A signal event in his early years at St. Paul's was his "scream fest" with a new head of the school with whom he

> locked horns and came out of it and now I'm kind of the golden boy with him. The screaming rocked the school house. Really. Really yelling, absolutely. At one point I threatened to walk out, right there and that turned it around. I always confront. I really believe in confronta-

tion. I will chase a guy all over school until I can confront
him. If I feel we're not talking, I'll keep saying, "What's
the matter? Why are you pissed off? Are you pissed off"?
If "Yes," then "Damn it, let's talk about it." Fairly aggressive about that. Always works out. It's incredible. I can't
think of a time that it hasn't, not one.

Remember six foot three inch Rich towers over most teenage boys and
his hefty 240 pounds can be quite persuasive.

His Wife's Views of Him

Rich does not view his marriage or himself with quite the same eyes as
his wife. For him, their communication is good. They do a lot together,
including acting (she is an actress). Like him, she's achievement-oriented
and finds people who are not talented to be boring. Rich is intrigued by his
wife's computer-mind. "She does the *New York Times'* crossword puzzle in
twenty minutes, as fast as she can print." She didn't want to work, but if she
did, he would be willing to do the housework, "not so much cleaning but the
child-rearing. I could accept it because I really feel her personhood in her
talents and would like to see her realize them more. We respect each other
as outstanding people."

His wife views him and their marriage with sharper eyes. She began,
"He is so high-pressured himself but doesn't think anything is wrong. He's
very volatile." (Rich says "Loud.") I asked about Rich's tenseness that she
said came out in screaming temper-tantrums, like those of his father. They
happen only within the family, not at school or with the students.

> Some things I do I know annoy him. He hates it when I
> like to sleep. (Rich goes to bed early in the evening; she
> after midnight and then sleeps to mid day.) He gets up
> after eight hours and looks in the mirror and says, "Didn't
> get my eight hours today. I have a tired look" though it
> may be only five minutes less. He has a thing that eight
> hours are essential to sleep.

"You've lived with him for eight years. Have you noticed any changes?"

I put a can of unopened evaporated milk in the refrigerator upside down. He said it should be right side up. I said, "Don't be foolish, who cares? You just can't care so much about such stupid things." He is not like that now which is good because I could not have lived with that. That would have been terrible.

"You say he yells a lot?"

Yes. He would stand at the top of the stairs and scream for the kids to come up. The kids were constantly yelling all the time. I said I couldn't live in a house where there was that much noise all the time. It's very hard for Rich to be calm but he has really tried not to yell. We used to have to fight in a closet when we lived in the dorm with very thin walls. In the closet we whispered. I got terrible headaches. Awful. It was really rotten. Now in our own home it is delightful.

"Anything else you are not too happy about?"

I get perverse and he gets real perverse with me which isn't such a mature attitude but sometimes you have to prove your independence. My trouble and his too. He is extremely dependent on me and on his own family. His parents fought all the time and he was probably very insecure. He asks my opinion on things all the time, which isn't always right. I tell him he should make his own mind up. He doesn't like to do this. He asked me whom he should vote for and I told him he shouldn't be voting. "That's the trouble with this country. People like you who vote the way people tell them to."

"Any other way he has been changing?"

"He constantly worries all the time about what other people are going to think of him. He's now getting enough confidence that he's beginning to think he can make up his mind."

"He's not a hostile person?"

> Oh no. I've never met a person so unhostile. He ought to
> be a little bit more hostile for his own good. He's much
> too trusting. Then he's always disillusioned if anything
> happens although nothing very much does. People trust
> him. He's very gullible. He'll believe almost anything.
> He's getting better about that.

Still wondering about his self-definition as a Jewish mother, I said,
"He fancies himself to be a Jewish mother."

> He is. I tell him this all the time. He nags; he does all
> those things like they do. He worries about everything
> constantly. But he's very supportive that way. He re-
> ally wants me to be doing things. He is constantly telling
> people how marvelous I am, which is a little hard to take
> because it is not always true. He's wonderful that way
> and loves his children. He really does. He likes doing
> things that children do. Enjoys children's games. He
> plays games with the boys in the dormitory. He's always
> talking about sports and hockey with them and inviting
> them for walks. He isn't an adult with them. He tells jokes
> and enjoys being an adolescent.

I then asked, "Where does he get the time to do everything he does?"
"That's it. I don't know. I never met anyone that does more with every
minute of their day. He doesn't let a minute go by that he isn't doing
something."

Before visiting Rich and his wife in their early 30s, I had prepared a written summary of his test findings. Fragments of it were that his vocational
choice integrated very well his values, temperament, and personality. However, since senior year he had become more concerned about affection, love,
security, and issues of dependency and sexuality, with increased potential
for experiencing more anxiety and tension.

Growing from Early 30s to Mid 40s

By his forty-fifth birthday, the direction of Rich's basic personality growth
seemed to be set. Yet, signs indicated that he was on the cusp of change. His
basic identity as a wordsmith was not at question, though he was evolving

away from editing students' compositions to writing his own articles and books full-time. While still a teacher he felt he was outgrowing St. Paul's adolescents to teach a national adult audience by his speeches and writings. As a Jewish mother he would always love and worry about his children. But they were changing; he would have to learn how to let them get out from his immediate control to stand on their own feet. He remained a married man but his commitment was wavering as his wife became an alcoholic.

Evolving Identity

I remain unclear why Rich endured so much pain to get his Ph.D. in linguistics from the University of New Hampshire. He had had wispy dreams of being a university professor but basically he wanted to learn more about English. To fulfill his Jewish heritage? For status? For pride to be the first St. Paul's teacher to get a Ph.D.? He felt himself being drawn into the narrowing scholarly world that had its own expectations of how he was to grow. Its focus could make him increasingly irrelevant to his expanding audience. The Ph.D. route was gut-wrenching. He had to take "bastardly field exams" in American *and* English literature which required that he absorb 300 pages of literature a day for months. Fulfilling his classroom work, writing newspaper columns, coaching, meeting the needs of his family, and keeping to an expanding speaking and writing schedule had its predictable effects: what he called "a near nervous breakdown," perhaps a mid-life crisis in his late 30s?

Rich was only one of two people accepted into the graduate program each year. His identity eventually expanded to be a doctor of philosophy: he was most proud that he had earned his Ph. D.

Expanding Audience

By his early 40s, Rich was answering three or four letters a day from his readers. He was serving as a consultant to a national commission. He was slowly being drawn out of St. Paul's to act on a more public stage, which he loved. Each of the study's participants had rated the strength of eighteen needs and how much they had changed in the past decade. His strongest needs remained to be widely recognized, well-known, in the "limelight," and to achieve, create, accomplish, and succeed in the world. (Already very strong, they became stronger in his 50s such as being autonomous, in control and being one's own boss, having and exercising power and influence, and competing aggressively with men.)

Shortly before he completed his doctorate, he was appointed departmental chairman, the youngest in the history of the school. Many academic departments are not filled with clones of Mr. Chips. They are potential minefields of older, self-protective colleagues and ambitious, competitive younger scholars. With the best of naive intentions, Rich tried to create an egalitarian, democratic, loving, and harmonious department out of crusty individualists. His publicized successes, absences from the campus, and efforts to get his colleagues to rethink what an English Department should be doing must have strained his relationships. His satisfaction with his vocation as a teacher at St. Paul's slipped to below the average for the men in the study. He was most dissatisfied with his collegial relationship with whom he saw little prospect of friendship. Rich received a lot of national adulation but none from within his school. His 20-year love affair with St. Paul's school also slipped. "My feeling is that staying will be tough; the current community is going to be an alien place for me."

He was slowly getting ready for more expansive, greener pastures.

Redefining a Jewish Mother

How does a Jewish mother—in fact, any mother who loves her children—let her children go? Most probably she doesn't, unless her smothering creates so much resentment that her children's rebelliousness becomes too painful to hold on to them any longer. Rich began to define himself as a Jewish father, though what that is I don't know. Make what you will out of Rich's comments about his kids.

"My son had great difficulty here (as a student). I taught him chess and poker; he now blows me away."

"How is he supporting himself?"

"He's nineteen; he sporadically has a job as a poker runner. Poker-playing is a dead end street. Like swimming with neurotic fish, and it is illegal besides. He's most alive when gaming, when he talks about chess and poker."

When visiting us some twenty years later, Rich spontaneously and proudly told us his son and oldest daughter are champion poker players and have won first places in national contests. He thinks of his son as one of the world's best poker players who collected $608,000 in the 2002–2003 world Pokertom.

His daughter "has been the winningest woman ever in the World Series of poker. She makes an excellent living as the featured player at an on-line betting site." In 2004 she became the world poker champion, winning two million dollars.

His youngest daughter is a poet; she has published a book of poems and recently completed a family memoir titled *Poker Face*.

Rich rates his relationship with each of his three children as quite close. He wrote that "I kvell [Yiddish meaning having great pride] for all three of my kids and feel unalloyed delight that they too are doing what they love."

A Wavering Marriage

Rich says he tends to be insensitive to cues others give that something is not right. He was so preoccupied with his career he apparently did not notice his wife becoming alcoholic until his mid to late 40s.

> I felt the black water of depression lapping up at my feet. I could scarcely tie my shoes in the morning. I had a tremendous fear of contact with people. I felt things were falling apart at home. Tremendous fights, terrific disorder in the house, problems with the kids, particularly with my son. My wife and son fight like hell; yell about a lot of things; many of the fights are justified, for he is pretty much withdrawn when home. If he didn't come home for the next five years, my wife would not be upset. I could guarantee that. I am delighted when the kids are here. If we had money, my wife would like to move out of here when the kids are home.

Whether true or not, these and other comments, such as her never kissing the children, must have hurt him more deeply than he has admitted consciously. [When preparing this chapter, I called her. She is proud of her children's accomplishments, works with her son on his business affairs, and visits each several times a year.]

Despite what he called his incipient "nervous breakdown," lapses in memory, and depression, Rich persisted with his athletics, teaching, and writing. He asked his students if they had noticed anything different about him. They said, "No." Maintaining his daily life and efficiency was a truer measure of his mental health than his self-diagnosis of a possible nervous breakdown. A mature person maintains his intellectual efficiency when working with very troubling and threatening personal issues. Less mature persons fall apart.

Rich's feelings toward his wife were changing. "Aside from at times powerful sexual feelings toward my wife, I just don't know how much genuine fuel there is inside the furnace of my body, something I can really feel as when I type those manuscripts."

He tried to spend more time with his wife, to go away together, to bridge the gap between his unrepentant permissiveness and her disciplinarian attitude toward the children, but to little avail. Eventually she recovered with the help of a detoxification center and as of my interview was completely alcohol-free. He had gone to Al-Anon and accepted that he had been a co-facilitator of her alcoholism, though again I remain unclear how he had changed his behavior—if at all.

Growing from Mid 40s into His 60s

Three growth-enhancing events occurred as he approached his fiftieth birthday: his divorce from his wife, remarriage, and his departure, though not without some nostalgia, from St. Paul's school.

His Divorce

The stresses of living with an alcoholic for seven years told on his marriage. Rich had always been irritated that his wife's brilliance was left fallow; they disagreed continually about how to rear the children; she never liked St. Paul's, his love. They both agreed they had married too young and it was time to separate as friends with an equitable financial settlement. She "went off with a fellow actor; she invited me to go with them." He declined the offer. They remain good friends without the irritations.

Remarriage

When speaking at a Mensa meeting (the society for intellectually gifted persons), he noticed an attractive woman in the audience. On a return visit, he saw her again and introduced himself. They subsequently married and had been married nine years prior to my next visit. They are soul-mates.

> The two of us are an incredible power as a couple. She makes me feel great. We are two hearts beating beat to beat. This is the one. Physically we smell right. Our religious, political, philosophical goals match and yet we are different.

And to "What has been the best thing about your relation with your wife since our last visit?" he answered, "Wonderful closeness with another human, that wonderful balance between independence and altruism."

Separation from St. Paul's School

His frequent absences and annual 100 profitable speaking engagements raised the issue of what was he doing for the school. "I realize these church-boarding schools rely on a monastic commitment and lifestyle. Would I be writing wonderful things or be wandering around the countryside with seven kids in tennis shorts for another decade?" He had started performing in a two-act play which he had written and given at the school. Few students or faculty came. At other comparable private schools, the entire school turned out to see it. The St. Paul's creative writing club never asked him to speak to it. Rich got the message; he left, I think with regret, and has never been asked since to return to speak to or work with the school or department. But the neglect hurts. So he created his own thriving consultant business.

Every person had been asked during each interview to give five one or two word associations to each major period in life as fast as he could. In his mid 50s, he replied to "Late middle age approaching eligibility for social security," with "Where I am now. Best time of life, growth, excitement, joy, and some bodily slowing down." Retrospectively when 65, he rated this period in his life to be the happiest. He described it as "productive, learning fulfilled, respected, loved, and good second marriage."

Understanding Rich's Maturity

Rich's PSQ scores of maturity spark a troubling question and interpretive uncertainty. When in his mid 40s, Rich ranked 15% within the group in his maturity. He matured rapidly in his 50s to reach 75%. I was surprised and puzzled trying to understand Rich's unusually low self-rated maturity in his 40s. Barbara has shown us that exceptional success and productivity do not always imply mental health or maturity. Is Rich providing us the same lesson? Given his achievements by his 40s, why did he describe himself to be so much less mature than others much less accomplished? Both Barbara and Rich are compulsively driven to achieve. Rich calls himself a "compulsively creative" person. Are they holding themselves to too high and unhealthy expectations of perfection and so are overly sensitive to their failures to reach them?

Or could the PSQ be a less valid measure of maturity for such perfectionists? Chapter 2 reviewed the consistent evidence, replicated in numerous groups of academically achieving young men. It is a valid predictor of maturity and adult effectiveness, however one wants to define either. Might a closer analysis of its results enrich our understanding of Rich? Recall he completed the PSQ after several years of severe stress and depression through his late 30s and early 40s. The MMPI suggests that he may be subject to manic-depressive swings in mood which, while not of pathological scope, could lead him to exaggerate his emotional state. Signs of a manic personality are an exceptional but compulsive productivity driven by high energy that needs multiple outlets such as those Rich had created for his. Some clinicians believe such furious activity when turned outward protects a person from, in Rich's words, the "black waters of depression lapping at my feet."

I compared the PSQ items on which he changed most from his 30s to his 40s for clues to why he had rated himself as so immature. A recurrent theme was his increased immaturity in his relationships with women, probably reflecting his deteriorating relationship with his wife. His least mature score in his 40s was his lack of autonomy from others' influence; that suggests a low sense of self and of self-confidence. Sensitivity to other's opinions, persistent efforts to create a good impression, and valuing harmonious relationships may be offshoots of uncertainty about one's acceptability. He showed greatest growth in his 50s by disagreeing with items like, "What I think of myself is easily influenced by what my friends and family tell me." However, by his mid 60s he had not been able to sustain that growth in autonomy. He reverted to his former sensitivity to others' opinions and acceptance by others.

Causes of Rich's Maturing

Rich selected the most influential contributors to his growth into his 40s to have been his first wife, graduate school, and type of occupation. Conflictual as was his relation with his wife and as painful was his graduate school experience, he described their effects as primarily maturing. What he did not select to have changed him were his children. Many fathers did. Did his rigid permissiveness protect him from conflict with his children and so from their potential spur to him to change?

His Brilliant First Wife

> She does have different views about discipline with the children. She does take a harder line that has rubbed off on my behavior. I do look now for a little more structure with the kids over the years. I am less amorphous about that [Awareness values]. And the wisdom she has passed on about controlling other people. I try to control others less [Autonomy relations]. I try to be more sensitive to others, which is a function of her sensitivity. How well I get along with her affects more how I get along with others [Awareness but Immature Autonomy relations]. I've learned from her that I'm less convinced that what I do is out of sheer altruism. She says there is a payoff for every thing and that may be true. An emotional payoff that is not meant to be selfish, but a payoff [Awareness self, values].

Type of Occupation

> I define myself by what I do. As a teacher that is my main professional identity here.[Stabilization self]. I define myself less in terms of my profession now in what I would like to think is a healthy way. I don't feel I have to spend every minute at the occupation [Autonomy self]. I feel I have a greater depth and understanding of students, but am not sure that is due to my occupation or age [Awareness relations].

Rich continued:

> I am less obviously innovative in my methods and am more concerned with depth [Integration cognitive]. On the other hand in the past ten years I have been into media and computers, which is innovative [Integration cognitive]. Much more concerned with the reading process. I have been at it for twenty-one years, so you begin to become a bit of a gray eminence [Awareness cognitive; Stability self]. More and more I want to be the best teacher around. I have published a lot. I want to be a great English teacher [Stability values].

Graduate Doctoral Program

> Really professionalized that great romance I had with language for my whole life so that has become a really dominant mode in the way I look at life and organize my perceptions [Integration cognitive]. Has made me aware of language [Awareness cognitive]. Here are these noises we are making and suddenly I hear them in a different way. It changed what I do in the classroom that is my life. I look at literature much more in terms of language now [Autonomy cognitive]. It is the image of a computer card. It showed me how much I loved language and that I could really handle it [Awareness self]; it gave me additional self-confidence of what I can do [Stability self]; it gave me a tool to share with others. I was really needy of that. It has led to all this other stuff in the community. I just feel more valuable throughout [Other-centered self].

Why did Rich show such great resilience to bounce back from his low point to 75% within the group in his late 40s and 50s? My hunch is that his manic type of personality, supported by the companionship of mutuality with his second wife, as well as continued career recognition, were driving the equilibration.

Rich had a heart attack in his late 50s. Though it was apparently not incapacitating, he now rates his physical health to be good, not excellent. Like others in the study he has begun to feel tired more frequently and put on more weight; he has more back trouble and reduced sexual desires. Vocationally he is very satisfied except with the demands of his career on his time and with his income though he is well-off financially. Ideally, he would like to work half-time. He is extremely happy with his marriage and generally very satisfied.

What Insights Does Rich's Life Show Us about Healthy Growth?

Driving ambition to succeed, when too single-minded, unbalances a person's healthy growth and can undermine maturing in other sectors of one's life.

Commitment to a transcendent calling provides a bulwark against potential vocational collapse.

Control of one's mind when reinforced by a calling or vocational commitment is a cardinal strength of mature persons.

When supported by a mutually fulfilling relationship, resilience can lead to resumed and even greater healthy growth.

Dedication to the growth of others, as in teaching and parenting, is both a cause and result of maturity.

High achievement is not equivalent to exceptional mental health though mental health may contribute to some types of achievement.

Commentaries

Two themes, important to Rich, provide an illuminating perspective to the results of the entire group: SAT test scores and the importance of fatherhood to a man's maturing. When adult, his exceptionally high verbal and quantitative scores opened Mensa's doors.

SAT Scores

Rich's life-long preoccupation with his SAT scores, parents' anxiety about their children's SAT scores, and American obsession with them as a marker of a school's quality should be moderated by what SAT scores predict.

Research on adult competence and mental health suggest that students, especially males, who have high SAT scores, may be vulnerable to failure as an effective adult unless they have developed the character attributes now known to contribute to success.

After citing anecdotal evidence I briefly summarize what I discovered about the vulnerabilities of highly talented young men. [I limit my comments to men for I had no access to the women's college files.]

Some Anecdotal Evidence

The chief justice of one state's supreme court wrote me that the courts' judges had become very discontent with the quality of lawyers appearing before them. They had crafted a resolution urging law schools to place less emphasis on the law aptitude test and more on selecting for "strength of will and character." He asked me how to do this.

Deans of a premier research-oriented engineering school believed their talented students would fall apart when they graduated from their protected environment. "They know nothing about people. They don't even know that the opposite sex exists."

For decades medical schools have selected for high intellectual talent. Thoughtful voices question whether academically talented persons turn out to be good healers and ethical people. One prestigious university's medical school's students have been called "sociopathic zombies"; its bright young doctors refuse to work in poor urban and rural areas to "repay" taxpayers for supporting them in medical school.

And then there is Enronitis which shows us how damaging psychopathic, highly talented persons can be to the integrity of business and Wall Street.

Some Research Results

Longitudinal studies are essential to assess fairly how people turn out and to identify the causes of their success.

I have found that when compared to less verbally gifted boys more gifted ones' Verbal SAT scores reliably predicted Terman IQ scores thirty years later. However, as adults verbally gifted boys were

  * less mature, e.g., lower self-esteem, less well-integrated and accurate self-concepts, less empathic, and felt not well understood by persons they were closest to.

- more interpersonally immature, e.g., judged by colleagues to be more distant and tense.

High quantitatively gifted adolescents also shared similar attributes thirty years later. They were also

- more inhibited about talking openly and frankly about their feelings, had fewer warm and intimate relationships, and did not feel understood by others.
- judged by their peers to have less integrity.

I have summarized elsewhere (1994a) other researchers' studies that support these findings. Statistical generalizations report only what may be probable, not what is certain. My study had some exceptionally high-scoring adolescents who turned out to be exemplary adults of interpersonal and ethical maturity.

Rich's insensitivity to his wife's emotional state, low self-confidence and need for others' approval are a few of the signs of the potential limitations of his high verbal talent.

Importance of Children to Paternal Maturing

Rich early defined himself as a Jewish mother but later as a Jewish father. His wife confirmed his love for and playfulness with his kids. In his 30s he selected his children and role as a father to rank fourth in importance in affecting his maturing. As they became teenagers and adults, he felt they had become friends with "whom I talk pretty intimately and share values and stories with." They also opened his eyes to alternative life styles to give him a "sense of the sweep of life" and how "you can't control others with any great significance."

How important were the men's children and their role as fathers to their growth? How did their children affect their healthy growth? (Heath, 1978b)

Regardless of how I defined "importance," e.g., frequency of selecting a parenting determinant in the interview as highly influential, fatherhood was moderately important but not a salient or decisive cause of the men's maturing for the majority. The non-influenced fathers (who selected no parenting determinant) were more maladjusted, rated themselves to have matured less since college, and had less mature self-concepts than fathers who had been influenced.

Maturing Effects of Fatherhood

Are fathers more mentally healthy than non-fathers, as Erik Erikson had proposed? He claimed that fatherhood contributed to the resolution of the generativity stage of adult development and so to continued mental health. Generativity means caring and accepting responsibility for the growth of increasingly different persons. Comparing the study's fathers to the non-fathers showed they had not differed in mental health when in college but they did in their 30s. The fathers were reliably more mature and competent on 11% of the personality measures. They were also more physically as well as psychologically healthy, well-adapted vocationally, more satisfied with their marriages, and enjoyed sexual relations more. So Erikson's claim that fatherhood may enhance maturing receives some support. He may have misjudged its relative contribution to continued maturing, however. Chapter 1's commentary reported that the personality of one's partner and type of occupation are more important to highly-achieving professional men like the ones I studied.

Fatherhood does not affect cognitive and non-familial maturing. It can cause increased awareness, other-centeredness, and integration, but not autonomy. The men's children furthered the maturing of the men's selves, values, and relationships. (Heath, 1978b)

The fathers' vivid, even eloquent, and insightful comments show how influential fatherhood can be for some men. (I list its effects in order of their decreasing influence.)

Increased Awareness

Effects on Self   "I've considered myself a very unflappable placid person who is difficult to rile or get to. I found that is not true. They can get to me."

"Being a father made me aware of the strength and almost primitive nature of feelings that I had not really expressed before but I can express with children—feelings like anger and resentment." [Amen!]

Effects on Values   "It's damn hard to explain to a child why what I say or what society dictates is right or wrong."

"I'm far more conservative in sexual mores with my daughter. You feel protective."

Effects on Personal Relations   "In my son's case, the things I want him desperately to do, he tends not to enjoy. The things he wants to do and gets out and does are the things he enjoys doing. Suddenly the reasons for rules and regulations become clearer."

"If I crack down too hard and am too strict or expect too much of them, I can see them withdrawing. I am then able to modify my ideas about child-rearing."

Increased Other-Centeredness

Effects on Values   "The feeling that you have toward a helpless baby and later growing child of enormous protectiveness and affection and love and wanting to shield and insure happiness for her can't help but make you feel a little better and more home-conscious and less pleasure-oriented too."

"I'm concerned for people other than myself. You become oblivious to your self. For the first time in your life, your self really drops out of your own thinking."

Effects on Personal Relations   "He has taught me that because he is tiny, little, and inexperienced does not mean that he is stupid or insensitive. Brought a greater sense of empathy and sympathy for him."

Increased Integration

Effects on Self   "I can be more emotional and more loving too. It is very easy for me to express love now and I don't think I could have done that four or five years ago."

"Makes me feel very proud of myself that I can handle all of this. I feel very self-reliant, capable. I feel almost as though I can handle anything if I can handle this."

Effects on Personal Relations   "I have had to take children into consideration. I am more objective, realistic, and sensitive to whatever the circumstances are. I have had to think of others as opposed to just of myself."

"I'm able to accept people for what they are."

Effects on Values   "I have become more conservative politically because I am looking out for him more in the future. If I don't do something about it now, if I don't pay attention now, I am not helping him in his future."

"I'm learning a lot about my own power plays [Awareness self]. He is teaching me how important it is to keep a flow of caring and compassion going even under the most trying circumstances."

The fathers' comments confirmed that the model of maturing compre-
hended the principal effects of paternal parenting. As I found when studying
the effects of college on students' maturation, most reported growths could
be mapped into the model.

Chapter 4

BUCK:

GROWING BEYOND DENIAL ON THE WAY TO WHOLENESS

"I don't like to think about unpleasant things so
I push them out of my mind."

Buck was only one of two men who continued to mature consistently from his early 20s to his 60s in spite of four severe catastrophes: By 1977, Buck's engineering corporation which he had built closed down; his respected father had died several years earlier; his wife had divorced him; and he had been diagnosed with diabetes, a sentence, in those days, of approaching handicaps. Why did he mature more than every other man between his early 30s and mid 60s? Note the slow evolution of a stronger integrated self as he faced the consequences of the catastrophes. The commentary examines the relation of ethical virtue—Buck's honesty and integrity, his most enduring adult traits—to maturity, success, and repressed femininity in masculine males like him.

I had not seen Buck, now 32, for eleven years. When we met at the airport prior to his catastrophes, I immediately recognized him, even though he was much heavier, wore dark glasses to protect his contact lens from the Arizona dust, and dressed in a non-matching worn coat with his tie askew. I had not recalled him as being reserved and taciturn but after we got to his country club for dinner he became more his familiar friendly self. I had always enjoyed Buck but occasionally found his deliberateness in responding to be off-putting. On the way to the motel where he had reserved a room for me, we went by way of his unpretentious factory, a long large metal building along a railroad siding. As we walked through it, I noticed he did not greet or speak to any of his men.

Buck has always been cooperative, sensitive to my reactions, dependent upon me to keep the conversation going and interviews on track. Though he said he enjoyed the interviews he had difficulty identifying and reflecting about the effects of the causes of the changes he selected to be most influential.

Family History

Buck cared for his parents to whom he was attached and whom he respected. He kept in touch with each once or twice a week as long as they lived. He never felt they rejected him nor let him down. His childhood familial environment ranked eighteenth (fairly high) among the men's families in possessing the attributes that research had found were favorable to a child's maturing: loving parents respectful of their child's individuality with firm expectations of how he was to grow.

Like most of the study's men, Buck felt emotionally closer to his mother than to his father. She was an affectionate, emotionally expressive friend with whom he enjoyed being; he would be very willing to assume responsibility for her if she ever became ill. From both parents, but particularly his mother, he got a "feeling of a family, a relationship that is incredibly strong," one reason he persisted in trying to keep his own family together during his marital difficulties.

Buck's belief that he was more similar to his father than to his mother may have contributed to feeling his father understood him better. His father was also a successful manager of a manufacturing company. To the incomplete sentence stem, *Remembering his father* he replied, "I still am in awe of his accomplishments." His influence lingered on after his death, particularly affecting Buck's financial attitudes. More than his mother, his father had excellent health, was energetic, socially out-going, ethically concerned, open to new ideas, and, like most other fathers of the men, not self-disclosing nor as emotionally expressive as the men's mothers.

Though Buck did well in public school and participated in its activities, his parents agreed he should go to a prestigious boarding "academic machine," in Buck's words. He felt his high school years were

> tough; I worked hard and yet didn't feel like I learned anything. I felt I was dumb. I should have been a little older. The way they had the curriculum cranked up I needed more maturity to get something out of it. If I had been more mature, I would probably have told them to jump in the lake.

Peeved by an obnoxious roommate, one freezing winter night he locked him out on their room's balcony, only to be discovered by a passing dean. Required psychiatric treatment did not lead to remorse.

Buck fell far below his academic potential. He consistently scored in the bright normal intellectual range; his SAT scores met Haverford's requirements; his quantitative scholastic aptitude was 99%. Despite ranking 220 out of his private school's graduating class of 235, he had learned more than his class rank suggested, and what he thought. He scored above 85% of high school juniors nationally on English, advanced math, and physics achievement tests. His counselor identified his principal traits to be a lack of pretense, personal dignity, self-depreciation, unteachableness, English papers characterized by a sense of realism, and then an unspecified "devastating conflict within him." What tipped the admission department's scales were not his aptitude and achievement scores, so he told me, but his father's friendship with its director—an example of his self-depreciation persisting into his 60s?

At Haverford he also did not live up to his potential. He did solid B work in his engineering courses, but failed a physics course. He graduated with a C average. His high school's academic demands had been so rigorous that when he encountered the college's, he was so "wrung out" he was only ready to enjoy the college's freedom and have fun [unspecified!]. The engineering department rated his intelligence and emotional stability to be good, personality excellent, his determination fair, but his originality poor. Ironically Buck turned out to be a creative engineer who has secured several patents.

Buck was selected by members of the administration and his peers as an exemplar of poor personality organization. He had achieved some notoriety by getting into an argument with a maid and submitting to the administration a photograph of dirt in his room after she had cleaned it. The college records indicate the picture showed much too much dirt to have come from one room. He made maids "nervous" and was tagged as a chronic complainer. Roy Schafer also classified him as poorly organized from his Rorschach. Buck's images were blandly and seemingly benign: However, images like bugs underneath butterflies, masks, traps which "if you got in there you wouldn't be able to get out," entangling spider webs, even dirt suggested to Schafer suspicious tendencies which the maids surely would have agreed to and which his freshman MMPI also suggested.

Vocational History

Buck had known what his career was to be long before college. His father had encouraged his mechanical talents and interest in electronics that eventually led to his participation in the emerging computer revolution. His temperamental identification with his father probably shaped his vocational inclinations. As a 17-year-old, his character was similar to successful managers of production, personnel, and credit, public administrators, scientific farmers, senior CPAs, aviators, and engineers. When seen in his early 30s, his interests had become more focused and applied. His temperament and interests at that time were most similar to more masculine, professional, scientifically and technically trained persons working within organizational or bureaucratic, authority-structured occupations.

After graduating as an engineer, he married, had two children, and went to Harvard's Business School where he did not do well enough to be invited back. When I asked him in his early 30s what his greatest accomplishments had been of which he was most proud, he immediately answered "building a house" which he enjoyed doing after his Harvard experience.

> It was a tremendous experience; I learned a great deal about my own interests, my perseverance. I did all of the electrical work, plumbing, heating, most of the dry walls. We sold the house for a substantial profit. The people who are living there now are very happy which is another way of being satisfied, if someone likes what you have done.

Building the house also taught him how much he enjoyed

> creating and bringing something into being that wasn't before. I have a very strong urge to do this. I am constantly developing or getting ready to develop a new product. I can control the actual effort but I can't control

> my urge to create. I see new products all the time. That's
> the way it is.

So much for his engineering faculty's rating of poor in originality.

By now, Buck had developed the confidence, perseverance, and creative urge to manage his own manufacturing company, which by the time I visited him had twenty-three workers. His company served the needs of the area's farmers, selling them thousands of sprinkling systems that he had designed and redesigned until they functioned reliably. "We had a series of frustrations that literally drove everyone out of their minds. Yet we kept pushing. I felt like I wasn't easily defeated by failures. I didn't consider them as failures but as development problems."

The reputation of the company's products for reliability, endurance, and service led to their distribution nationally and internationally. To take care of his expanding customer base, Buck became a pilot to fly to where he was needed. The company was turning its inventory over fourteen times a year. Raw materials occasionally remained in the factory less than twenty-four hours. And he kept designing other products, like rear bumpers for trucks and parts for all-terrain vehicles. His business consumed his energy with predictable effects upon his marriage.

He had rated himself as not very happy because he was worried about the economic direction of the country and its effects on his company. His company used a great deal of brass and stainless steel; he bought 30% of it from Japan because of its higher quality. Though his was one of the larger companies in the town dependent on bank loans, financing for purchasing his raw materials had become worrisome. Prompt payment by customers had become an irritating problem for him to deal with.

> I was completely unprepared from my personal experi-
> ence with the premise that people will deliberately
> attempt not to pay their bills. I've had to cope with this
> ever since I started this company. It's an idea and a phi-
> losophy that is completely foreign to my background. I
> was unprepared and still find it extremely difficult to dun
> a customer, to call him up and ask why in hell he hasn't
> sent the damn money to us.

Buck recognized that people-problems were the bane of his presidency and that as a manager he was not always skilled in working with them effectively. He believed he was not sensitive to the needs of others or responded as a leader should. When problems arose, as when two employees could not work well with each other, he preferred to close his eyes and let them work it out on their own. On the other hand, he dealt more decisively when ethical issues arose. He had consistently rated his honesty and integrity to be among his most distinctive traits for each of the four decades that he had described himself. To the incomplete sentence, "I value most," he wrote, "honesty and integrity." When he discovered two of his employees charging for their services, which he had been paying them to provide, he fired them immediately.

Despite the recognition and prestige of being a president of a company he had created in his town, Buck was dissatisfied with his vocation. He ranked 20% in satisfaction among the study's men. His colleague agreed that he was not well-adapted to his vocation; his scores about Buck ranked him similarly. I was perplexed. Why was he so dissatisfied? His paternal history and identification, similarity to successful men in applied occupations, and educational history pointed to his current occupation. Uncertain about the reliability of Buck's scores, I examined why his colleague rated his vocational adaptation as he had. Unexpectedly, he was neither "very" nor "quite" satisfied with how well Buck was adapting to his work. Of the eight attributes of work his colleague was "somewhat" dissatisfied with, several puzzled me even more: fulfillment of his responsibilities, temperamental suitability for his work, and degree of personal involvement and dedication to his work. I had no clue about how to resolve my puzzlement.

However, Buck's vocational story does not end here. Not until I interviewed his wife twelve years later did I learn why his colleague rated him as he did.

I asked my standard interview question, "To feel you have lived fully, what changes would you have to make now for the next ten years?" Not surprisingly Buck replied,

> To feel that way in ten years I would have to devote a great deal more time to my family. I don't really see my kids except in passing on the weekends. I should spend less time at work and more time playing.

He said nothing about his wife.

Causes of Maturing from Graduation to His Mid 30s

Understandably Buck's dedication to his company left little space in his life for other events to affect him. His constant lament was that he had not been prepared to be a manager. He had no doubts about his technical proficiency; he had many about his people-skills. His type of occupation, occupational way of life, and occupational demands to play a role provoked him to change. His company provided him the means "to do what he wanted to do," which was to design and improve new products [Integration cognitive]. He "does not dread going to work now" for creating is "really fun" [Integration self]. Because his occupation's way of life required him to make decisions about other people, he became more aware of and responsible to them [Awareness relations; Autonomy self]. His role as a president "thrust me into the outside business community" and its customs against "which I rebelled inwardly and occasionally outwardly. I delight in wearing work clothes" [Autonomy self].

Fragments of Report of Tests about Growth Since Graduation

The psychological tests confirmed that Buck had changed since entering college but they also raised questions about how accurately he knew himself and how well integrated he was. He had become much more focused in his interests, which could make him highly effective. But if he encounters disappointment or crises he might not have strong secondary alternatives. I noted:

- he had improved in taking different perspectives toward a problem, so he has the flexibility of mind to create alternative creative options.
- he no longer seems to feel trapped, caught, not fully in control of himself, powerless, as he seemed to feel when a junior in college.
- he has been developing strong intellectual, analytic efforts to master himself and his emotions but such focusing may be inhibiting his feelings, so he might well feel emotionally dead at times or much less passionate than he knows he could be. Such inhibition could limit his empathy for others.

I concluded that "I do not see him so locked into his patterns that there isn't movement or change. He is open to growing and may be aware of this movement himself."

Growth from Buck's Early 30s to His Retirement

Buck's catastrophes had all come to a head four years prior to my visit in
his early 40s. The rate of his maturing had steadily increased with no further
disruptions or retreats; so I take a broader view of his growth from his 30s to
his 60s. His pre-visit questionnaire alerted me to the four catastrophes that
had befallen him in his late 30s.

He was waiting for me at the airline gate when I arrived. He had lost
about thirty pounds as a result of efforts to deal with his diabetes. He looked
gaunt. His hair had noticeably thinned and grayed. His face had aged to
make him look older than 43. His manner was similar to my previous
visit: initially diffident, impersonal, and matter-of-fact, then friendly,
always cooperative, and generous in making living and meal arrangements.
We worked until midnight, began early the next morning, and worked until
my afternoon flight.

Vocational Catastrophe and Recovery

Escalating oil and natural gas prices had done him and his customers in.
Farmers had switched to dry land crops so did not need irrigation equipment. He blames himself for failing to anticipate earlier the economic
effects of the oil crisis and alter his product line. He wondered if his marital
problems had so upset him that he hadn't thought clearly about his options.

I asked, "What choices might you have made differently?"

> We really weren't doing that badly in comparison to other
> businesses. Our performance was quite good. We were in
> a miserable market and just assumed the whole thing was
> worthless and maybe I had thrown out the baby with the
> wash. If I had had more confidence in my ability when
> we had shut down, we could have gone off in a different
> direction. Out of this I learned I had some good people
> working for me, far better than I thought at the time. I
> really feel I didn't give them enough opportunity to show
> what they had.

Though he had closed the factory, he himself continued to repair and
replace parts when customers requested his help.

He began to think that he was not made to be a president but someone who created visions and strategic action plans.

> I might have been more comfortable if I had been in charge of the technical part of the company creating new products. I should have left management to those who really enjoy doing all of the things managers must do with undercapitalized small companies dealing with people who don't want to pay their bills.

He succinctly described his business philosophy, illustrating his commitment to excellence:

> Whenever I have gone back to my core beliefs I've done well. I've always believed in delivering more than I was asked. I've found customers have been very supportive in giving me more things to do or paying me more in some cases, even overpaying me. They felt they were getting more than what they paid for . And I landed up becoming friends with most of my former customers.

Closing his factory was one of the straws that bent his will. He retreated from the community where he had had economic clout, been on several community boards, and had the reputation of making things happen, "not just wishing them to happen." For three years he was in a "slump" and began to reemerge when approached to become a partner in the creation of a foundry which two years later went bankrupt because of under-capitalization.

Buck's knowledge of computers led to consulting jobs in the late 80s and 90s. He joined another manufacturing company's technical division where he created two processes, which he patented. For example, he created a knife for sawing very cold objects without heating up and shattering. He has now retired though still dreams of other projects he might design.

Marital Catastrophe

Buck had married Anne, a Mount Holyoke graduate, after his graduation and remained married for seventeen years. Anne was the only child of a successful executive whose early death had left her a small trust fund but its income would not support extravagant expenses. When asked what were the best things about his marriage, he spontaneously said she "is a social animal, a fantastic social asset. She meets people beautifully, she's exciting, vivacious, fun to be around, fun to be with."

My next question, "What is not quite so good about your marriage?" tapped into a continuing complaint about money and sex.

"She spends money on things she doesn't need. I told her you can wear a dress more than one time. If she bought a dress that she absolutely didn't need, I have in the past made her take it back. She sends them back, pouts, and then accepts it."

"Anything else?" I asked.

"I'd like my wife to be sexier. More responsive as she was earlier." She agrees but she doesn't know why or says she doesn't."

According to Buck, for their first six years of marriage they had had sex two to three times a week but after that less than once a week. Anne has a different memory. By his 40s he still got great enjoyment from sex and wished they could return to the frequency of their first six years. But he sensed there was more going on than he knew for a fact. I asked him to identify the six most important attributes of a sexually fulfilling relationship and then rate how much he and Anne showed each. He felt he was very honest in their relationship; his wife was not honest at all. Similarly, he rated himself to be quite spontaneous, open, and considerate; his wife somewhat open but not at all spontaneous and considerate. They also differed in their attitudes about sexual fidelity. He believed it to be very important that each of them should be 100% sexually faithful; he believed she didn't believe this at all. While he had been occasionally unfaithful, he felt she had been quite frequently unfaithful.

Buck, as was his way of dealing with a potential conflict, "looked the other way" to pretend his suspicions were not true. He was getting angrier until he no longer could ignore his hurt. The telephone company forced him to act. It called to ask when was he going to pay his huge phone bill. He asked for a copy. Someone had made numerous calls to Reno; he had made none. Tracking down to whom the calls had been made led to a close older friend of his who had moved away several months earlier. Inquiries at the airport confirmed that his wife, known to the agents, had frequently flown to Reno.

Buck belatedly said he should have probably done something sooner and gone ahead to get a divorce. "It was a ridiculous struggle to keep it going. I was just unable to recognize the problem. I assumed her interest and goals were the same as mine. That was not right. I was very much mistaken."

Interview with Anne

Buck had given me permission to see Anne and to share anything we had talked about. Anne told me I could tell him anything except about her and "the man in Reno;" she referred to "the man" throughout the long interview. In thirty-six pages she colorfully illuminated what Buck had failed to describe, though what was true for her may not have been true for him.

To my question why she married Buck, she replied that he had all of the qualities one would want: tall, physically well-built, handsome, great mind, good sense of humor, aggressive, but, resignedly, "not real sensitive but one can't have everything." She bemoaned that he was not demonstrative or out-going; he would go wild if she kissed him in public. But with children he was fantastic. "I wish he would treat me like he treats our own daughter. He hugs her and picks her up; very tender which is really adorable." Buck is inhibited about saying nice things about Anne who has to "dig and dig" to discover what he thinks about her. She learns what he thinks from other people to whom he has spoken.

Primed to talk about sex, Anne began within ten minutes to contrast their feelings about sex.

> I'm basically an animal with a terribly strong sexual drive.
> Though tender, loving, and gentle, Buck is not passionate
> or exciting any more. It is no longer exciting to see this
> man on the "john" and the same man around every day. It
> is different and exciting with somebody else.

Because Buck was so uptight she couldn't tell him how he could perform better. She said she had an Electra complex, being attracted to older fatherly men and Buck was not fatherly. Nor is she motherly, not like Buck's mother to whom he is attached. Pregnant by the second month of their marriage, she was not as sexually interested as he might have expected. "The first two years I was not too great. Then we got to the third year and by this time we were so far apart, not only sexually but every other way. You see how it just went down hill." Buck's single-minded focus on the factory left her alone and frustrated.

"How would you want Buck to have been different?"

> "Make him more an animal, more demonstrative, less
> disorderly, more dependable. He was not with me when
> I went into labor; he was selling a sprinkler to a farmer.
> Make me feel more safe with him."

I asked, "I don't understand. More safe?"

Apparently, he had become increasingly more suspicious about where she was going at night, accusing her of having "hot pants" for the man she was bedding, which was true but she wasn't going to confirm that. One night when she came home late from a friend's house, he demanded she tell him where she had been. Buck had a Puritan view of women as delicate. She provoked him by telling him, "rip my clothes off" which she knew he never would. But he did beat her, which became the ostensible cause for her suit to divorce him. He didn't want a divorce. She knew that by his frantic reaction to her fake suicide attempt swallowing sleeping pills. It was the only time Buck had lost his cool, which persuaded her he could feel intensely about her.

The other reason Anne decided to divorce Buck had also not been mentioned by him. In her words, "I live with this brain who does nothing but stay in bed and then play cards all evening." He would rise late in the morning, go to the factory from noon until two in the afternoon, then go to his club where he gambled with older men for hours. When first married, she resented that he would leave her alone, especially as she got pregnant one month after their marriage, to gamble on the weekends. He apparently won more than he lost.

Another unexpected bombshell was that his father owned the business and had had his first heart attack while building the factory. She said he had run out of money and had to take in partners to get the funds. Buck agreed to run the factory, which he felt obligated to do for his father. Anne praised him for how hard he had worked.

> He does everything for his father; he is going to do what
> his father says all the way because that's the way he is.
> Actually I would like to have a son like him. I wouldn't
> do what he does for my family. I'm too selfish. Of course,
> it is coming to him as their only child; maybe that is why
> he is doing it.

Though Buck's father had died shortly before his divorce, he had never talked about it with me. As he had said, "I don't like to think about unpleasant things so I push them out of my mind." Had his three-year "slump," triggered by the precipitous closing of the factory and divorce, also been a delayed reaction to his failure to mourn his father's death? As close as he had been to his father, why had he not selected his death to be a more important influence than only one of the twenty possible causes of changes in his values that he had selected? He had selected his divorce to be the most important cause of his change in his values and view of self. Failure to mourn can cause persistent unhealthy physical and emotional effects long after the loss or death of a loved one.

Anne's comments about Buck's gambling, paternal backing of the company, his reduced involvement in his company, and precipitous closing of the factory answered but had not eliminated my puzzlement about his low vocational satisfaction. Despite his varied vocational experiences ranging from managing to consulting to working in a company's technical division, Buck had never ranked his vocational satisfaction above 20% from his 30s to his 60s. His satisfaction did increase 22% from his mid 50s as he approached retirement though he ranked near the bottom of the group in his overall satisfaction with his work. Buck's colleague agreed about his dissatisfaction, especially with the way he met his responsibilities and degree of his personal involvement. He questioned Buck's temperamental compatibility with his position as manager. Was Buck's gambling signaling his disenchantment with his vocation? Was closing the factory an unconscious way to break his close tie to his father to strike out on his own?

The relative stability of Buck's dissatisfaction during his varied working years suggests that his level of satisfaction was more a function of his character than of his type of occupation. The supporting evidence? Recall his school said he was a "complainer." Buck expects excellence of others, even maids, and more tellingly of himself. His MMPI suggests he is a depressive personality who tends to see the glass half-empty rather than half-full. He rated himself consistently to be more pessimistic than optimistic, not emotional or cheerful. Of the 112 ratings he made of his vocational adaptation over forty years or of the 230 ratings of his personality over thirty years, he rated only three percent as very satisfying or positive. Does describing himself negatively come more "naturally" than rating himself positively?

Marital Recovery

Eight years after his divorce, Buck married Alice, a divorcee with two children. For the first time in the years I have known him he rated himself and relationships very positively. He is extremely happy. They almost always agree about their goals, values, and how they make major decisions.

"Why do you rate yourself to be very highly satisfied and fulfilled with Alice?"

> I feel loved but I'm not sure why. [That persistent self-depreciation!] We seem to enjoy lots of the same things. I was pretty self-sufficient the last time we talked. She has lulled me into being totally dependent on her. She is such a wonderful person in every respect. We are partners. She is a communicator. She has accepted my limitations. Just been supportive in every way.

Buck is correct. When first married to Alice the strength of his emotional dependence on her was non-existent. In his 50s and 60s, being taken care of by her was his strongest need and the one need that had strengthened the most, probably because of his increasingly poor health.

The effects of diabetes complicated their sexual relationship. Though impotence is one of its most reliable effects, he has found ways to "convey my feelings of love and respect. I am perhaps more sensitive than I ever was. Maybe that is not going to be enough but I can talk about almost anything with her."

In his 60s, he feels very comfortable talking with her about every interpersonal topic except his dreams, socially unacceptable desires, failures, and greatest insecurities about which he is only slightly less comfortable sharing.

Because she is so accepting, Buck can volunteer "I am very comfortable with her because when I am with her I am with me." Does this succinct perceptive comment tell us that Buck himself had become more self-acceptant and so a more integrated and whole and mature person?

Health Catastrophe and His Future

Diagnosis of diabetes from an insurance examination in his late 30s had caused an undercurrent of worry ever since. When I saw him in his early 40s he felt his physical health was good, in his 50s fair, and since that visit, poor.

He consistently has occasionally felt more blue each visit. He progressively finds he can't concentrate as well and has less stamina and sexual desire. Since other non-diabetic men report similar changes, physiological aging may be aggravating diabetes' effects. Buck tells me persons with diabetes can not get a pilot license according to FAA rules. He had hoped that Alice would get her pilot's license. She demurred. He no longer plays tennis though he is not clear how to separate out the progressive effects of diabetes from those of aging.

Buck is now apprehensive about the loss of his peripheral vision and other visual complications that might lead to progressive blindness in one or both eyes. He now must limit his driving. Alice drives him in the evening. Also he has abandoned his favorite hobby of fly-fishing. He ranked fly-fishing in all of the major trout streams of the world as his seventh most important wish for retirement. He rated the probability of achieving that wish as low; he can no longer hold his own when fishing with a friend. He can't spot a fish and cast with his former precise visual-motor coordination.

His most recent worry is his diagnosis of a progressive neuromuscular disease that results in a loss of skeletal muscle control. It eventually leads to a permanent vegetative state requiring assistance with all motor activities.

Understandably, he now rates his emotional health to be poor. Though happily married, he is quite dissatisfied with his life and is not too happy. He is beginning to face his mortality rather than avoid it as he did in his 50s. In his 40s he said he would dread being told he had one more year to live. In his 50s, he would accept death. He completed the incomplete sentence stem, *Death* . . . "is now much closer." To understand his intuition about how close his death might be, he rated the age when he felt each of thirty typical events might occur, such as premature loss of job, serious illness of a child, enduring handicap. He believed 44% of the possible events would occur between 60 and 64, the latter his current age. He expected that assuming more community responsibility and discovering faith and the meaning of life would occur before his 75th birthday. (His felt limit of his probable mortality?)

Causes of Buck's Increasing Maturity

When assessing his growth from graduation as a senior to his mid 30s I had predicted he would be open to continued growth. Buck's four catastrophes cascaded over him in his late 30s making him exceptionally vulnerable to change—but in what direction and how? When I returned home from my visit to him in his mid 40s, I summarized my observations and intuitions about my visit: His problem is that he is not very reflective so his awareness of himself may be somewhat inaccurate. I thought he might benefit from counseling or some intimate type of discussion. He is eager to explore a deeper relation. I felt quite moved to see his growth. I told him how fond I was of him and said he had my strong vote of confidence in him and his future.

He was unable to respond.

When visiting him in his 50s, I felt he was "more alive and glowing than I remembered him." As always, he was courteous and cooperative; "more able to reflect about how he had been changing." He continued to take every opportunity to move away from himself personally to talk about his interests: contribution of carbon dioxide to the greenhouse effect, his project to improve the efficiency of making dry ice, his stock market coups that had made him quite wealthy. I summarized my impressions afterwards: Insightful and when pushed was even illuminating. He was quite high. A very different manner than twelve years ago. A lot of vitality though he says he can't sustain activities. However, his wife has to call him to remind him to come home at nights because he is so consumed by his work.

Of the greater variety of determinants of his maturing into his 50s, interpersonal ones associated with his divorce rather than occupational ones had more maturing effects: divorce, personality of his ex-wife, and children.

Divorce

Buck's divorce had many disruptive effects; yet, any disruption of long established patterns of values and relationships provides the opportunity for new growth, as occurred for each man. For Buck, his divorce showed him that he

> was no better or worse than a lot of people which made it easier to understand how people can get themselves into a mess. [Awareness relations and self]. It certainly made me less critical, more tolerant of other people's problems [Other-centered values]. I get along better with people, this sensitivity, this shared experience [Other-centered relations].

Personality of Anne

> She caused me to reexamine a lot of values [Awareness values] and made me make a major attempt to understand why she did what she did. She didn't turn out to be the kind of person I had thought. She didn't need much sexual attention and to discover her fairly wide range of sexual activities really surprised me [Awareness relations]. It caused me to reexamine my own values about what two people might choose to do [Awareness values].

Children

Buck provided a consistent set of values so his children knew where he stood. [Stability values]. He has learned "about how they face their problems and tried to solve them" [Awareness relations] and so became more understanding and acceptant, even tolerant [Other-centered relations]. He had been shocked to discover that his daughter was not like boys. He never learned how to anticipate when she might react. "Her mood changes were illogical to me. I didn't know how to react" [Immature integration relations].

Extracts of Test Findings of Changes Between His 30s and 40s

Interpretation of Buck's changes from his 30s to his 40s challenged me. [I had not given him the Rorschach nor prepared a summary analysis for my visit in his 50s.] Though he reported consistent maturing on his PSQ, he also reported increased pathology on his MMPI which was not confirmed by his Rorschach. MMPI's items more transparently describe negative attributes and symptoms. A self-denigrating person can secure unhealthy scores due more to his character than to some active, underlying unhealthy process. So I gave greater weight to his PSQ and Rorschach than to the MMPI changes, a judgment supported by a subsequent healthier MMPI pattern of scores thirteen years later.

There has been an almost dramatic maturation since some time prior to his mid 40s. He is certainly a stronger and less vulnerable person now than his view of himself seems to suggest. Still may be locked into some old views of himself as not being worthy and of being overly self-critical. The opening to this growth has been a growing acceptance of a more feminine, warmer, emotional side of himself that has resulted in a firmer sense of self-esteem, a growing sense of personality integration that may not yet be a part of his self-concept. He may find this growth occurring in his relations with men with whom he may feel more at home. He is much freer of former limiting, even paralyzing, inhibitions so I expect he will continue his growth. He has the emotional resilience to withstand temporary defeats and a drive to press ahead is now emerging. Only now he may be at the threshold of his talents—including interpersonal—that he always had but which have been screwed up by cutting himself off from his warmer emotional side. There is too much life and vitality in him at the moment to allow more conscious dismal views of himself and his future to undermine their evolving realization.

[Until I finished writing this chapter, I had not made the connection between these comments and his TAT story to a blank card in my last visit to him in 1996.]

> The picture is of two men doing what we are now doing. One of them is really enjoying it. Perhaps for the first time ever in his life he is enjoying doing this. I guess I am looking at myself. I seem to find it more and more intriguing what I want to find out about myself. In some ways I was afraid to find out. Now it is me and I can't do anything about it and I might as well. I think you are enjoying it too. So it is kind of a happy picture. And I guess you are probably going to stay after and be here in ten years. You can't quit now.

What to Learn from Buck's Story

Maturing can continue throughout middle age.

A happy and favorable growing-up environment does not guarantee continued maturing.

Denial blocks awareness of pain that potentially could initiate more healthy growth.

Reflection about self and relationships is essential for continued healthy growth.

Self-acceptance of positive strengths is not easily earned when what to accept contradicts a long-held socially reinforced idea of what a man should be.

For a man, fashioning an integrative and stable vocational identity is critical for his healthy growth.

Companionable and mutually non-defensive marriages are a major condition for and impetus to continued maturation during middle age.

Commentary

Like the majority of men in the study, Buck, while raised an Episcopalian, and accompanying his wife to their Baptist church, did not think of himself as religious. Also like most of the men, he thought of himself as an ethical person. He consistently rated honesty and integrity to be his most prominent traits. He struggled much of his adult life not to be honest about himself—even his strengths. He also had avoided, denied, and repressed what was unpleasant. To spontaneously admit, "I was afraid to find out," be "intrigued" about how to discover himself, to accept what he hadn't wanted to face as "me," to enjoy the process, and to feel "happy" sharing with me told me how mature he was becoming.

Table 2.1 identified the core ethical values I believe describe a mature person: honesty, compassion, integrity, commitment, and courage. Every major religion values such cardinal virtues though one does not have to be religious in its conventional sense to be virtuous.

What is the character of ethical men and women? Are they in fact more mature than less ethical persons? (Heath, 1994b)

Character of Ethical Persons

Virtuous men and women are indeed more successful, happier, healthier, and more mature than unethical ones. Unquestionably, old-fashioned virtue does pay off in most of the good things of life, such as marital happiness, parental fulfillment, sexual competence, and, for men, vocational satisfaction—but not higher income.

Also, more ethical people do differ from less ethical ones in their character. They are more cheerful, optimistic, decisive, energetic, and reliable.[1] Their peers believe they also are sympathetic, tender, open, and loyal. They seek out new experiences and willingly take risks to continue growing.

And finally, it may be easier for more feminine men and women than masculine ones to be virtuous because virtue is rooted in interpersonal strengths more typical of feminine than masculine persons. This controversial but important generalization must be examined more carefully.

Ethical Behavior and Gender

What attributes define a masculine person? A feminine person? The men's and women's partners, closest friends, and colleagues rated them on the PTS. It included twenty traits other researchers had found described masculinity and twenty femininity. (Bem, 1974) The men were reliably rated to differ from the women on eight of the masculinity traits, e.g., analytic, independent, dominant, aggressive; the women differed from the men on ten of the femininity traits, e.g., sympathetic, sensitive to other's needs, understanding, eager to soothe hurt feelings. Neither gender was rated to score higher on the opposite sex's stereotypic traits than the gender's sex itself.

Though women are rated on an ethical index, defined by its core traits of honesty, etc., to be more ethical than men, it is not their gender but their femininity that predicts their ethical behavior. Similarly, it is men's femininity that is associated with their judged ethical behavior. Of course, women and men have both masculine and feminine traits to different degrees. The androgynous person has more of each on which to rely while adapting.

These ethical and gender differences have been traced back to thousands of public and independent middle and high school students. To be ethical, males must be androgynous. Females don't need to be androgynous to be ethical since masculine strengths are irrelevant to being ethical. Given the more sharply constricted American meaning of maleness than of femaleness, typical masculine boys may be less educable than girls for moral education. (Heath, 1999b)

Buck's temperament, reflected in his occupational preferences, was consistently masculine. He and judges rated him to be at the fifth percentile in femininity but 35 points higher in masculinity—one of the largest differences among the men in their 40s. The equilibrating principle suggests if Buck had matured the discrepancy would become much less, which by his 60s had dwindled to only three points. Though he and his judges consistently rated him high in honesty and integrity, they did not agree about his other ethical traits. His judges believed he was very compassionate and courageous; he didn't. Was his self-depreciation getting in the way of accurately understanding himself again? Significantly, the themes of his changes were increasing awareness, other-centeredness, and integration of himself, values, and relationships—the ground out of which ethical sensitivity grows. What was Buck afraid to discover about himself? What many masculine males in American society are afraid of: their repressed "feminine" emotional compassion unreflectively defended against by a rigid masculine persona to others and to themselves?

Chapter 5

⸺⊷◉⊶⸺

Susan:

Mothering a Great Santini's Three Sons

"I have no desire to prove I can do everything—
to be a super woman."

Susan is an example of many women dominated by oppressive husbands who stifle their healthy growth—often unknowingly and unintentionally. This chapter describes how both women and men unconsciously have been programmed to act in culturally approved stereotypic ways that block the healthy growth of each or both. Her renewed growth came as a consequence of counseling and her divorce. The commentary examines the maturing effects of a woman's stereotypic maternal role.

⸺⊷◉⊶⸺

This book features those who changed the most on the PSQ. Among the women, Susan had grown the most from her early 40s into her mid 50s and then into her 60s. Her scores on the PSQ portrayed her as more immature than any other woman in her early 40s; she had cried during much of our interview. However, she had matured on the PSQ by 45%, more than any other person, woman or man, by her 60s. She bubbled with joy when I called her a model of change. She is a healthy and sane example of many women in the study who liberated themselves during the heyday of the women's lib movement.

  She warned me upon my arrival in January 1983 at their ranch house that she had been unable to complete the questionnaire. It was too emotionally upsetting to describe her sixteen years of marriage to Alan. She had married him immediately after graduating from Goucher College.

82

"I may break down unable to continue," she said. We were not strangers; I had interviewed her about her marriage with Alan twelve years earlier during Time 3. She is a warm, expressive, open, and emotional middle-aged woman whose short black hair was streaked with gray. Both she and Alan had agreed to a "sexual moratorium" until my visit. Isolated and lonely due to frequent airforce moves, she claimed she had not talked with anyone about their marriage. Both seemed to expect the marriage would continue. Alan was willing to have no sex to remain married. Given his highly visible position as a colonel in the airforce, it was a matter of pride that his men not know of his marital and sexual troubles. So Alan had refused to talk about them with counselors but was as eager as she to talk about his troubles with me. We had been friends since his sophomore year. The interviews went much longer than planned. I remained an additional day to be with them.

Susan's Family Background

Susan gave no hint that she was estranged from her own parents whom she loved, really cared for, felt independent of, and equal to. Her mother had a "breakdown" into depression and was hospitalized when she was in high school; she attached herself to another "mother" while her own recovered. Both parents supported her, giving her freedom to make her own decisions, which she in retrospect believed had been too much. Her mother had allowed her to fly to Las Vegas to visit a boy friend that developed into a "situation that scared me." Like many women in the study, she wished she had been closer to her parents, especially her mother. To the Incomplete Sentence stem, *My mother and I*, she wrote in her 40s, "have a warm and friendly relationship" and in her 50s, "are closer now than we've ever been." To, *When she thought of her mother, she* wrote in her 40s, "wished she'd had a happier life" and in her 50s, "hoped she'd grow old just like her." However, when Susan was in her early 60s, she altered this description of her feelings about her mother. She had wished that her mother had been more affectionate and caring. Near the end of her mother's life, Susan had confronted her about her regrets. They became reconciled.

Susan knew she was her father's favorite. To, *My father*, she wrote in her 40s, "was warm and understanding—only to his children" and in her 50s, "was special to me and I wish he could see me happier now."

She raised her boys the way she was raised: treated them fairly, listened to and respected their opinions, responded differently to their individual needs, and demonstratively gave them a great deal of affection—all values that proved to be aggravating sources of conflict between her and Alan.

Two themes capture many of the changes she underwent in maturing from her 40s to her 50s: her relationships with her sons and her liberation from what she felt to be an oppressive husband. Since our beliefs define reality for us, I focus on her reality, not Alan's.

Child-Rearing Conflicts

As military families know, their futures are not fully their own to make decisions about. Alan and Susan had moved eight times by their mid 40s; Alan had assignments ranging from two to thirty months abroad. Susan was essentially a single parent much of the children's growing-up years. By carefully managing Alan's salary, she got by. But unlike other military wives she persisted in believing she should, and wanted to, stay home to take care of her three boys, each born within two to three years of each other. Alan wanted her to get a job to support the family—a continuing aggravation between them. Susan stubbornly resisted. "My kids come home with the most god-awful ideas of what they are going to do, where they are going to go." Perhaps recalling her experience with a too permissive mother, she said:

> I need to be around now more than when they were younger. They are not bad kids. There are too many kids who come home to empty houses but end up in wrong places. Alan thinks I should lay down the law, tell them what to do and what not to do, rely on them to use their best judgment, and punish them if they do wrong. I don't see it as that simple. They don't have the experience to use that judgment well.

She continued:

> I told Alan I feel like I am the family and he is the guest that comes to visit now and then. He is always busy. He has his projects. He does not participate in routine functions of the household. I fear this will not change if I get a job and I have no desire to prove I can do everything, to be a super woman.

"What are some of these routine functions?"

> If he would check on lights at night that would be great;
> but he falls asleep. When boys are out at night, he goes
> to sleep and I have to stay up. He feels it isn't necessary.
> The oldest is only fifteen. I did tell him if garbage has to
> go out, if he sees it at the top of the steps, he should take it
> down. He was very upset one morning when in uniform,
> and said he wouldn't take it down. I have told him to
> participate in the dirty side.

She told the story of Alan leaving one morning and then rushing back to demand she tell him where his wallet was. After all, she is responsible for the household and should know where everything is.

As trivial as such incidents are, I thought Susan cited them as examples of a basic male attitude of what the role of men and women have always been and should be. Fathers should be stern; mothers nurturers of all their children (even big ones!). Reflecting how she was raised she said that Alan

> is too hard, expects too much of the boys. I also don't think
> he knows their different personalities as well as I do. What
> will upset one of them won't upset another. I don't think
> they need to be treated with kid gloves but their differences
> in sensitivity need to be recognized [A theme my wife has
> reminded me of more than once.]

In spite of these gloomy examples, Alan enjoyed his relations with the boys and their friends. He and Susan volunteered to be cub-scout leaders. She appreciated that he assumed this responsibility for raising her boys. Alan was the only father willing to take his den camping and on nearby trips. Other boys started to leave their own dens to join his. When Alan moved to the next station, his den collapsed. No other adults were willing to become leaders. She continued:

> We are good parents together. Always backed each other
> up. Very good team. I have the patience and compassion
> and he has the expectations and energy and enthusiasm.
> A good father has to engender a little fear. He might just
> come over and let them have it. He commands a lot of
> respect. When he says something they do it on the double.

The first one who is in trouble gets to me first, and then
tells Alan. We complement each other very well.

Twelve years later she rated she had been highly satisfied and fulfilled
as a parent, but not "very" highly satisfied. The boys were now in their 20s.
They lived nearby. Two were married. They had a "great sense of fairness"
and were very ethical. She felt they dealt with her as an adult; their relations
with their father were more deferential, even apprehensive. Her identity as a
mother who was 90% responsible for raising her children was shaken by her
youngest son's flight from home the week of his senior year's final exams.

"Shaken" is my interpretation inferred from how long and detailed she
talked about the incident. She introduced the story by saying, "I relied too
much on fate as I listened to other parents' horror stories." Walt had left in
the middle of the night with no warning at the urging of his girl who had
planned to run away from a difficult home situation. Susan and Alan heard
nothing for a week. In the months that followed they heard every two weeks
by way of a postcard with no return address. Walt and his girl had rented
an apartment, gotten jobs, and stayed away from their parental homes for
months. Finally, the two fathers found their children, who refused to return
home. Walt's girl, bored, soon tired of their adventure and returned. Walt
felt his "fate had been sealed" and refused to return. Later he was convinced
by the mother of a friend of his to return. The school made adjustments so
he could graduate.

Walt never explained why he left. Susan thought he had been the only
son who had stood up to Alan. He had refused to continue being a football
hero and go out for the team in his junior year. "I suspect he was afraid his
father would kill him." His older brother asked how did he ever get away
with what he did. Walt's stubbornness and self-assertion later were tested
when the airforce released him from active duty because of the occurrence
of asthma. Walt was indignant. He had had an exceptional record and had
been promoted to be responsible for training other airmen. His appeal to be
reinstated was turned down by several airforce boards. As was his right, he
appealed to the Secretary of the Airforce who ordered him to be reinstated
to his former position.

How did her wayward son turn out as an adult, the ultimate test for Susan
of how well she had done? He's married and working. But she said, "Walt is
still trying to please his dad. His wife told him he is trying to show his dad

he can do it." When Susan left Alan, who took the divorce very hard, Walt "went to him to hold his hand and tried to get him to talk about it. He drags his dad away from his work to go golfing with him." The fruits of patience may ripen very slowly.

The study's men and women spontaneously and most frequently cited patience to be necessary when rearing a child. Susan identified "ability to listen, consistency, sense of humor, firmness, and patience" in that order as the five most important. She rated herself to have considerable patience, Alan none.

"In what ways have you been a good parent?"

> I accepted the kids as small human beings with their own lives to lead and was just there to guide and direct and instill some sense of what the world is all about and how to make your way in it. They always discussed problems with me. They'd say, "Don't tell dad." I would keep on that child's back until he did tell dad. We discussed how to work our way around the problem, what price to be paid, and what would be the consequence.

To a question about her feelings about death, she said, "I'm an acceptor of fate. When raising three kids you have to be. I was the one who said you could go skydiving to one of them. He then said, 'Here you are trying to get me killed.'" [Shades of her mother's permissiveness?]

A Troubled Marriage

Alan? "A good parent, yes, with some flaws. As a friend for me, he isn't. As sexual partner we have entirely different ideas about sex." She, along with six others of the forty women, rated her marriage as fairly unhappy. On a questionnaire, assessing marital adjustment, she ranked fourth from the bottom among the women. Most of the time she regrets she married Alan; we "get on each other's nerves." They almost always disagree about their leisure time and sexual relations. "I've discovered to my horror that I am much happier when he is on assignment away from home than when he is here and I made the mistake of telling him. I am more comfortable when he is out of town for three or four days."

"What was his reaction?" I asked.

"His usual reaction is silence."

Their frequent moves didn't help.

> We live in two different worlds that barely meet any
> more; he doesn't take the time to know me. He is one of
> those who doesn't really enjoy women, who are uncom-
> fortable with the other sex. He really feels that what he is
> interested in is what I should be interested in. He has his
> hobbies and expects me to spend some time working with
> him on them. He sees things as right and wrong, black
> and white, and I can see six sides to every story.

She shares her refrain with most women in the study: their husbands'
inability or reluctance to communicate their feelings. "I see no emotion in
him, except anger. I don't get angry, I simmer for a long while. He explodes
on every occasion and gets it out of his system. I can't handle it. He gets
angry at very simple things. I fall apart."

Sexual Incompatibility

It is in bed that Susan's frustration found its most intense voice. She believes
they are not well-mated sexually at all. She is not sexually attracted to Alan,
finds sex boring, would prefer to have had sex no more than once or twice
in the past three years, and has had no sexual desire in the previous nine
months. She is unsure that she has ever experienced an orgasm. Susan has
tried to avoid sex by going to sleep before he comes to bed. Her menstrual
periods were becoming irregular in her early 40s but she had not yet had hot
flashes or other signs of an approaching menopause that might account for
her lack of libido. She never had any menopausal symptoms. A doctor she
had consulted about feeling stressed said she had completed menopause.

What troubled her most was that she "craved affection" but Alan was
rough, not affectionate, and showed no tenderness toward her. He is uncomfortable just holding her hand, though he is very affectionate with his boys.

> I sometimes think sex is a physical activity to keep him
> in shape. He sees no reason if I am mad at him why we
> can't participate in sex. For Alan, love is sex and love is
> therefore intercourse. He needs more sex than I want. He
> thinks I must be masturbating the whole time. That is not

true. I feel intense guilt because we have so little sex. I am
disappointed in myself but I feel relieved that we have put
the whole issue aside. Alan startled me. He believes our
marriage is a lot more positive than our sex relations and
ability to communicate. We can survive without those.

Three episodes suggest Susan was more sexually responsive than she
realized about herself. The first happened when her oldest boy claimed she
acted seductively toward his friends and asked her to stop it.

The second episode occurred while a scorekeeper for a boy's baseball
team; she was attracted to a 15-year-old heavy hitter. They visited each
other's homes, could "communicate without saying anything" and start a
conversation in "mid air." She was puzzled by her feelings about which she
felt a little guilty. Since she was moving to another base in a few months,
she was not concerned that she might "make a big fool" of herself.

The third episode was potentially more serious. When she began to work
at the officer's club, she was attracted to a young man who worked in the
kitchen. He was a "sad sack," ignored by his family and lived by himself
like a hermit. They talked about sports.

> I pushed too hard to become friends. He left his job
> and wrote a letter to his boss charging me with sexual
> harassment. I was totally floored; we had never even
> touched each other, but because everyone knew him to
> be strange, the charge was dropped. Alan knew about it
> and was very comforting for the first time and supported
> me all the way.

So her responsive potential was there; it just needed to be released from
Alan's controlling oppression.

As her children began to leave home, Susan realized she needed to
search for activities to keep her busy. Participation in a singing group and as
a receptionist were enough to forestall a depression. She entered counseling
which eventually led to her divorce. She very happily remarried several
years later. She discovered she was not frigid, as Alan had charged and she
had believed. That she is "sexually arousing to someone else came as a great
amazement, a great miracle."

Causes of Her Maturing

Counseling

The psychologist made me focus on myself [Awareness self]. I knew I had to please myself, but I didn't make that a priority. She brought that into the forefront as something I needed to focus on [Awareness and Integration values]. She suggested separating myself from the family for several months "to have a chance to be with myself and put my priorities up front. What kind of needs did I have that weren't being met? Could I meet them within my present relationship?" I explained to Alan that I didn't want it to be permanent. She recommended I go to a public place where it would be safer in case he got very angry. I did and never have been so scared in my life [Autonomy self]. He didn't say a word for two weeks; perfectly civil; never said a word in the car. Alan refused to talk with the counselor.

Divorce

A lot of freedom to be myself [Integration self]. I didn't know what myself really was until I divorced Alan [Awareness self]. I was doing a lot of things because they were expected of me because I was trying to please my partner [Immature Autonomy self; Other-centered values]. I could come up with a long list of things I didn't want to do but couldn't come up with a list of what I wanted to do. I'm more open and friendlier than I used to be [Integration self; Other-centered relations]. If I were with a group of women I'd make sharp remarks that would come out unbidden. I'd make end runs around subjects. Am now much happier to go into a group of people. It is easier to find something to say [Integration relations]. I value honesty a lot more [Awareness values]. I wish I had been honest with myself and with Alan. If my kids have a problem with their wives, I'm telling them to get it out.

Remarriage

> Gave me confidence I can make reasonable decisions
> [Stability self]. Allows me to live my own life [Autonomy
> self]. Have learned I must be an individual before you
> both bend to a partnership [Autonomy self; Integration
> relations]. Have to have your own life outside of marriage
> [Autonomy relations].

"Doug, I wake up every morning feeling joyful."

She later told me that after her divorce, Alan continued to try to control her, telling her not to participate further in the study. They remain distant friends to talk about their boys.

Maturing from Her Mid 50s into Her Early 60s

Susan continued her maturing and by 61 was the most mature person in the study. She feels more resilient, especially in not allowing arguments with either male or female friends to disrupt her relationships; she also has become more independent of lingering child and adolescent trials.

I could find no persisting dark clouds in her life since her divorce and remarriage whether in her health, community activities, friendships, or familial relationships. She now had a very sunny life. Her physical and emotional health remain excellent. She keeps physically active by joining a gym, exercises an hour three to four times a week. She does not smoke and often drinks only wine. Like others of this age, she feels occasionally tired, struggles with her weight, and has reduced sexual desires after an uneventful menopause. Increasingly she feels her feet tingle and become numb and her hands cold, probably enough to make her dream of becoming a snowbird, spending winters in warmer climates and taking cruises.

Susan continues singing in a chorale group and summer musical theater and is more active in her Episcopal church. She continues to be quite content with her job, works full-time as a manager, earning $52,000 a year. She expected to fully retire by 70 though she wouldn't mind working only 50% of the time, if she were financially secure.

She has several female friends to whom she feels quite close; she is satisfied that her friendships match her desires for the ideal relationships. She is extremely happy with her marriage; though quite a good partner to her husband, she feels she is not as good a sexual partner. Like Barbara, and others you will meet shortly, she does not enjoy marital sex as much and as frequently as her husband. Her history of sexual attraction to other males may be repeating itself and cause her some future troubles. Unlike other women she has developed a close friendship with another man but does not feel comfortable talking to him about her attraction. Fantasies of having a "romantic fling" ranked sixth of her ten most wished-for daydreams; she has no expectation the "fling" could happen. Given Susan's strong identity as a mother and family person, she might find such a "fling" to be too severely troubling for her to allow it to happen.

Being a good parent and grandparent has always been Susan's highest value. She is proud that her children, even Walt, now in their 30s, are in managerial positions. She values Walt's optimism. Despite "many setbacks, and his "deep love" for his children, she worries he "will settle for work beneath his capabilities." She also worries about her other sons finding their own niches, staying where they are too long and not pushing themselves, being happy and "able to love again."

I had asked each person, if they wished, to share "any words of wisdom about growing healthily through adulthood." What had Susan learned from her continued maturing?

> Growing up can be a crisis period in everyone's life and growing up (maturing) does not always occur at a particular point in a timeline. Speaking for women in general, we seem to look for a partner long before we have completed our growing up and thereby generally end up crippling ourselves, and hurting any more personal growth in the process.
>
> While it would be wonderful if we could continue growing while connected to a partner, it doesn't seem to happen that way. And what growing or changing does occur is often in a negative way.
>
> Women and men must determine who they are, and find an independence, a balance point, before they can share a part of themselves with someone else.
>
> It just took fifty years out of my life to realize this!

What Lessons to Draw from Susan's Story?

Deeply engrained gender roles can suppress healthy growth for men as well as women.

A visible sign of maturity is joy to be alive.

Parental attitudes most conducive to children's healthy growth are love, respect for a child's individuality, and firm expectations.

Differences in affectionate and sexual needs not discussed can lead to a dead marriage.

Don't let unhappiness go unspoken in a relationship.

Commentary

Not surprisingly, motherhood and children were more central to women's identity than fatherhood was to men's. Chapter 1's commentary shows that the demands of being a mother for women in their late 30s ranked second in their influence and in their late 40s ranked ninth; interestingly children ranked eighth in influence but twelve years later, second. Why this reversal in influence? Babies and young children can of course be stubborn, even defiant, but they still need maternal nurturing and mothers still have control. According to the study's mothers, modern teenagers, especially their daughters, are another problem altogether. They can be distressingly confrontational, not just irritatingly argumentative but also physically testing their escalating independence. Barbara suffered her daughter's merciless criticisms and sought counseling; Chapter 9's Elise sent her rebellious daughter away to a boarding school. Susan's son ran away from home with his girl friend to try living like an adult.

Like fatherhood, motherhood furthered the awareness and other-centeredness of the women's selves, familial relationships, and values. Their children had marked maturing effects on their minds, an effect not cited by the fathers. Motherhood's effects were more instrumental, managing, and teaching; fatherhood's were more emotional and expressive. Note the difference in tone between chapter 3's fathers and this chapter's mothers' descriptions of the effects of being a parent. I list them in declining order of frequency of citation.

Maturing Effects of Motherhood

Increased Awareness

Effects on Self   "I have learned that I can be easily frustrated. Taught me to relax, that life is not as difficult as I have tried to make it. I have learned I can handle kids. I don't have to wait for daddy to come home but I can make decisions. It is good to feel that way."

"I was much less patient than I had known before and they brought out all my vices."

Effects on Values   "Because we have three female children I have to be very clear about what being a woman means to me and not expect them to accept that as their total picture but to give them something against which to work. They may make other choices. That is fine."

"Having children has changed my values. Generally, I am very liberal about them, like drugs, alcohol, abortion for other people but not for them."

Effects on Personal Relations   "Parenting teaches you to live intimately with other people. Taught me something about respect, privacy, communication, sharing, listening, and patience. All these skills that I was learning as I was raising children are part of other relationships that I've made."

Effects on Mind   "I have had to constantly assess what my effect is on my children and what I can do. I can't simply react. I have to understand, reassess, and talk with other people."

"I need to really know what the hell I am talking about to communicate with an adolescent. One really needs to know the subject because the children by adolescence are so sharp they will pick up any loose pieces, any weak points."

Increased Other-Centeredness

Effects on Self   "I have become less self-centered."

"Makes me feel very proud of myself that I can handle all of this. I feel very self-reliant, capable. I feel almost as though I can handle anything if I can handle this." [Stepmother of two adolescents, mother of one child, and a baby on the way.]

Effects on Personal Relations   "I have had to take children into consideration. Be more objective, realistic, and sensitive to whatever the circumstances are. I have had to think of others as opposed to just of myself."

"I'm able to accept people for what they are."

Effects on Values   "I have become more conservative politically because I am looking out for him more in the future. If I don't do something about it now, if I don't pay now, I am not helping him in his future."

"I'm learning a lot about my own power plays [Awareness self]. He is teaching me how important it is to keep a flow of caring and compassion going even under the most trying circumstances" [Awareness values].

Effects on Mind   "Am more apt to realize that if they have a problem, even though I don't perceive it as a problem, if they have it, it is a problem. It is no good trying to talk someone out of a problem, trying to convince him that a problem doesn't exist. Problem is there so I must deal with it."

"My adolescent daughter makes me read more of their kind of literature, makes me aware I must keep up with their thinking, likes and dislikes, not to compete but to be able to understand, talk about and communicate. If I didn't know what they are listening to and reading why would they want to talk to me. I don't want to be shut out of that part of their lives."

Chapter 6

MARY:

TRANSFORMING HER SELF INTO
A MODERN WOMAN

Transformation: "Be a Christian in all that I do."

Like Susan, Mary had been a people-pleaser until she faced its unhealthy effects. Her life-long commitment to her singing, Christian faith, and a close female friendship provided the emotional stability on which to build a more mature autonomous self. The commentary explores the effects of the concurrent women's movement whose tenets Mary did not accept but which provided the cultural justification for her self-assertion.

December 21, 1990

Dear Mary,

I have your last letter and July card by my side. They bring back memories of our wonderful visit and the great insights you gave me about how so many women were moving as a result of the liberation that the women's movement brought them, even though they, like you, may not have thought of themselves as part of its more radical fringe. Of all of the women in the study, you are one of the exemplars of how so many other women have found a way to grow beyond the typed role they were raised to play, to find your own path.

Mary was a featured exemplar not automatically selected because I had only one of her PSQ scores and could not determine the amount of her change. Mary had scored slightly above the women's average in her late 30s. However, her interviews revealed her dramatic change and so she was selected because of her contribution to understanding a female's healthy growth.

Interview about Her Husband

My notes about my first visit with Mary, when she was in her early 20s and engaged to her partner, remind me once more how first impressions do not always predict the future very well. I squirm now at my judgmental attitude.

She is a pretty blonde who speaks like the Texan that she is. She is in an MA program in music, hopeful of becoming a professional opera singer. She was sweet, nice, but one might get bored rather quickly when with her. In terms of insight and intuition, I just got the impression of great thinness. She didn't seem to have the subtly or depth, certainly not a psychological mindedness. Almost one of those "dumb blondes" one reads about, at least in terms of anything intellectually distinctive. Apparently they haven't talked about their relationship or very much about themselves, so not a self-revealing, self-confiding kind of relationship. Probably both depend more on external events rather than on themselves as a source of conversation.

How wrong these impressions turned out to be! I selected her as an exemplar of maturing because no other woman so dramatically changed and was aware of how much she had grown. By her mid 30s she had become more self-reliant, able to assertively stand up for her beliefs, be much more decisive, and feel in control of her own life.

The only attribute of her partner that she identified as the "best thing about their relationship" was "our ability to share with each other. I would really say him more with me than me with him so far." He always attended her performances, but since he was a professor of classics writing a book she cannot share as directly in his life. She never called her future husband by name, only as "husband," so I will also.

"What things about your relationship are not quite as good as you would like them to be?"

"Very little negative I want to change about it. I really like it the way it is." [Love is blind?]

I then asked, "If you could change one thing about your future husband, what would it be?"

> I'm really groping for straws. Sometimes being abrupt. We were at church where we both sing in the choir. I had been waiting for him to take communion with me. It didn't work out. I said I was sorry. He said that taking communion with someone else wasn't the purpose of communion. It was important to me. He said, "Don't worry about it." It upset me for two days. I made an unexpected visit to his office and told him how I felt, that I disagreed with what he said, and he said, "This is the way it is going to be." He didn't realize how I felt before. Didn't realize it mattered to me.

I asked, "Do you feel he has trouble understanding how you feel?" "No, not usually. I am very expressive and will say quite readily how I feel. He keeps within himself much more than I do."

I then explored how her husband-to-be expressed his feelings. "Affectionate?"

"In little ways. Not actually giving, more indirect but does come out."

"Anger feelings?"

"I don't know that much about it. I don't really know."

"Dependency and needing people and support?"

"This is what I think, and he would say completely differently. He feels he is completely independent. I think his relationship with his family is a very close one. We stayed with his family for two weeks this summer. He is a very devoted son."

"How would you describe his relationship with his mother?"

"He's her first born. She does not interfere, absolutely doesn't."

" Relation with his father?"

"I'm not so sure. I didn't get to know his father very well. They seem to get along very well."

"Ever see him sad or cry?"

"No, never."

"What are some of the ways in which he is a good partner?"

> He's extremely intelligent. First thing that attracted me about him because he was someone I could respect. I met

him at church in the choir. At this point I was too young
for him. He didn't ask me out for a date. Didn't want to
have a student dating a professor. He's considerate and
sort of contradictory.

I pursued their relationship by asking if there were any times in the past
they didn't get along with each other.

"Not really."

"If difficulties do occur, who takes the initiative?"

"I probably do. There are so few cases."

"Many women feel they are not as good fiancees as they would like to
be?"

"No. My singing ego."

"What are some ways you have been a good fiancee?"

"Little things. I bought him a pipe just to say 'I love you.' I like to please
people I care about—try to."

"How does he support you?"

"Last February I was getting bottled up, and I exploded because the
teacher was putting pressure on me. I walked off the stage in tears. He
walked in at that moment and gave me his shoulder to cry on. Support when
I have needed it."

"Do you sense any underlying opposition or irritability?

"No."

A record! The shortest interview I have given in the entire study. I was
grateful it was over. Only twelve years later did I understand how helpful it
would be as a baseline for understanding her growth.

Interview when Mary was 35

I did not look forward to my interview with Mary. There were only a few
clues in her completed background questionnaire that alerted me to what
she would shortly flood me with: another record, but this time of pages and
pages about her changes and their reasons. She rated

- her relationship with her father-in-law to be as tense and strained as it
  could possibly be.
- the birth of her second baby to be the most unhappy, stagnant, and
  empty time since her early 20s.
- her emotional health since her late 20s and early 30s to be poor.

- her satisfaction teaching music in an elementary school to be very low.
- her marriage to be very unhappy but her sexual relations to be very enjoyable.
- her strongest needs were to cry when depressed or emotionally moved, and then to feel emotionally close to others, be sexually attracted to males, and to succeed vocationally.
- her strongest wishes in declining order to be a "Christian in all I do, a better wife, mother, daughter, and teacher."

Relationship with Father-in-Law

Mary was primed to give me a detailed recital about her "transformation," as she called it, as soon as I had asked the first question, "What were your experiences that contributed to the recent years being so productive and happy for you?" Paradoxically her ratings about the years had been so unhappy and empty that they almost fell off the scale.

> It was the happiest [sic] period in my life. It was most difficult to go through, but having gone through a very difficult period and being at a different stage now and being at peace with my self and my destiny is why I feel it was so productive. We don't grow when things are peaceful and calm. It has been a period of great personal growth.

Three years after she had married her husband, he went on leave to work ten hours a day, six days a week, on his book. He had promised that they would have their own apartment. Instead, they returned to his father's home in New York during the middle of winter where Mary was "stuck" alone with her father-in-law most of the day. (Her husband's mother had died four days before their marriage.) Mary had lost her first baby and was now pregnant again. She was apprehensive about another miscarriage.

> All my life I had been a people-pleaser. I went out of my way to not rock the boat, to make the other person that I was dealing with feel good, to the point I didn't know how I felt or what I was thinking of. Sort of based my identity on pleasing others. His father is like nobody I have ever known in my whole life. Didn't know what to

do about it. I met someone who couldn't be pleased no matter what I did. I felt that I had never been treated by anyone the way he tried to control my entire existence. If I were sewing, he would put a book in my lap and say, "Why don't you read!" If I didn't take my walk because I was pregnant he would nag me to walk. I had never met anyone like him and I hated him. I couldn't cope with him. I needed to get my head in order, because he would blame me for something horrible that went wrong with my baby. I was very disturbed about my relation with him and my husband.

"Why about your husband?"

"Because they are so much alike. I knew it was irrational." Mary then talked at length about being in a doctor's office. As another mother entered, her son smashed his finger in the doctor's door. The mother said she, herself, was to blame, which horrified Mary. Mary later told her husband who said, "The mother should have been more careful. It shouldn't have happened."

I went straight through the ceiling. I told him, "I'm fighting a battle with myself to protect this child. Accidents will happen. Hopefully nothing serious, but you had better never blame me because that is something I can't handle."

She sought counseling from their minister to examine her fear that her husband would be like his father,

and that could haunt me. The real problem didn't have anything to do with my father-in-law but with my husband. Dead or alive, this man's ghost could haunt my relation with my husband for thirty years from now. I had to deal with my feelings about his father so I would learn how to deal with the parts of my husband that are like his father. I couldn't admit to myself that any parts of my husband were like his father. I couldn't stand his father.

Puzzled, I asked, "How did you get to believe the year was so productive?"

I came to grips with my father-in-law situation without
dealing with him directly but dealing with my feelings
about him. I didn't want to hate him. I realized he is as he
is, and I am who I am. I didn't have to allow him to do
things to me and my family I am not comfortable with.
I decided I was going to deal with it directly instead of
smiling and harboring resentment. I feel he did me a
favor, though at times my anger would come back.

His favor to Mary was to give her a backbone, to learn how to assert
herself, and not always please others.

Birth of Second Child and Emotional Collapse

Mary had had a thirty-three-hour, painful labor so she was reluctant to have
another child, especially as she was becoming "very, very involved" in her
burgeoning career. She had had a difficult year following her first son's birth
and anticipated another child might have the same effect. She liked to keep
everything in "neat little packages, boxes, where I can handle them." But
she couldn't keep her pregnancy and its effects in a box. She had a lot of
diarrhea, allergies, and periods when she was out of control with a "deep
fear of the delivery I wouldn't admit to anyone. The last three weeks I
walked the floor hysterically, absolutely terrified of going through another
thirty-three-hour labor. I prepared myself for another horrible time." But
her baby fooled her. Her son came so quickly she could have had him in
her bed. Her "package" was now under control—so she thought. But one
month later, "I absolutely became a basket case. I had anxiety attacks at four
in the afternoon and cried for four hours every afternoon." Reading a book
about postpartum depression convinced her she was "mentally ill." Her
nose became stuffed up, and she thought it was what was driving her crazy.
"I wanted to die; I couldn't cope with everything, and I was falling apart."

Her husband again suggested she seek help. She sought out another
minister and with his help recalled that she had been working on her career
interests in the late afternoon by teaching music. She learned if she kept
busy in the mid afternoon the attacks might lessen in frequency. They did.

Career Conflicts

Mary called herself a "perfectionist, an achiever, overachiever in school." She was an all-A student. She worked hard on her voice and took every opportunity during these up-and-down years to sing. She had been the director of music and pianist at a church, which she loved; a stage director at an arts festival; a participant in local civic yearly chorales; Maria in *Sound of Music*, and later Mimi in *La Boheme* singing opposite a Metropolitan opera star. Since her marriage, Mary had given private singing lessons to children after school. She told her husband,

> I was very frustrated by having no time in the late afternoon to be with my son, taking him to baseball practice. I need to be free. I want to be with my child. My life has changed with a school-aged child. My needs are different. I'm going to do something about it instead of worrying about it the next ten years. I'm just going to quit.

Mary lived her music. It was central to her pre-transformational identity. To just quit violated who she felt she was.

> I never will give up music. Since the day I was born, I never ever questioned it; it was so inevitable. If I close down some things, there are new areas that might happen. I don't know what they are, but I know it will deal with music.

So she took a part-time position teaching music in her son's private elementary school.

When I saw her, she had been "drained" of all ideas about how to reach children she found to be "unmanageable, disinterested, and disrespectful." A month earlier she had given a stern talk to her fourth grade children, some of whom complained to their parents, who in turn complained to the head. Calling her to his office, she heard in no uncertain terms that she should not bad-mouth the school, give no other such talks to the students, and not talk about the children with the other fourth-grade teachers. Highly indignant, not just indignant but incensed and still fuming—she was not going to be shut up. She had decided she would never teach there again.

My questionnaire had arrived which, so she claimed, took her a whole day to complete. It spurred her to review what she wanted from life. Rating her vocational satisfaction showed her just how dissatisfied she was with teaching. Only one other woman and four other men in the study were more dissatisfied. Mary's only sources of satisfaction were her competence, quality of her work, social and ethical practices of her work, and degree of involvement and devotion to her work. She has never taught since.

Marital Unhappiness

Marriage became the principal playing field on which Mary, and most other women, explored what her future identity was to be. Conflicted about her career commitment, her belief in the sanctity of marriage, and her love for her children, she was tormented for years about how to create a healthier integration. I respected her for her courage to make the choice she eventually did.

What was her evaluation of how good a wife she was? I asked.

Mary responded, "Quite good."

> I don't think I'm as good as I would like to be. Because of this stage of transition what I would have thought was a good wife is no longer what I think a good wife is. I think I'm a better wife, but a better wife is not a doormat who just makes dinner. At a real deep level I care enough to force some of the issues out. It isn't pleasant on the surface. We don't get along as the world sees it. But it's a more positive thing than when I was trying to follow all the rules. In the long run it is healthier for me and for the relationship to do what I am doing now. I'm not just sitting there humdrum and saying that is the way it is and not doing anything about it. I started with me, not him. I changed me to make a better wife than when we were living parallel lives. He definitely knows I am there now. He can't miss it.

"What's his reaction?"

"Not as much as I want. Sometimes I wonder what it will take to ring his chimes. He did react to the broccoli."

The Broccoli Incident

Last fall I came home late. He likes fresh vegetables. The night before I had a main dish and broccoli. I put the leftover broccoli on the table. He said, "Are we having broccoli again. From now on I want you to alternate a green vegetable one night and a yellow one the next." He wanted to make rules for me to follow. I'm a busy lady with much to do. I felt I had walked on eggshells for years to follow all of these little rules to keep him from becoming mad. It is an abuse of his authority and his rights, but I've always tried to do what he wanted. I told him as long as I was the cook, I was going to plan the menu. He could either eat it or leave it. The following night on purpose, with premeditation, I cooked broccoli again. He didn't speak to me for forty-eight hours. For the first time in my life I was assertive. I meant what I said. I did something. I just didn't follow his rules.

The Junk Drawer Incident

I bought some office supplies to use at church. I put them in my junk drawer in the kitchen. He looked in the drawer and accused me of hiding things from him. I should put things where people can find them. What if he needed the pens and didn't know where they were? So the following day I put stamps in his desk drawer. One morning a week later, I heard profanity coming from his office. I have told him 1000 times that not only am I offended by his profanity but it chips away my feelings about him. But he doesn't change. Anyway, I asked him, "What is wrong?" "I can't find the postage stamps. There is so much junk in this drawer that I can't find anything." So I put the ball in his court. I said, "When I put the stuff in the kitchen drawer you accused me of hiding it from you. When I put stamps in the desk drawer you rant and rave because the junk is in your way. I would really like to please you.

> Obviously you don't know what you want. When you
> decide, let me know. In the meantime I am going to do
> what I want to do."
>   I am not getting pleasure out of this. It is my way of
> coping with it and saving my health. It is his problem.

Mary continued, "He wants absolute control over all aspects of our lives.
He emotionally is abusive because he is so critical of me and our son about
small things like the broccoli."

"What are the ways he is a good partner?"

> His practical knowledge keeps my emotional excess
> in check. He is a very good father, willing to baby-sit,
> does his share of the housekeeping without grumbling.
> Whatever else has happened, we have never had any
> sexual problems that I am aware of.

She felt they were quite well-mated, greatly enjoyed sex, and had as
much sex as she wanted, about ten times a month. She rated both of them
to be spontaneously playful and open in their sexual relationship, were not
uncomfortable or guilty about how they satisfied their sexual needs, and had
not been sexually unfaithful.

Emotional Infidelity

When younger, Mary had had a close male friend, an organist and "sensitive
soul," who had said he was in love with her. He was like her husband: bright
and non-emotional. She did not love Stan, whose father was a Lutheran
minister. He called long-distance to invite her to give a recital at the dedication of a new organ. She accepted with her husband's blessing. He knew
Stan and was willing to take care of the kids for several days. "Nothing was
wrong on the surface but I felt everything was wrong. I was totally innocent
of any incorrect thought, though deep down I knew Stan cared for me. My
husband did not know that."

Mary invited her best friend, Paula, to go with her, for which she was
thankful later. Her recital went beautifully. "I felt I was a little bird who had
been let out of the cage. The performer part of me wanted to be free of the
other part of being a mother and wife." Stan lived life intensely and was going through a difficult time with his father. Mary's "heart went out to him;"

she wanted to comfort him. She had fantasies for several weeks of wanting to "fly the coop and leave my humdrum existence and go off into the sunset with Stan. I could not cope with the way I felt for two weeks." She had held nothing back from Paula about her relation with her husband.

Though very comfortable sharing most everything with Paula she was less comfortable sharing her sexual desires, socially unacceptable dreams, and financial affairs. (IC) But now she withdrew from Paula. "I really didn't want anyone to know what I was feeling. I made some telephone calls to Stan; needless to say I was feeling a lot of guilt."

However, Paula very quickly knew what Mary was feeling. How was Mary to integrate her family, her wavering number one priority, with her need for career success and what I sensed were very strong sexual needs ready to spring into consciousness—if they already hadn't done so?

What Did God Want Mary to Do?

> I couldn't live sitting on an emotional tight rope very long without losing my mind. One evening Paula called in tears. She knew I was at a crossroad, at the brink, that I had no choice but to make a decision because my feelings were too strong to ignore. So I had to come to terms with them in some way. Paula told me, "You have the feelings on this side and other responsibilities over here. You have to make a choice." She is very practical and lays it down one, two, and three.

Paula knew,

> You can fly the coop and trade one hell for another. You are looking at that with rose-colored glasses; it isn't going to be that way, but if it is what you want, then choose. I know you don't want to hear this. The only concrete absolute in our lives is God. You can ask God what He intends you to do with your feelings.

Mary then paused to reflect about what she really wanted.

> What I really wanted was a perfect relationship with a person on earth. I really wanted and believed it was still

out there. I came to a screeching halt because I realized
for the first time that relationship did not and was not going to exist. What I was doing and feeling was wrong. It
comes down basically to what is right and wrong for me.
What I was tempted to do was not going to fix anything.
It was going to create other problems. It was ridiculous.
I didn't sleep a wink. I was in sheer torment. Next day
was Sunday. I went to church and felt closer to God. I
prayed. The following morning Stan called. I said things I
shouldn't have. In my heart it was infidelity. I don't know
why but in the middle of our conversation I said the only
thing I can do is to find what God wants me to do, and
I have decided. First time I knew I had decided. With
God's help, I had to discard permanently any relationship
with any other man. Something was controlling me and
I needed help. I did discard it. I have forgiven myself.
I didn't do anything that was all that horrible but its
direction would have been horrible. At that moment the
doorbell rang. It was Paula. She said "You look as if you
have found peace." I felt it was a shattering experience
and yet I was emerging stronger from it than I ever had
been. So I knew what I had to do. I had to talk with my
husband. It was the beginning of taking responsibility for
my self. I am going to base my life on what my Christian
principles tell me is the right thing to do. Stan didn't like
my decision. My decision was permanent and definite. I
let go of this fantasy which was my big dream, but I did
it and I am glad.

As Freud said, less mature persons resort to unconscious repression;
more mature persons, like Mary, use conscious suppression to control
unruly impulses.

Mary decided her relations with her husband and children were her
primary responsibility. She let go her childhood dream of becoming a great
opera singer as being too much a "self" thing. "The balloon burst; I don't
feel bad about it; I feel relief." Her relationship with her husband remained
a problem. She decided she was no longer going to be so aggressive, like

initiating sex, but give him space to reveal more clearly his own needs. She had never defined herself as part of the women's liberation movement. Instead she decided to be a Christian in everything she did as "a wife, mother, daughter, and teacher."

I asked Mary to talk about the roles of women and men from a Christian viewpoint. I was curious because I knew she would never march in a woman's liberation parade.

> Now more strongly than ever I believe in a husband's authority in the home and a wife's position. I think they are separate and distinct roles. I don't think you qualify them as 50-50. What I do and he does are almost the same as what they were. I have certain unstated responsibilities, as he does. They come very specifically with his sex role. I have come full circle back to the same spot, but now I base what I do on different reasons. I do it for my identity, and I do it now because I feel it is right. I really think my entire identity and growth are intimately related with being a woman and that is why it isn't a problem. I have a very specific scripturally-based idea of what a woman's role is at home and in all other areas. I feel that my greatest freedom is to be myself when I am in the proper relationship to my husband, when I am "under the umbrella of a husband's authority." As women discover that to try to be a "man" in the work force doesn't really answer their needs, which is what I think will happen, the pendulum will swing back to a more traditional family.

"Where does your husband fit into this view?"

> He's able to get through because he thinks this is the way a man should be. Be emotionally controlled, maintain a sense of maleness, keep stiff lip, and not show any feeling. And he does that. It interferes with his growth because it keeps people at arm's length. He does not allow other people really to reach him. I think this eats away at him all the time and comes out in rage over trivial things. He is a very frustrated husband who throws smoke screens

to protect himself from the real issues. He doesn't want anybody to know if he has a problem; he doesn't think he has any, but he continually flies into a rage if something breaks. He can't handle it.

Mary then reflectively continued with a feeling of regret:

He used to hold himself aloof from real emotional expression. He loves our son. I know and he knows it intellectually, but he can't get through that brick wall. I feel it is a protection; his way of coping. He builds the wall and unfortunately he is behind the wall and the rest of us aren't. I could sing sweetly in church but wasn't really supposed to do anything profound. I have grown beyond the bounds he had set for me.

Causes of Mary's Growth

The intriguing question now is, "How did Mary, raised to be a people-pleaser, develop the stronger, more autonomous person she became?"

Father-in-law

The first painful cause was her run-in with her father-in-law. She very succinctly said of its effect:

I don't feel obligations for things that are out of my control and will not allow someone to impose that obligation on me. When it is indeed my responsibility, I accept it but when it is being imposed on me as my responsibility, I will not allow that other person to make me feel that it is" [Stability self; Autonomy relations and self].

Close Friends

In talking about Paula, her close friend, Mary identified a principal reason why counseling can be effective. Acceptance by a non-judgmental but respected person encourages self-acceptance.

I have learned to be myself and not be afraid to be that even though somebody else might not like me. [Autonomy relations; self] Paula likes me, she accepts me, knows me very well. I'm okay. Paula understands. It is mutual for Paula [Other- centered relations and self; Stability self]. That is our relationship in a nutshell.

Physical-Emotional Health

In another nutshell, Mary summarized the effect of her

bleak period when I was a non-person and not growing, when I was not emotionally healthy and definitely not physically healthy. It is a sense of mental stability, well-being, that I don't have to be bothered thinking about whether I am going crazy at four o'clock this afternoon, which leaves my mind free to pursue other things, because my mind isn't bogged down" [Stability and Autonomy mind].

October 9, 1987

Dear Doug,

Life circumstances have opened up my life somewhat from the "narrow focus" you discovered five years ago. Problems with my husband in our marriage reached a crisis last April, and I was surprised when he agreed to therapy. We have both been in individual therapy since May with separate clinical psychologists who share a practice. The results have been nothing short of remark-able, at least for me. I have worked very hard, and about two weeks ago made a major breakthrough. I'm going to go "all the way" this time, and the process is becoming far less painful and much more exciting than anything I've ever done. In my desire to become healthier in relating to others, I have received a special bonus. I have discovered that I am extremely interested in studying psychology! So you see, my interest in the work you are doing, of which I was fortunate to take part, is now meaningful to me in a far different way than when I did it. My husband has saved everything you ever gave him, so I am devouring the material with great interest. He is making progress too, but since my realization that my life depends only upon what I do, I'm not worried about it. My life depends upon the outcome of my therapy, not his!

Thanks for getting us involved. I'm so glad we were.

Sincerely,

———•·•———

December 22, 1988

Dear Doug,

Our lives are much better now than when you last heard from us. Both of us are still in therapy after being very bad. Our marriage is now more solid and better than ever before! We have learned how to deal with our problems. Individually we still have a lot of work to do, but we're doing it and life is pretty good these days. [She continued to say she was applying for a program in counseling psychology and an internship in music therapy.] Do you detect a note of enthusiasm as I tell you about this?

I hope you are well. I would love for you to come to see us again sometime. This time we could talk "shop."

Best Wishes

———•·•———

June 29, 1990

Postcard

I am performing Mimi in *La Boheme* this summer with a tenor from the MET! Am still in school and love it. Did not get into psychology program but am in music therapy, the perfect integration. Husband is okay; kid is great.

———

Mary divorced her husband in 1992 with an amicable settlement. She had a surgical operation for malignant melanoma on her back that had already metastasized. She had another operation to remove some thirty cancerous lymph nodes under her arm. She then had difficulty breathing, and cancer was discovered in the lining but not air sacs of her lungs. For four months she was confined to her bed taking chemotherapy.

February 26, 1994, I flew out to Texas to be with her, if only for the half-hour she said she could tolerate, to thank her for the gift she had given me. She was in bed with a white hat on that she shortly took off to reveal she was completely bald—no longer a blonde, certainly not dumb. Oxygen tubes came out of her nose; she had become puffy around her face and obviously had little energy. During our half-hour she kept looking at the clock, which alerted me that my presence might be drawing down her scarce energy reserves. She wanted to let me know her cancer history, how she had begun to work as a music therapist at a nursing home and the next day had collapsed.

She maintained her hope; she was determined, not a person who gave up, and with God's help she would overcome her cancer. She had come to terms with her possible death. Calling it a "miracle," she had sung the twenty-thrid psalm in church three weeks before she was diagnosed with cancer of the lungs.

"Would you like to hear it?" she asked.

"I'd be honored."

She had no difficulty hitting the high notes with poignant feeling. I abandoned myself to the tears welling up. I thanked her. I kissed her on her cheek, gave her a farewell hug, and left her. My eyes were blurred.

March 29, 1994, I had a premonition about Mary so I called her husband. He said she had died last night. She had to go to the hospital a week ago. She had been scared about what was happening. She had to be doped her last days because of the pain. Her family had been with her. He felt sad.

Mary's Contribution to Understanding Maturing

A strong foundation to one's identity can develop very early and provide a basis for mature self-assertion.

A deep religious commitment can bolster will-power to resist sexual temptation.

Close, caring, but confrontational friendships can spur maturing.

A devastating painful challenge to a habitual interpersonal style may turn out to trigger the initiation of more healthy interpersonal growth.

Young adult behavior may not be prognostic of later adult growth.

The capacity for maturing may vary from one person to the next and depends on genetically influenced personality traits, like decisiveness, energy level, ego strength.

Commentary

Mary's transformation from a person-pleaser to an assertive person in her own right provides the opportunity to summarize and interpret the study's reliable findings about women's healthy growth. My interpretations may not hold for the daughters of the middle-aged women I have studied. Why? Most of the study's women were raised into adulthood prior to the feminist movement and its cataclysmic effects on the meaning of being a woman. Young women now have options for living their lives not as readily available thirty and forty years ago.

Mary, and other women like Susan, told me that a woman's maturing has been more conflicted than men's. Their biology, parental enmeshment, and overdeveloped feminine interpersonal strengths blocked their maturing. While still affected by their biology, today's girls and younger women are growing up freer of former parental and stereotypical feminine interpersonal limitations. *Morale, Culture, and Character* (Heath, 1999b) describes girls' growing androgyny due to greater opportunities to develop stereotypic masculine strengths. They can be even fighter pilots or presidents of Fortune 500 companies or basketball stars to their children![1]

If you are a woman, I hope my efforts to make sense of the women's results won't inflame you. Harriet, my wife, doesn't like them. Her reaction is, "At least women are trying to grow. Men aren't." I'm not sure where that leaves me. Other women already have proposed similar ideas, for which the study now provides the scientific support. I shall briefly review the evidence and then describe in more detail why the women matured as they did in their adult years.

Biological Influences

Women share similar recurring biological experiences, like menstruation, pregnancy, birth, nursing, child-rearing, and menopause. These experiences strengthen and reaffirm a communizing rather than individualizing identity. The consequences of developing such an identity are numerous and pervasive: the development of interpersonal skills that further communal harmony, language that is sensitive to and articulates feelings, and values that conserve social rather than promote individualistic traits and competitive roles. Too-developed communizing strengths can block the development of individualizing potentials and so hinder maturing.

The suggestive evidence? Compared to the men's judges' ratings, the women's judges reliably rated them to be more interpersonally feminine, e.g., warm, eager to soothe hurt feelings, understanding, sensitive to others' needs, etc. Women's bodily health and adolescent personalities did not predict much about them as adults. This suggests that gender and over-socialization into typical feminine roles may have suppressed or obscured their individual talents and needs which might otherwise have predicted their individual adult differences.

Parental Enmeshment

Women but not men remain emotionally close to and enmeshed in their families of origin far into their adult years. They also look back for support more to their mothers than men do. Worldwide, fathers do not expect their daughters to "get out on their own" as early and in the same way that they expect their sons to. They early expect their sons to roam, explore, climb trees, get drunk, gamble, race cars, and generally "get into trouble," and model such behaviors. Fathers also have a biological ally. After all, testosterone is an assertive, intruding, penetrating, risk-taking hormone. So boys are often goaded to learn how to cope, achieve, and master themselves on their own. Chapter 9's Dave expected his becalmed windsurfing son to get himself back home on his own; his wife, Elise, didn't. She went to get him.

For centuries, girls have been raised to stay home. The consequences of such enmeshment are, among other things, valuing security more than risk-taking and reaffirming a prescribed identity rather than fashioning one's own. By not testing themselves against a rich variety of challenges, other than interpersonal ones, they do not discover and expand new interests and develop latent, particularly assertive, strengths. Although Mary's mother was not authoritarian, she did not encourage her to become independent. Neither of Mary's parents encouraged her to participate physically in outdoor activities.

The suggestive evidence? Women satisfied with their vocations or serving their communities as leaders share few character traits because they have not been raised to succeed in those ways. Parents continue to contribute more directly to their adult daughters' than to their sons' successes. Fathers influence more their adult daughters' than their sons' vocational success. Two reasons help explain why women continue to be more affected by their parents than men are.

Women are more sensitive and responsive to parental cues and expecta-tions than men are. The women's parents occupied more of their daughters' emotional life space than they did of their sons', as the interviews and tests showed. The women valued their parental (even parent-in-law) relation-ships more than their husbands did. They also did not feel as understood by both parents or act as equals with them.

Most women felt divided about and distressed by their mothers with whom they still felt like children. More than the men, they felt that their mothers had rejected them when younger. Also, the women disagreed and argued with their mothers much more than the men about almost every topic, most notably about sex and ethical-religious issues. When we are so emotional and unsettled about our relations with another, that person can affect us in singularly enduring ways. In contrast to the men, few of the study's women had "freed" themselves of their mothers even by their 40s. One 41-year-old woman said that she still "wanted more" from her dead mother. Another middle-aged woman still simmered and fumed about her mother, whom she wouldn't allow to visit her grandchildren. By their 50s, most of the women of the study had made peace with their mothers—though grudgingly.

Furthermore, the women's parents continued to influence their daughters because they were in flux, unsure of their future, and searching for a more comfortable identity. By their mid 40s, with only a few exceptions , the men had themselves together. But many of the women, like Susan, had not. Mary had fashioned her identity earlier than most women. If we are unclear about our priorities, and who we are and want to be, we may be more vulnerable to continuing parental influences. When we are unsure of or have not tested ourselves in many different ways and found our path, we may reach back to find support from our families. We "call home" more frequently.

Overdeveloped Interpersonal Strengths

Typical feminine interpersonal skills like compassion, understanding, and sensitivity to the feelings of others contribute to adult success. The study showed such skills to be also critical to men's success as marital partners. (Heath, 1994b) Some writers about women believe that their interpersonal skills and values are the pinnacle and the measuring rod of female moral and personal growth. The study's adult women resoundingly say otherwise. The core of their maturity and well-being is their stability and autonomy, not their other-centeredness.

The ideal of equilibration warns us that every outstanding strength can be a potentially fatal weakness if it is not integrated with other strengths. The commentary on Rich told us that scholastically talented but interpersonally immature males are at risk of failing in their familial and vocational roles as adults. Or too self-sufficient autonomy, as occurs in men, not integrated with other-centered interpersonal skills, as for Susan's and Mary's husbands, can produce an arrogant and self-centered narcissist who fails in his familial roles.

So also, over-developed feminine interpersonal skills can block continued growth, as occurs in some women like Susan. When such potential strengths are not integrated with a strong and independent sense of self, they can produce a conforming adjustment but unhealthy adaptation. Women have always faced unhealthy trade-offs for adjusting. Women are more depressed and have lower self-esteem and self-confidence than men. The negative effects of being raised to be a woman who pleases and conforms to others' expectations are several. Interpersonal adjustment bars discovering individualizing strengths that might disrupt harmonious relationships. One's self-worth depends on others' approval. So maturing remains blocked and well-being elusive. Again, Mary's "people-pleasing" identity is a good example.

The suggestive evidence? The women's peers judged them to be more compassionate, sensitive, and understanding than the men's peers rated them to be. Regardless of how I measured the women's and men's maturity, mental health, and happiness, not their interpersonal strengths but their stability and autonomy consistently were at their center. Stereotypical feminine strengths are necessary for some forms of adult success but not as critical to maturity and well- being.

Androgynous men and women who are roughly similar in socially de-fined masculinity and femininity are mature and healthy persons. Women's and men's mental health is predicted by some masculine qualities, though not by core qualities like aggressiveness, competitiveness, and forcefulness. It is predicted by strengths characteristic of autonomy and stability, like self-reliance, courage, decisiveness, and self-confidence, every strength Barbara, Susan, and Mary had developed since they had begun to par-ticipate in the study. A psychology of women that ignores such strengths to overemphasize their interpersonal ones risks entrenching women's past psychic oppression even more; it will undermine women's potential to be healthy and happy individuals. The meaning of a woman's maturity and well-being has to be much more complex and multidimensional to be faith-ful to how she grows healthily.

As long as women fulfilled their traditional feminine roles, they could adjust successfully to being wives, mothers, and lovers, roles their mothers had modeled and prepared them for. Those who wished to work could be satisfied in a limited number of nurturing vocations, like teaching and nurs-ing. They did not have to modify their feminine identity in such jobs, for their interpersonal skills contributed to their vocational success. Until the late 60s, therefore, the values of the women's parents and their upbringing matched those needed to succeed in their traditional roles.

But the world changed in the late 60s in ways the women had not been prepared for. They discovered they had been raised to play a social role that did not fit many of their talents and needs. They became enigmas to them-selves because many had not discovered who their "real" selves were. They did not feel strong inside themselves. They told me, "All I am is an empty eggshell." "I am a wife to my husband, a mother to my children, a daughter-in-law to my mother-in-law. I don't know who I am." Or, in the words of an unexcelled leader of the League of Women Voters and other community groups, "All I am is a collection of roles put together by a committee."

None had talked like that in the 60s when they were in their late 20s and early 30s. Twelve years later many women told me that they had no strong sense of themselves. They had identified with their other-centered interpersonal roles at the expense of discovering and developing stable and autonomous selves.

I could not trace the roots of the women's mental health back to their parents or their adolescent personalities because neither had prepared them to develop the strong autonomous selves that are the core of a mentally healthy woman. The study's non-results mirrored the women's transitional steps away from identifying with a prescribed social role and toward fashioning a more centered and independent self. Unhappily, some modern women, in their pursuit of their autonomy or other stereotypic masculine competencies, so violate their sense of wholeness to discover their communized selves have become impoverished and their lives sterile and meaningless.

Chapter 7

CHARLIE:

A SURGEON'S DRIVING PASSION
AND COMMITMENT

"Life is a struggle. I enjoy that."

Charlie had never been able to assert his autonomy from his Jewish parents until they died, though he took small steps to do so. His marriage to a "Jewish princess" had devastating effects; it precipitated a major regression for years. His passionate commitment to surgery and idealistic desire to create a better society preserved his sanity, but what contributed to his resumed maturing?

Charlie ranked third highest within the group for amount of maturing from his early 30s to mid 40s. He changed more on five other preliminary measures of change than anyone else, both self- and judge-rated ones. He was within the middle range of the PSQ measure of maturity. One more record distinguishes him. Only four men became more immature between their senior year and early 30s. Charlie was one of them. He actually regressed the most. His searing marital dispute accounted for 50% of the decline in his PSQ scores on its items about his relationships with women. He is also an exemplar par excellence of maleness, consistently scoring higher on a stereotypic measure of masculinity (ranked second) than on femininity (ranked last) than any other male in the study.

He is an exceptional surgeon with a fierce dedication to social causes, most recently to the rights of women and blue whales. You need his replies to five incomplete sentences (SCT) to understand his feistiness.

To be successful, he wrote, "I must do meaningful things."

I value most . . . "doing something I strongly believe in."

My conscience bothers me if . . . "I don't act out my beliefs."

At this time in my life (mid 50s) . . . "I am still working for new battles to fight any worthy cause to support."

During the next few years, I . . . "will fight for choice."

Please don't dismiss him if his causes are not yours; he is a complicated person to understand: a tough-minded individual with a good heart.

Parental Programming

Charlie's grandfather immigrated to the states in 1906 during a pogrom. Charlie's father opened a bakery. The religious teachings and practices of his grandfather and parents didn't take; the remaining part of the Jewish mystique did. Charlie definitely disagreed that religious beliefs underlay his whole approach to life, that religion is important because it answers many questions about the meaning of life, and that he thinks of himself as an intrinsically religious person committed to living a life based on religious beliefs and practices. However, Jewish ethical and social values did take, strongly so. He rated himself a very honest, deeply ethical person of integrity committed to ideals and principles. "Here I am an agnostic but when I heard Israel took the Western Wall back from Jordan, it broke me up. How do you explain something like that?" Part of that mystique is Charlie. He is a social activist and Zionist, willing to defend justice and go to Israel to work where needed. "I'm now part of the American Physicians' Fellowship. If there is another disaster I will be on the first flight over there."

He was deeply affected by his parents' expectations of what he should do with his life. While he knows his parents loved him, he felt his first twenty years of adulthood were darkened by their expectations that he marry a Jewish princess which he finally did. He fulfilled his parents' expectation (he claimed he was "programmed") to work hard at an elite college (which he did), become a surgeon (which he did), and earn a lot of money (which he did though not until after twenty years). He repeatedly said their expectations never included having "any fun"—which Charlie claimed he never had had until after he had divorced his first wife.

Charlie's feelings about his parents were accurately mirrored in his replies to the incomplete sentences: *My mother and I . . .* "had a wall between us" and *When he thought of his mother, he . . .* "wished he had been more assertive." And to *My father* he wrote "was a magnificent self-made man but with very narrow vistas" and to *Remembering his father, he . . .* "wished he had stood up to him."

He felt neither parent understood him and that both moderately disagreed with him about his feelings about his marriage and his views on politics and money. His father was more exercised about how little money he was making as a surgeon than about whether he enjoyed his work. Even by his mid 50s, Charlie still felt like a child when with both, would like to avoid them but really cared for them. While he appreciated their insistence that he get a good education and his mother's encouragement that he enjoy music, opera, and literature, he would not assume responsibility for them in their older years. Charlie is being honest about how he really felt; he felt "horrible" having such feelings. [No other member of the study felt so strongly.] "In my last talk with mother, I was in such agony because I couldn't give much emotional support." His guilt flowed from his feeling of obligation to them: "They sweated blood to get out of the depression, to put me through college, and contribute to medical school."

Why Charlie married in his first year of medical school is not clear, though he said later good upper-class Jewish boys married early to be able to have regular sex. He rued that he missed the sexual revolution that began ten years later. He locates all of his subsequent unhappiness to have begun with this early marriage to a Jewish princess and the arrival of his first of three children within the year, preventing him from bumming around Europe having a bash. An inner voice complained bitterly for the years that he never "got to sow his wild oats." He called them "his lost years."

For the first sixteen of his adult years he lived under his parents' shadow. His mother died a year after his father died. One week after her death, he felt free for the first time in his life and initiated steps to divorce his self-centered wife. More later.

Medical Career

Charlie's career began as a freshman pre-med student at Haverford College. His verbal SAT score was somewhat below that of his peers, but his quantitative and achievement test scores put him in the top 10%. His academic record varied but settled into the mid Bs. His chemistry departmental chairman rated his determination to be excellent; his emotional stability, intelligence, and originality to be good; but his personality to be fair. Charlie did not pay much attention to the social graces or what others thought about him.

His medical career began at Philadelphia's Hahnemann Hospital. He completed his internship and part of his surgical residency at the hospital. He worked every other night for four years and every summer, with the predictable effects on his marriage.

Charlie said doctors had "the highest rates of divorce, suicide, mental illness, drug, and marital problems" of any profession in the country. Of the study's original eleven doctors, five are still married to their original spouses. Of the five, only Barbara and Jim have never had the serious problems that surveys measure. Of the eleven, only Jim and Charlie rate their current marriages to be very happy.

Before completing his residency, Charlie's "seven year itch" and desire for adventure led him into the army and Vietnam, where at the age of 28 he was responsible for 100 medical personnel. His Haverford's freshman and Vietnam experience had been his happiest years. No longer being nagged at home, nobody bothering him, running his own show, he enjoyed the opportunity to do a lot of surgery on trauma cases. He found the Vietnamese to be very grateful which showed him that he was not as "cold heart" as he thought he was.

"A Vietnamese came in and almost bled to death from an ulcer. I got the x-ray and sent him to the operating room where I got him through everything. As he was walking out of the hospital, his wife came over and embraced me. That is satisfying."

But Charlie didn't get his "bash." Because of his programming he "couldn't enjoy his time off. Just a mental block for me to go into a bar in Taipei and pick somebody up. They were there for the taking." Charlie was driven to keep busy. By his mid 30s he had had no vacation in ten years. He said of his work, "I did an outstanding job when I was in military service and always look back on it with a great deal of pride. Surgery is the field that has the most to do with the fate of a patient."

"What are your strengths that make you such a good surgeon?"

> Good technical skill and good physical stamina. Ability to place family and friends and everything else second. When I'm in the operating room I can be there for ten hours and not think about any other problems, and then

they hit you when you walk out. I can shut it out, one of
the characteristics of any surgeon. I was able to function
with rockets blasting outside without worrying about
them. Aggressive. Got to take the bull by the horns some
times. If a guy is bleeding to death and somebody wants
to fool around, you've got to say "do or die" sometimes.

Returning from Vietnam, he completed his surgical residency in Brooklyn which Martha, his first wife, hated. He passed his boards. Certified as
a surgeon, he began to search for a position. His wife now wanted her say
about his career.

Deteriorating Marriage

Wife's View of Charlie and Marriage

I asked Charlie during our Time 3 interview if Martha would like me to interview her. After considerable hemming and hawing they agreed. I visited
her at their home during a snowstorm; she said she was cold. I offhandedly
suggested that perhaps she was anxious, which she didn't deny. She was
plain with a tinge of red to her dark hair. They rented the house about which
she was fastidious but also apologetic. Initially tense and bottled-up, she
loosened up as we progressed. I did not sense any hostility towards Charlie,
only resignation and a touch of defensiveness.

For Martha, the children are the best things about a marriage that has no
companionship. He comes home so tired they can seldom go out. "We all
have certain illusions and ideals and life isn't like that." She would like to
change Charlie's personal habits. He forgets to hang up his coat, falls asleep
in front of the TV, leaves his socks all over the floor, forgets to call her when
he is delayed, and other "petty annoyances." They are deeply in debt.

I then asked about how he handles his feelings, like anger.

She bitterly replied:

> I don't feel he has any feelings. Very rarely gets angry
> except at his mother. She probes, pesters, annoys. She
> is Mrs. Portnoy. She hated the book because it was so
> dirty. He needs my family but not his. His mother doesn't

let him alone. She asks what is he earning, when did he leave, where is he? We can't look a gift horse in the mouth. If we needed money it's there. She is relentless.

"Is Charlie affectionate?"

"With me in public, no. Won't even hold my hand when someone is in the room. When I was seventeen, he used to bother me. A status symbol. He has pet names for the kids but doesn't kiss them. I would like him to come home and kiss me."

"Sad feelings?"

"No. Never have seen him cry."

"Dependency?"

"He doesn't have any. He's self-sufficient. He's not jealous of anyone or anything. He's very content with his lot."

"How is he a good husband?"

"Terrific father."

I did not pursue the unanswered question about being a husband to follow her lead about his fathering.

He cares for and enjoys his children. He allows me to live my own life, which I need. I could not be at the beck and call of a man. Can't sit in a room with his smoking, like when he is listening downstairs to his 4000 taped records. This is something we fight about. Both of our sons have very high IQs. Husband is too tired to sit down and explain something to our sons when they ask questions. The oldest son's teacher said our son "was an excellent student but is not associating with his peers." Charlie blew up and humiliated me in front of her. "Why does he have to associate with his peers and fall into this mold?" I blew up on the way home. "It's not important to you because you have only one friend and that is sufficient, but that is not the usual way of life and people are important." That was the trigger that took us to a marriage counselor. We were able to reduce our mutual tension but the counseling led to an "armed truce."

Charlie's View of His Wife and Marriage

He too said "the kids" were the best part of their marriage.

"What else is good about it?"

"Not sure. There must have been at one time."

Again, the standard interview question, "What is not quite as good as you would like?"

"Everything. Sex relations. We don't communicate."

Charlie then opened up the issue that would lead to his eventual divorce: Martha's dependence on her parents required them to live near them in Philadelphia and also to his parents, whom he wouldn't mind being 10,000 miles away from. She had hated the two years in Brooklyn.

The issue came to a head when Charlie got a good job in New Brunswick and signed a contract. But she refused to go and leave her parents. Martha's refusal

> set me off; I became hysterical and tore the place apart. Of course I put it back together. I then saw an army poster with, "Your Uncle Sam still loves you." I signed up without asking her and was assigned to a nearby base where I got back on track professionally. She refused to move. She was implacable. We separated for the first time. She got a lawyer who terrorized me. He wrote letters to the base commander complaining about me. I chickened out and moved back and commuted, which was agony. My father was unhappy about our separation. My parents' view of divorce is about 40-years old.

For three years, Charlie warred with Martha who threatened to set her lawyer after him again. He claimed she was bleeding him financially by sending their children to an expensive Hebrew school and squandering her allowance. She was being what he called a "classic JAP" (Jewish American princess) holding on to what security she could get.

While he continued to work and to live in their house, he had lost enthusiasm for his work. He blames her for his failure to advance professionally during these years. When she told him her lawyer had died,

> I told her that one half of my wishes had come true. Really an overwhelming hatred. She is a very vicious

psychopath and able to live off the productivity of other people. She has never gotten active in anything and not tried to find any work. I came close to a nervous break-down. I felt very humiliated. She had enough allowance on which to live. I moved to the base and came home to sleep over the weekends. I made a feeble attempt to have sex and she said I had to earn that again. Six months later she wanted sex and I told her she had to earn that by join-ing me at the base. During this separation, my father was dying of lung cancer and then my mother died of heart failure. She made my life so painful I couldn't properly mourn their deaths.

He immediately filed for divorce after his mother died, knowing that his wife would make him "pay through the nose. It has been worth the aggravation."

He associated to this period, "totally unmitigated disaster; professionally strangled; financially wiped out; no companionship or sex; board certifica-tion the only good thing about that period."

Healing, Resiliency, Resuming Growth

Nine months after what I called a "comedy of our calendars," I visited 44-year-old Charlie and worked with him in his basement near his secret locked room. Preferring solitude he would recover from his exhausting schedule and marital strife by retreating to this room. There he relaxed and listened to one of his legacies, "the world's greatest private record collection of historic importance."

Concerned about his over-weight, Charlie had been on a rigorous program, losing thirty-five pounds, stopping smoking, jogging every day, minding his health more consciously. He had rated his current physical and emotional health to be excellent: his irritability had decreased though not his excitability, his sleeping troubles and depression had almost disappeared. His mood was upbeat. Looking forward to our visit he made every coopera-tive effort to make it go well. We had a most affable visit.

By preference, Charlie seeks solitude. He was the most alone of the study's few lone wolves. Except for one son, he had no friends in whom he confided. He never had talked even with his current wife about some of the topics he wanted to share. He used the first hour of the interview to rehash the years of his previous marital war, a necessary emotionally healing catharsis. After the death of his mother and divorce from Martha, he had had his delayed "bash."

> I had a ball, dated a lot, doing anything I wanted, as well as working. My idea of a bash is not just being a playboy. I can't take leisure as much as I love music. More than a week I would go crazy. To me leisure has to be earned.

I thought, "A rather subdued bash to suppress for twenty years!" He continued:

> Professionally, I have no question in my mind. My ex-wife held me back. I was a competent surgeon, and I went from being competent to excellent. With her off my back, knowing I had my own life, I went to being an outstanding surgeon. I can hold up with the best. That is why I am getting this job at one of the country's premier hospitals. I'm damn good. I'm now chief surgeon at the base hospital and have increasing administrative responsibilities. I hate to say I am a beneficent dictator. I do not do unto others what has been done to me in the past. I answer to only one person—the base commander and he gives me a very long leash.

He had been appointed colonel and was looking forward to becoming a brigadier general. Curious, I asked again about what he had learned were the strengths that led to his excellence.

> You have to have guts to do something very decisive very quickly. Not vacillating at a critical time; when in the heat of an operation you don't get infantile. You say, "I want this and I want that." Actually I rate surgical judgment more important than technical facility.

I asked, "What choices did you make in the past that slowed you down, blocked the development of important potentials?"
Without hesitation, Charlie said,

Getting married at 21. Getting tied in. People change a lot from 20 to 30. I've made only one bad decision in my life. I like my life. I accept the struggle. You find yourself in a happy situation as a result of the earlier unhappy situation. If I didn't have that unhappy relationship, I wouldn't have this happy time now.

His associations to "middle age" took a 180 degree turn from those about his 30s: "chance to re-look at your whole life and not get self-hardened into firm patterns; time for renewal; not get self locked in; enjoy certainly many good things."

From his position of new-found strength, Charlie decided to solve the alimony issue. His first wife had rejected his earlier proposals. "She says I married her. I am hers for life." Eventually she settled for one-sixth of his gross income. On his first check to her he had written, "Let there be peace." He had not missed sending her one check.

Free at last, Charlie looked to the future. He ranked again his daydreams and hopes and the probability of achieving them, beginning with:
- Make general in command of a hospital (50-50)
- Drop last alimony check into my ex-wife's grave (Very low)
- Continue good second marriage (High)
- Maintain good relationship with children (High)
- Collect all Toscanini recordings (High)
- Become full professor at a medical college (Very high)
- See all children successful (Very high)
- Help contribute to the moral majority's destruction (50-50)

He's very satisfied and happy with his life, and rates his second marriage to be a "very happy" one.

Remarriage

Charlie married Naomi, a Jewish divorcee with two children. He was very clear that his profession was his number one priority. "I told Naomi what destroyed my first marriage. Wherever my career goes is where I go and you have to understand that." She agreed to support his professional goals. They share similar tastes and interests in entertainment. They each have good relationships with each other's children. He only wishes she would make choices from a menu "more decisively."

For the twenty-one years of their marriage, their sexual relationship has enjoyed cloudless skies. In his mid 40s and late 50s he thought they were very well-mated, both greatly enjoyed sex, had sex six times a month (which was about as much as he wished), and believed his wife was quite considerate of his sexual needs. He rated her higher than he rated himself on the principal attributes that contribute to a fulfilling sexual relationship: openness, appeal, and warmth. Overall he rated his sexual fulfillment to be "very high."

His alimony payments are their only dark cloud; they are ever present in their marriage. His wife resents their payment and believes his ex-wife should work. (She died some years later.)

Charlie remains devoted to his children and satisfied with his role as a parent. When his daughter was fifteen, she drove him "nuts," which he attributes to his ex-wife's making him the "heavy" in the divorce break-up. Learning how not to raise children from his own parents, he has consistently believed for thirty years that parents should not interfere in their children's lives.

> I want the best for them, but they have to do it for them-
> selves. I want them to enjoy doing what they want to do.
> I have given them the opportunity to bum around Israel
> and be on a Kibbutz; my kids don't want it. I want my
> children to be liberated before and not after my death.

Growth from His 50s into His 60s

Once Charlie remarried and his children had left home, his maturing more or less leveled off in his interpersonal relationships. He had become increasingly bored with his work for the army and retired after a tour of duty in Desert Storm where he received a medal for his work. But Charlie was built to be restless and seek new ways to become involved in carrying out his convictions. Since listing his ranked hopes and daydreams in his mid 40s, he changed them by his late 50s. They prefigured how he used his medical expertise to further them. He ranked his hopes with their estimated probability of achieving them within the next decade:

- Become known as a warrior against religious fascism (High)
- See Choice secure (50-50)
- Leave wife secure (Very High)

- Travel to the great opera houses of Europe (Very high)
- President of Planned Parenthood (Low)
- Know grandchildren (Very high)
- Around the world trip on the Concorde (50-50)
- See demise of Islamic and Christian fundamentalism (Very low)
- Come to terms with conflicts with late parents (Low)
- Largest private collection of historical recordings in the world (Low)

Charlie had traveled along an increasingly liberal road since he had resisted Haverford's Quaker liberalism, volunteered for the Vietnam war in 1967, and actively campaigned to elect Nixon President in 1968. I never would have predicted he would campaign for President Nixon and forty years later dream of becoming President of Planned Parenthood. Charlie took a hard-nosed attitude toward reality; he was not an ideologue. He traced his attitude about abortion back to 1971. He had seen a family destroyed when its daughter, who had been gang-raped, couldn't get an abortion and committed suicide.

The year he retired from the army he learned how to do abortions and began to work actively for Choice by moving several times a week to different clinics. For five years he successfully avoided assassins and fire-bombers as he performed more than several thousand abortions.

Causes of His Growth

Death of Parents

> I sorted out the good values that I kept and the ones I didn't think were so good, I didn't [Integration and autonomy values]. I made up my mind I was going to overhaul everything in my life. That might look very cold-blooded [Awareness and autonomy self]. Like calling the lawyer one week after mother died. Again, no doubt my parents had my best interests in their hearts. The change is in my reaction to my parents' expectation that I owed them something because of what they did for me. My children have no strings on them—either legal or emotional [Other-centered value].

Women's Liberation

> When I was in medical school gynecologists were the
> worst in relation to women. I believe women have
> full rights to everything [Other-centered values]. I've
> observed them doing great jobs. Being in favor of
> women's rights is part and parcel like being against the
> Moral Majority [Autonomy values]. My ex-wife was not
> at all a woman's libber. Her programming as a Jewish
> princess was to be totally nurturing and taken care of, and
> get insurance from dead husbands. Twenty years ago I'll
> be the first to admit I would not have been too overjoyed
> going to women doctors. Now that doesn't bother me
> in the least [Autonomy relations] How would I like a
> woman boss? I don't know. I have had no experience. In
> taking on these issues, I have tried to extrapolate them to
> apply to all situations [Integration cognitive].

Parental Role

> Made me much more tolerant of some things than I was
> [Other-centered values]. It is all part-and-parcel of how I
> was programmed. When things come up, I try to reflect
> on what I had been through at that time [Awareness self].
> If my son comes and thinks about taking off a year, I wish
> I had had the guts to do the same thing. Son didn't take off
> but he had the choice.

Charlie admired his younger brother who had defied his parents to have
his own "bash" while wandering around Europe after college; he always felt
guilty he had not had the guts to do the same thing. In a negative way, his
public opposition to right-to-lifers and others may be a remedial compensatory effort to undo his earlier lack of guts to stand up to his parents.

Charlie's Maleness

Other clues help me understand Charlie. On a widely-used test of one's
masculinity and femininity, he scored as the second highest man in masculinity and the lowest one on femininity (BEM). The difference between

his two scores was the largest of any of the men in the study. He thought of himself as an aggressive, decisive, self-sufficient person willing to take stands, but not as affectionate, yielding, sentimental, and eager to soothe hurt feelings, among other stereotypic traits of masculinity and femininity. His strongest needs were to achieve and succeed, exercise power and influence, be widely recognized, and have thrilling adventures. His weakest needs were to have harmonious and cooperative relationships, to emotionally depend on women, and be affectionately demonstrative with anyone, whether female or male.

Rorschach confirmation of Charlie's maleness.   I compared Charlie's Rorschach responses given when 20 and 32 with those given when 44 to identify his less conscious changes. The comparisons did not include any other information I had about him nor any subsequent Rorschach. In his late 50s, despite three years of letters and uncounted telephone calls, I had never succeeded in contacting Charlie directly to interview him and give him a fourth Rorschach. I had attributed this second "comedy of our calendars" to his going underground to avoid those who objected to his abortion activities. I worried for years that I might some day read that an anti-abortion fanatic had assassinated Charlie.

The results of my comparisons made more than twenty years ago surprisingly confirmed and rooted more deeply his maleness in his sexuality. The major changes I detected were

- consistent continuity in his personality, but some decrease in productivity in more personal areas, such as his relationships with mother figures.
- moving to incorporate in awareness more phallic-aggressive impulses without anxiety which he himself equated with ambition and achievement, e.g., saw many more rockets taking off, which he claimed were phallic symbols. I noted colloquially that he "really has found his penis which he is asserting in all its authority."
- more conscious self-acceptance of his sexual potency.
- more readily aroused hostility which he was struggling to control by fantasy and negativism.

I felt he had good control and defenses to cope with his intensifying phallic-aggressiveness but I questioned, "Where is his tender side in his relationships with women?" Might not such a pattern of extreme personality scores suggest he will experience future difficulties feeling empathy for and understanding the inner world of women, especially more feminine ones?

Might his future well-being depend upon discovering and integrating, in Jung's terms, his anima—his least developed needs, his more tender side?

Approaching Death

In 1998, Charlie had a major stroke that left him sexually impotent and incapacitated to do surgery, though he had continued as a consultant advising women about abortions. He is now more feeble, indecisive, and restricted in his physical motion. In the fall of 2003, I finally met Charlie again and Naomi. At lunch, I was surprised about how well he looked. "That's what people tell me but I'm at the bottom inside," a comment he repeated several times. He is weary of living, spending much of his limited energy to just survive, primarily watching television. He no longer listens to his precious records. While he reads the daily *New York Times,* his wife is unsure how much he comprehends given that his attention span is now quite limited. She does not believe he can recall events accurately and so does not trust his replies to my recent survey and PSQ, neither of which he was able to complete. He no longer has a cause for which to fight. Life has become a different kind of struggle that he no longer enjoys. He is collecting sleeping pills.

Since my last visit, Charlie gave up his struggle, swallowed his accumulated sleeping pills, lost consciousness, was discovered by his housekeeper, rushed to the hospital, revived with no obvious after-effects, except for a deep bitterness that he had failed to end his struggle.

Charlie died peacefully three months later from a lung complication.

What Charlie's Life Tells Us about Maturing

Over-developed masculinity can block interpersonal maturing and undermine today's marriages.

Too great discrepancy between one's masculinity and femininity can have regressive non-integrative effects and be especially harmful in heterosexual interpersonal relations.

Passionate idealistic commitments to serve others and society mark more mature adults.

Following an imposed religious path not emotionally owned can produce severe conflict and possible regression in health.

Maturity needs genuine freedom to become what maturity could become.

It may not seem worth holding onto life when passion and commitments have died.

Commentary

For men, chapter 1's commentary identified the personality of their spouses and type of occupation to be the two leading causes of maturing into the early 30s and mid 40s. Their type of occupation ranked fourth in influence during their 50s. For women, the personality of their spouses and their parental role and/or children were the two most important causes. Type of occupation was sixth and eighth in influence during their 40s and 50s respectively. The rapid increase in the number of professional and managerial women now working full-time may alter the relative importance of their professional and parental roles. Some professionals may spend 60 to 70 hours a week working for 40 or more years; many may devote more than 80,000 hours during their adult years to their occupations, more time than they spend with their partners and children. That's a lot of time for an occupation to work itself into one's personality.

What are an occupation's effects on maturing, especially during the early years of adulthood, the 20s and early 30s, the most receptive period for change to occur in adults? I rely on the men's reported changes since I had not studied the women's until their 40s. Research has shown that the effects of maturing vary among occupations. For example, professional and managerial men are happier and more content with their work than clerical workers are. The study's highly educated professional men are homogenous enough to identify their professions' effects. (Heath, 1976)

Researchers on occupational effects have been bedeviled by a major methodological flaw, a flaw also shared by studies on the effects of schooling. They have not used a comprehensive model of healthy growth to assess the full scope of an occupation's, or schools' and colleges', effects. The consequence is that no statement about their *most* important occupational effects can be made. (Heath, 1980) As chapter 2 suggested, the study's model of maturing comprehends every effect found in studies of change in different groups. Three judges scoring the men's interviews for occupational effects found no effect or change that could not be scored using the model of maturity's categories.

Three questions frame this commentary: 1.What are the principal maturing effects of professional occupations on men? 2. Principal immaturing effects?

3. Do different professional occupations differ in their effects on their members' mental health? The men did not differ enough in age or education from national samples to be atypical of professionals generally. (Heath, 1977b)

Occupations' Mature Effects on Professional Men

The men had matured reliably from graduation to their early 30s so it is reasonable to ask, "How had they changed?" Their occupations had had maturing effects in every category of the model of maturing except in their familial relationships, which were vulnerable to occupations' negative effects. The occupational maturing effects of men's professions were in order of declining prominence:

Increased Other-Centeredness

Of Mind   Charlie believed that surgery had increased his analytic skill and judgment.

A specialist in international law said his job required "impartiality and openness to arguments from all sides. You learn to look at problems from more than just a narrow point of view."

Increased Integration

Of Mind   A novice opera director said, "In dealing with a piece of music, scoring, and staging it, I am dealing with specifics and fitting them into a larger whole. It's just a huge amount of knowledge that I never had to cope with before."

Increased Stability and Autonomy

Of self   Discovering that they were in fact competent professionals stabilized the men's identities. A teacher spoke for many when he said,

"I know I can do something well professionally which is not always certain when you are starting off. That lingering self-doubt that you may be doing something that you are technically able to do but not emotionally able to do well."

Charlie learned he could do surgery even with bombs going off outside his medical tent. As an army surgeon he saw "a lot of horror without upsetting me. I was surprised to learn I could live like an animal and not let it bother me."

Increased Awareness

Of Values   As a Vietnam surgeon, Charlie "saw so much destruction I developed a higher respect for human life. I began to think about capital punishment in a different way." He later attributed the "liberalization" of his values to his experience in performing surgery with very different people.

A lawyer who worked with poor people said his occupation "radicalized my political beliefs and showed me really close up the oppression in the country. Taught me to value people even more; showed me the need for struggle."

Of Relationships   Charlie performed surgery on people he never would have met. He had to learn how to deal with them. As a consequence he became "interested in people," including enlisted men with whom he, as their commanding officer, learned to get along with well. [Other-centered relations]

Other surgeons said surgery taught them to become more sensitive to and sympathetic for patients. "You have to be aware of people and sensitized about what is going on with them at a very personal level. If I had been a chemist or physicist, it would have been a lot easier to continue on being what I was."

Finally, a teacher summarized the effects of his teaching this way:

"The fact that I am a college teacher just about determined 95% of my life. Teaching is a personal relationship. Communication with students and colleagues demands a kind of mentality or attitude about other people. One cannot afford to be too self-seclusive. [*sic*]

"Has changed my interpersonal relationships to a great extent."

Occupations' Principal Negative Effects on Professional Men's Maturity

Professional occupations' maturing effects do not come without a price, especially for highly achieving and ambitious persons. While the men reported about six times more mature than immature effects, their occupations' absorption of their energy and time had pervasive negative constricting effects on their mental health. Their social, recreational, sexual, friendship, and community relations were most frequently adversely affected during the men's 20s and 30s.

- "I don't have much time to spend with other people, to socialize. I am not developing as richly when I don't have much time with other people. I feel inhibited at many levels."
- "The tensions and pressures get to me; they take their toll in terms of not being responsive to my wife."
- "My work has been so over-taxing that I'm just not up to carrying on social relationships, even carrying on conversations. I'm bushed, tired, and irritable due to the stress of my business."
- "My occupation has decreased my energy for other pursuits and desires. At the end of the day I do not have the desire to do anything else."

Sixty percent of the men's wives noted the inhibition and excessive self-control of their husbands. While probably more the result of the men's socialization as males, reduced energy has its effects. The following comments of their wives were not rare: "It's hard to talk to him," "closed up emotionally," "He shuts up like a clam," "He's just not here. He tunes out."

While Charlie's retreat to his private music room was singular, falling asleep in front of the nightly TV was not. Might their absorption in their work "explain" why the men had one-third fewer sexual relations a month than Kinsey's most comparable highly educated group? Or why a surprising 47% had sought counseling during their 20s and early 30s? Or why their children meant so much to some fathers? Had their children helped them to rediscover and re-equilibrate their expressive and emotional selves?

Mental Health Effects of Different Professional-Managerial Careers

Charlie claimed that physicians have high rates of suicide, marital failures, drug and other unhealthy effects. I could not probe the meaning of his claim and his sources of information because of the incapacitating effects of his stroke. Nor could I find the evidence to clarify several critical questions. What defines "high?" When compared to a representative national sample? To similar professionals like lawyers and business executives? Lawyers and judges are alleged to have the highest incidence of depression in the country. (Harrison, 2003) Compared to similarly educated persons of what age? Are the unhealthy effects due to the type of person admitted to medical school? Does the practice of medicine, rather than law, make physicians more vulnerable to such effects? What types of medical and legal practice are more likely to create pathological effects? These and other questions quickly become prohibitively expensive, if not practically impossible, to answer with any certainty.

My study illustrates how the questions might be approached. Its longitudinal nature provides comparative baseline data for four small professional groups: 11 physicians, 12 lawyers, 17 college academicians and deans, and 21 business executives and entrepreneurs. None of these groups differed significantly from each other in their verbal, quantitative, and English achievement test scores upon admission to college. Nor did the four occupational groups differ in their mental health, defined by their freshman MMPI scores.

The similarity of the men's ages, college curricular requirements, other societal and cultural experiences such as the Vietnam War, and socioeconomic status limit any possible differential effect on their mental health. The study's comprehensiveness, however, makes it possible to search out other types of possible differences between the occupations that might contribute to the men's subsequent health.

Repeated administrations of the MMPI and PSQ measures of psychological health made it possible to examine (true, very crudely and only suggestively) if the type of occupation decisively contributed to a change in mental health. The physicians, lawyers, academicians, and executives did not reliably differ from each other in their MMPI-defined mental health in their 30s as well as in their 40s. This result was confirmed by the PSQ comparisons with only one exception. Whereas the physicians, lawyers, and academicians did not differ from each other in their maturity in their early 30s and also in their mid 40s, the academicians scored as more mature than the business executives at both times.

No statistical evidence suggests that any of the occupational groups improved in their mental health or maturity from their 30s to their 40s. The groups' statistical results do not, of course, invalidate the individual men's measured maturity nor reports about how their occupations changed them. I return in chapter 10 to argue that the decisive period for the healthy growth of adults is their 20s to early 30s.

I don't pursue further how type of occupation might have affected the men differently, given that the small size of the samples makes such explorations too risky to be reliable.

Chapter 8

—————>●<—————

JOSH:

SEEKING LOVING GAY FRIENDSHIPS

"Like anybody he needs people. He needs to be loved a lot."
Greg, Josh's partner

Josh provides an example of the potential maturing effects of Erhard Seminars Training (EST) that contributed to his ranking fifth among the study's men in the amount of his maturing between his 30s and 40s. While his sexuality seems to dominate his personality, its significance is not as a goal but as a route for him to create loving male friendships. This chapter and its commentary illuminate some deeper meanings of American males' relationships with men, one of the two personality sectors in which the study's men grew least as adults.

—————

Josh's growth through his adult years touched some of the themes of others like Rich, a member of Mensa, the society for the intellectually gifted. However, he was not compulsively driven to exploit his intellectual gifts. Josh slowly matured, like Buck. I had hesitated to include him as an exemplar since I had no information about how he might have matured into his 50s and 60s. However, the PSQ measure of his maturing was confirmed not only by his rated changes on the Personality Trait Survey (PTS) but also by the independent ratings of his friends and partner. Josh was an average mature young man who struggled more self-consciously than the study's other men with what his relationships should be and what it meant to be a male at a time women were redefining what a female was, a theme that Mary lived out.

140

Josh's father was a naval officer who died when Josh was very young. Sent to a boy's boarding military school, he later felt it was the unhappiest period of his life. "I learned a lot of things that shocked me. I was thought of as very prudish. I realized I had human appetites." The boys introduced him to sex. He began to become aware of his homosexual inclinations. Academically, he did very well, graduating first in his class as a National Merit Scholar. His associations to his high school years were "lots to do, parties, anger, uncertainty, seeking friends."

He felt "very close" to his mother who really cared for him and whom he enjoyed being with. Though they quarreled about his vocation, finances, and politics, he never told her about his gayness, though he thinks she may have guessed it. When she visited his home, Greg, his partner, hid Josh's dirty pictures of nude males in his own bureau drawer. Josh appreciated his mother's warmth, individuality and liberality, her openness to new ideas. She taught him to be tolerant of and open to different kinds of people. He regretted she never took the chance to make a career for herself. She died in a nursing home shortly before he took the EST training.

As would be expected of a member of Mensa, Josh scored at the ninety-ninth percentile on all of the college's measures of his intelligence. Though he worked diligently, he averaged only B+ in his academic work. He excelled in his major, mathematics, and received honors in German and Economics. He actively participated in extracurricular activities, especially drama, the students' newspaper, and on important student committees. Entering Haverford College intent on becoming a physician, he soon switched to law. His departmental chairman rated his emotional stability and personality excellent and his determination, intelligence, and originality to be good.

In his junior year he made a fateful "choice." He came out as gay, claiming it was a consciously deliberate choice at a time when gayness was not an acceptable life style among his peers. He defined himself as radically liberal on social issues like sex and drugs, but conservative in his politics and economics. Though an Episcopalian, he remained indifferent to religious practices.

After graduating he went to University of Pennsylvania's law school with a full scholarship and graduated three years later with a prize for the greatest improvement. Then he began a series of different jobs while he took evening courses in accounting. He clerked for an attorney, fixed up and rented apartments, and worked as an auditor in various city departments. Josh had gone into law to enter politics where he felt he could affect social policy. He had been introduced to Arlen Specter, a district attorney and later United States senator, who was interested in hiring him as an assistant. However, someone recognized that he had marched in a peace demonstration. Also Specter had gotten reports "about the kinds of people I hung around with, kinds of bars where I go which reflected on my moral code and sexual life." His job application was rejected. Believing that politicians needed to be married and have a family, he abandoned his political ambitions.

Originally interested in criminal law, he now felt 90% of the laws should be eliminated, including laws about sex, gambling, and liquor, anything in the moral area.

> Seems to me government is getting involved in all areas and should be more involved in education than prohibition. When I look back on my life, I see adjustment to morality as adjustment to ambition. I had lots of ambitions and fantasies as a child, and I guess as I have grown up I've seen them more and more as fantasies and escapes rather than things that are actually going to happen to me.

Eventually he found work with the state's Human Relations Commission where he worked on racial quota issues.

> What I do is work with companies who have low percentages of minority workers compared with the total percentage in the city population. I then visit the companies to persuade them to hire more. I sit down with companies and let them talk first and get them to explain their goals and why we are harassing them.

Because of the irregularity of the work and his need for a predictable income, he kept searching for a position that would fit his values and pay more money. Eventually, Josh turned to the individual practice of law, concentrating on bankruptcies and made a passable income. He never viewed his work as his calling, which in effect turned out to be his self-development and being a friend. Developing friendships with men became more important to Josh than personal ambition or the full use of his intellectual gifts, as Rich exploited his. I wondered if he did not downplay his intellectual talents because they got in the way of his friendships. Note the meaning of friendship to Josh as you read his story.

Excerpts from Notes about Visit to Josh in His Mid 30s

I met Josh at his home in Philadelphia's center city where I thought I was in a junkyard. He and his lover had been redecorating their house; the roof of the dining room was off, and all kinds of equipment were scattered about. We went to the second floor, which was a solarium filled with plants, some parakeets, and fish. Josh had put on weight and grown a beard and longer hair. More importantly, he was shy, reserved, quiet, and certainly not assertive or dominating. He was passive and silent. Though Josh thinks of himself as very optimistic, I sensed an undercurrent of sadness and lostness. He had remembered some comments I had made when I worked with him as a junior: "Be careful as a criminal prosecutor in court that you don't become a persecutor."

Josh did not spontaneously talk about his gayness but his partner, Greg, wanted to talk with me about it.

Greg—Josh's Partner

Josh talked at length about Greg, an unemployed artist, who had been in an automobile accident with him. Both were receiving a settlement that enabled them to buy their house together where they had lived for seven years. They thought of themselves as lovers who had frustrating communication problems. [Where had I heard that before?] Devoted to Greg, Josh paid for his upkeep, including liquor and ongoing medical bills. He said of Greg, "He is not very good about doing something he doesn't want to do. He'll only do it so long and then it becomes too much to continue." The only partially renovated house was a focal point of disagreement. Greg didn't carry an equal share of the work.

Josh continued somewhat mournfully,

> I'd like to be able to share my life with him in the things I
> like to do which I can't because we are just two different
> people. Another way to define 'communication' is by
> openness. I would like to be more open—just feel that I
> can't be because we are so different.

Josh felt Greg was very prudish, even puritanical, who objected to his smoking marijuana and inviting so many people to stay in the house with them because some of Josh's friends are "dangerous."

"In what ways have you been a good friend?"

> I've been able to comfort Greg with his problems and worries. He knows he has someone who will stand beside him. I put a lot of stuff on trust. You trust and you know that you are going to be disappointed many times but most of them will be small things. He gets very hurt when I fall short of the expectation. The old argument about truth and frankness. Ideal relationships should be absolutely frank. When I first met Greg I told him I'm honest and always tell the truth; then I realized that I don't really do that at all. I almost never give a direct answer. I've done this all my life.

Greg was a little skittish about talking to a "psychiatrist" but soon relaxed and spoke quite openly about his relationship with Josh. The interview turned out to be cathartic for him. He said he felt better as a result of talking with me.

I asked, "What is Josh's relation with his mother and sisters?"

> Josh is the last born and the only boy. I think he was spoiled. He gets along with his family beautifully. Like anybody, he needs people. He needs to be loved a lot. He has to have a lot of respect. If you catch him in a mistake, he will very seldom admit it. His cousin was getting married; his mother said he couldn't go to the wedding unless he cut off his beard, and she thought he would. He told her, "I didn't cut off the beard and so can't go to the wedding." She said, "All right; keep your beard."

"What are the best things about your relationship with Josh?"

> Josh likes to help people out. People are always calling him up and asking him to do this and do that and he'll do it. I think people take advantage of him. People ask, "Can you take me to the station?" "Could you pick me up here?" "Would you go over and feed my cat?" "On

the way over would you stop and get a bottle of soda?" It
goes on and on. He's loyal.

I then asked, "What things are not quite as good about your relationship?"
"He has a terrible stubborn streak and sometimes I might provoke it. I
don't like some of his friends' activities. If I say 'no' to drugs, he'll take
them anyway. I don't want any of that stuff in the house. He has smoked it
right in front of me."
I then explored why Greg didn't like some of Josh's friends.

> Some of his friends are not really good people. They are
> a bad influence. Drugs and sex probably too. They aren't
> up to his standards. He could meet much better people.
> They are a little low. A fellow is here now from Califor-
> nia. I thought he would be here for a few weeks. He said
> he thinks he'll stay for the summer. Josh doesn't seem to
> care. I don't feel that this is my place at all. I just stopped
> putting into the house. I've lost all interest right now.

Greg continued about drugs, which he doesn't want in the house. "Josh
doesn't main line, just grass and mescaline. Not speed. I made him promise
there wouldn't be any grass in the house. His friend here now has grass and
that shakes me up a bit."
"Why is Josh attracted to this kind of person?"

> He needs to be surrounded by people first of all. I don't
> like hordes of people at parties. I find things missing. I
> find people in my bed. I go upstairs to another bed and
> find somebody else there. Josh doesn't seem to care.
> Once he gets into the party and starts drinking, he just
> goes and goes and goes. He needs people.

"What else is not quite so good?"
Greg replied, "I would like him to be happy. No question. I would like
him to stop smoking pot, drinking. I would like him to take a little more
interest in the house and also his personal appearance too."
"Why do you think he is unhappy?"

> Well, me and the house. I'm unhappy and Josh wants
> to do something and he doesn't know what to do. It's

money right now that is getting me uptight and it's
getting Josh uptight too. He doesn't want me to worry
about money. He's worried about his job. Doesn't think
he knows exactly what he wants. Both of us are sort of
dragging right now. I just want to sometimes move out
and go away. I just feel so lost and don't know how to do
it. Josh wouldn't want me to go. Josh has to be pushed
sometimes. He is not aggressive.

"What is he like when he is drunk?"

He's a pleasant drunk. He talks and laughs a lot. Gets
very, very loud. Usually he is quiet. Starts talking about
very heavy things like Greek mythology, composers, tells
funny stories about them that are not printed in textbooks.
Things you don't get in high school.

I had completed my analysis of Josh's tests and had noticed a change in
his aggressiveness. So I returned to Greg's comment about Josh's aggressiveness to ask if he had noticed any change.

"He has probably gotten a little more aggressive to me. I think he has. He
has gotten a little harder, a little tougher. Tougher or calloused. Josh can be
stung once but he won't be stung again. He remembers hurts."

Greg then talked about Josh's drinking. He was not going to the bars as
frequently, had stopped smoking cigarettes, cut back on grass, and had not
"dropped acid in a long time."

"What are some ways Josh is a good friend?"

"Gosh. I can ask him to go down and pick up a pack of cigarettes, which
he doesn't like to smoke. But he'll go buy that type of cigarette. There he
is doing something he doesn't want to do. If anybody steps on me or does
something terrible, Josh will defend me."

Pursuing how Josh dealt with different emotions, I asked if Greg had
ever seen Josh cry.

Yes. He cries at a movie, over books. Once we had a
serious fight when I blew up and raged out of control and
started breaking things. He was crying and I had to help

him upstairs to bed. He wasn't angry. He was hurt and felt sad. He thought everything was all gone. I must have hit him so hard with whatever it was.

"Does he ever allow himself to feel dependent, to ask for help?"

Not too often. Sometimes I play mother, nurse, doctor when he has an illness, which is easy for me to do. I'll cook his dinner and take breakfast up to bed and mop his brow. He responds very well to emotion. He's pretty soft really underneath. He likes sex a hell of a lot more than I do. I think I'm undersexed. Sometimes I think he feels that I think he was responsible for it. Guilt there. Which he wasn't.

Greg used the rest of our interview to talk about his anxieties, a fight with his boss that resulted in being fired, and Josh's legal support.

Fragments of Analysis of Test Results in Josh's Mid 30s

I had written: Now there has been a marked reduction in the affective and impulsive intensity of his life. Feelings seem more mute, impulses less violent, sadistic, intense, even guilty. Been a quieting down, so that, in contrast to when he graduated, he seems to be a much more inwardly quiet person. Not as much tension and conflict or in as much direct hostile opposition to the world. A very noticeable change. The most singular new trend is the emergence of a strong need for security, to be taken care of, a safe harbor, a relationship in which to be cared for, a persistent passivity or expectation of waiting for something good to happen to him. This may tie up his energy in some depression.

Emotionally, he is sensitive and readily aroused, more acceptant of his affectionate needs for others. Is certainly concerned about people; is not isolated from them; he needs them too much. Under persistent emotional stress, with strong emotional input from others, he could well respond more assertively and in more masculine ways. Yet, there is a tendency still to fear hurting others and being hurt, and there remains the potential for relating but not with much openness or trust.

Growing from Josh's 30s to His Mid 40s

When I arrived at his new home, his current lover, Herb, met me at the door: heavily tattooed, shoeless, bedraggled, and carrying a drink. Josh had shaved off his beard, cut his hair, and his forehead had expanded. The scar on his cheek he had gotten from his automobile accident was now more prominent. He slurred his speech more noticeably and mumbled more frequently.

The house was more disheveled than Josh's first house. Six cats prowled through the house, leaving a noticeable smell. Josh loved plants and had so many I felt I was in an arboretum. The heavy furniture gave me a feeling of being back in the 19th century. The office was so small a second chair wouldn't fit; I brought Josh back to Haverford for our sessions.

Josh's Experience with EST

Josh had several friends who had taken EST's training and who had urged him to participate. Part of the training is to share the good news and encourage others to participate. Eventually another friend, who had been smiling much more than he ever had before the training, said, "We are good friends. I know who you are. I love you. I want you to do this training." Josh said okay. He had recently completed the training and now is interested in becoming a trainer himself. He is urging his current lover, Herb, to go to EST. Herb thinks Josh is "obsessed" by EST—commonly heard about "graduates" of the sessions.

Josh explained why EST has been the most influential cause of his current growth.

> I knew in some ineffable way that I was responsible for what was in my life. I knew it in a more magical or metaphysical way. From the experience of EST it fell out of my head into my gut and now I have been empowered to be me. The experience is not really about fixing me up and making me better but to be responsible for who I am.

I asked, "Well, who is Josh?"

The love I have for other people. I really want to be with other people, closely, lovingly, and intimately. Coming from a willful, impatient sort of background, I still have a tremendous faith to let other people be the way they are, to appreciate the qualities they have to bring forth. I discovered I had a great deal of patience really.

"I don't understand what you mean by 'willful.'"

"Like eating dinner, rushing to get to the desert. My mother and family are like that. Always looking ahead to see what is next rather than taking time to enjoy now."

Adam

Josh launched into a detailed recital of his lovers beginning with his "tragic romance with Adam" with whom he was going when breaking up with Greg, though they remain friends.

Adam was incredible. Had to have me. I really was split between the two: one night with Greg and another night with Adam. I wasn't particularly honest about it for a year or so. Then I realized that Greg was too dependent upon me. The house was a never-ending sink. I told Adam I would live with him and told Greg he could get off on his own. We needed to sell the house. In December Adam said he couldn't bear waiting for me to wind things up with the house so he moved to San Francisco. We wrote practically every day. Without a buyer by spring, Greg asked whom did I love more. I only answered, "You both and I need to live with Adam now." Adam then wrote in August that he had waited for me for three years, so would I be willing to wait for six months because he was going to India with someone to learn about meditation. It was a platonic relationship with no physical appetite involved. In October Adam's father died. He came back for the funeral. I went to the church. We went out into the woods in New Jersey, had sex that obviously affected him immensely. He had to return to California immediately.

Eventually I went out to California to live with Adam for a
month. I drank a lot.

Josh returned to his Philadelphia law firm to work on bankruptcy cases.

Herb

Josh and Herb had lived with each other for eight years prior to my next
visit. They had moved from one apartment for a week, to a house for a
month, to another apartment and so on for several years; they even had lived
for several weeks under a bridge. They are renting the house they now live
in and are considering buying it.

Josh is very happily Herb's partner. He values most highly Herb's
companionship, "knowing that I matter to him, the excitement of being
with him physically." Josh appreciates Herb's concern for his comfort and
his physical needs.

When I asked, "In what ways have you been a good partner?" Josh replied

> I have stuck with him. I supported him in having the
> things he wants in his life. I have moderated my demands
> to give him time to get around to them instead of insisting
> that they be done immediately. I provide space for him to
> live, encourage him to go for quality in his life, and I let
> him know I love him and that I know he loves me.

Josh is unhappy about Herb's insecurity and use of drugs and alcohol.
Josh is "much more casual" in his relationships. "I don't have the same
picture of fidelity that he does." He believes Herb has quite strong beliefs
that the same standard of sexual morality should hold for both partners, a
belief Josh does not hold at all either for himself or for Herb to hold. Though
only somewhat well-mated sexually, Josh gets great enjoyment from their
sexual relationship; Herb gets only mild enjoyment. They have sex about
eight times a month, though Josh wishes they had sex twelve times a month.
On Josh's list of the five most important attributes for a sexually fulfilling
relationship, he rates himself higher than he rates Herb on willingness,
patience, presence, desire, but not quite as honest in the relationship. He
rates them both to be very much in love with each other. Josh explained the
difference between their overall sense of sexual fulfillment this way.

I was much more passive with Greg and more active with Herb, which surprised me. I guess I think of myself as passive when thinking of the person I wanted. Now I'm taking a more active role in the sexual act. One of Herb's insecurities is he can't get into being the active partner, like masturbating me. I like being active with him. I find myself getting a lot more involved when I'm active than when fantasizing. I use fantasies a lot less to bring about sexual release than I used to. Seven to eight years ago I always used a fantasy. You do it and a while later you are ready to do it again, flesh against flesh or whatever you do to reduce the tension. There is something more than just the physical act of sex. One reason I enjoy sex is that it is a means of being with people. Just to sleep with someone in the same bed is as satisfying as having sex with somebody.

Josh's maturity remained within the average of the group. He matured only modestly in his awareness [Awareness self] but more in his acceptance of himself from his college days to his mid 40s [Other-centered self]. He matured little in his relationships with women and somewhat more in his relations with men.

Causes of Josh's Maturing

Not surprisingly his EST experience dominated his over-all personality growth.

EST Training Effects

Josh explained EST's effects by using some of EST's terms.

Experiencing people directly instead of through the categories or judgments I had about them. I have a much more complete experience of our commonality [Other-centered self]. It is who I am. The oneness of who I am. The potential of who I am. My visions of myself and my world have become available to me again [Integration cognitive and self]. Before I had shut them off in some part of my mind. While sitting in the room with the other trainees, I had the opportunity to be totally with myself. I really did think I was my mind to a large degree. That was my story. I discovered this for myself [Autonomy self].

Personality of Josh's Partner

My partner is warm and loving, so I'm able to express myself a lot more because of that [Integration self]. Am able to hold a lot of room for a lot of people through knowing him [Other-centered self]. He doesn't really fit my picture. His family background is from a funny area; he is not very classy. Because he is my lover I feel room to let these things into myself. I might otherwise shut them out due to my categories [Integration relations]. I can let people be the way they are. They have a contribution to make because of themselves and not because of what they represent [Other-centered relations]. Seeing traits in him that I could discover in myself, because if it is not all right for him than it is not all right for me, like his compulsiveness [Awareness of self]. I can try to change myself. Because I notice I don't like his compulsiveness and I have something like it, I had better clear up my own act, like drugs [Autonomy self]. He is a wonderful example of why I want to get that out of my life, which ultimately means helping him get them out of his life because he is in my life [Other-centered value].

Role as Partner

Josh continued to apply the insights he had secured from his EST experience.

Having responsibility for someone [Other-centered relations]. Having someone to whom I can express my caring [Other-centered self]. How to handle my anger [Awareness self]. Learned how I can get angry at people and how to make it useful to me [Awareness relations].

Learning about His Maleness

Following the interview in their mid 30s, the participants were interviewed about their changing roles as males or females. To the question of what should a man be, Josh replied,

> He should be independent, self-reliant, taking care of people who are dependent on him. I was definitely into "handling cases." I definitely looked upon men as needing to be taken care of by women. I can now see how a lot of that was internalized which I definitely was not aware of. I was liberated enough then to know it was all right for men to cry in appropriate circumstances but I'm sure my range about what was appropriate was more limited. I was definitely more concerned about how to appear to others. I thought I should have an image and a very rigid one.

"How are you typically male?" I asked.

> From a gay viewpoint, I am very typically male. From a straight viewpoint, how can I be typically male if I am not straight? Presupposes what a typical male is. I became aware of a lot of stereotypes in me when I was 25 or 26. I had a girl friend. She traveled with me and I had a good time with her sexually. I got really clear that women could enjoy sex like a man. My whole way of looking at sex before was that women did sex because it was a duty and men enjoyed it. That was one of the rationalizations for being gay. My experience was that there is a sexual revolution and I am part of it. EST helped me to accept women as human beings like me for we live in the same era. Like being able to be open about my sexual preferences with others who have little in common with me and working and sharing with them allowing them to express their appreciation and affection for me without being uptight about how to respond.

Excerpts of Summary Analysis of Tests about Josh's Changes to Mid 40s

I speculated that there had been a major self-defining event in young adulthood that led to avoiding or not fulfilling the more masculine, assertive, virile, potent, achieving potential he has. Instead, he lives out the more feminine side of his nature: the need for security and love without mastering the discipline to channel his potentials into more conventional ways. Perhaps the death of his mother and EST are now freeing him from a former self-defined identity, which means he is now beginning to confront formerly repressed parts of himself. It looks as if it is this more masculine, intrusive, aggressive, achieving self that is beginning to lay claim on him. He is now at a choice point as to whether he will dedicate his energies in more disciplined channeled ways to fulfill his intellectual potentials that may have lain fallow. Will he find a broad enough channel through which to pour his energies but which will also integrate the more immediate past with his psycho-historical past? Can he finally accept and integrate all of his character, as he said in his story to the TAT card portraying a man in a cemetery?

> One night he falls asleep and he is alone in darkness. He dreams he keeps walking deeper and deeper into the cemetery and finally comes to this massive tombstone in the shape of a cross. He doesn't want to read the name but he can't resist the compulsion that drives him. Seeing his own name he awakens with a cry of horror in a cold sweat. He realizes that what he has given up and that he has the opportunity to transform his life.

EST means so much symbolically to Josh because it represents the ultimate confrontation a person must face: Will he begin to grow into the full range of his potentials and so live, or will he block out and deny his strongest potentials and so in guilt die?

Because of the recent death of his mother, I now asked the standard interview question, "What are your feelings and thoughts about dying?"

> My thought is that it is a long way from now. My feeling is I'll never be ready and it is okay with me whenever it

happens because it will. I have a sense I used to have a lot of unexpressed anxieties about it. Ever since my mother's death they are not there any more. EST taught me to be willing to have them be the way they are. I now feel a lot more whole about it.

Five years after I had seen Josh, he died of AIDS. A colleague whom I had called said he had died with "great dignity." Herb had died several years later in anguish.

Josh's Lessons for Us

Failure to accept responsibility for one's own known talents can distort healthy growth.

Substituting sex as a goal rather than using it as a means for connecting with others can limit interpersonal maturing.

American males' identification of sexuality with affection results in immature interpersonal maturing.

Failure to integrate one's masculinity with one's femininity, regardless which may be repressed or underdeveloped, results in an immature self-maturation; androgyny is essential to interpersonal maturing with both the opposite and one's own sex.

Commentary

Josh was a marginal member of American society in two ways: he was intellectually gifted and his homosexuality satisfied his intense need for male companionship. The lives of those who live at the edge of a society's values can illuminate heretofore unknown and/or unhealthy vulnerabilities.

You might wish to now review chapter 3's commentary about SAT scores to better understand Josh's devaluation of his intellectual potentials in order to develop his friendships.

Homosexual Companionship

As Greg said of Josh, "he needs to be loved a lot." His sexual orientation provided the means, really the impetus, to secure that companionship which persisted for years with Greg, Adam, and Herb.

Few men of the study had close male friendships that persisted as long or were as close as the women's female relationships. Only 22% of the men claimed they had a close male friend. A national survey of American men reported similar findings, i.e., fewer than 25% of men said they had a close male friend. (Block, 1980)

Attributes of Ideal Friendship

While not differing from women in the attributes they wanted in their ideal same-sexed friendships, e.g., trusting, self-disclosing, affectionate, the women's friendships clearly reliably differed from the men's. In contrast to men, the study's women
- believed it is more important to have a close friend.
- felt more fulfilled in their friendships and so were less lonely.
- were more intimate with and closer to their friends.
- felt more affectionate and loving toward their friends.
- were more open and self-disclosing in their relationships.
- felt more comfortable sharing their greatest insecurities, failures, and feelings about their own parents. (Heath 1994b)

These differences persisted into the women's 60s.

Cultural Differences in Meaning of Friendship

American men are more conflicted about close male friendships than men in some other cultures. In 1965-66 I compared mature and immature Turkish Muslim, Italian Catholic, and American Protestant and Jewish men on the principal measures used in the current longitudinal study. To identify how the three cultural groups differed in the pattern of their relationships, I identified eight modes of relatedness ranging from aggression, independence, and avoidance to dependence, affection, and flirting, in ninety-six paired types of relationships, e.g., adolescent males with their mothers, fathers, brothers, females. Fifty judges from each culture rated their culture's degree of approval and disapproval of each mode of relatedness with each of the gender and age types of relationships. The results illuminated the problems American males, and men like Josh, have in their relationships. I list the most pertinent reliable cultural differences.

Compared to the Turkish and Italian cultures, the American culture was judged to be the most restrictive and punitive. It approved reliably fewer modes of relatedness with the gender-age categories. For example, it approved only more independent and playful modes of relatedness, especially for males, than either the Turkish or Italian cultures approved. However, both the Turkish and Italian cultures approved controlling, aggressing, depending, and being affectionate with more gender-age categories than the American culture approved.

In contrast to the Italian and Turkish cultures, the American culture strongly approves sexual seductive relationships in only five, at most, of the ninety-six types of relationships, such as sexual contact between 17-year-old males and females and unmarried 22-year-old men and women. Italian and Turkish males have greater freedom to roam sexually more widely.

The American culture does not distinguish as clearly as the other cultures do between sexual and affectionate friendships. Close friendships seem to imply sexual relationships for Americans. Turks and Italians are significantly less disapproving than the Americans of pubertal and young adult affectionate and homosexual or extramarital relationships with more diverse people. (Heath, 1977a, Appendix A)

Other studies report that Chinese male friendships are much more loyal than American ones. (Yeh & Chu, 1974) European and Asian friendships are widely believed to be "deeper," more personal, and more loyal. Australian men value very highly having a life-long male "buddy."

Are American males more uncomfortable expressing the qualities of ideal friends? I have written in greater depth about the meaning and character of American male friendships. (Heath 1994b) The men who had close male friendships were androgynous, e.g., understanding, loyal, warm, and sympathetic. They definitely were not macho, e.g., competitive, aggressive, dominant, or forceful.

Josh's intellectual giftedness and gayness may have made him marginal in the American though not gay culture.[1] (Mann, 2003) He was not marginal to the ideal character of a close friend.

Chapter 9

————»·•·◅⁄◄————

DAVE AND ELISE:

SURVIVING A SEXUALLY INCOMPATIBLE MARRIAGE
A TROUBLED COUPLE'S LONG ROAD TO HEALTH

"I am not going to help you care for the children;
the children are your bag." Dave

"When he is not here, I miss him. When I am not around,
he says he misses me. I believe him." Elise

Dave and Elise show us the graphic dynamics of the insides of a couple trying not just to survive as a couple but to create more fulfilling lives for themselves. This chapter's question is, "Why have they survived as a couple, given their formidable problems to overcome, when so many other couples split apart?" The commentary examines two of their formidable problems: their need for but lack of mutual sexual compatibility and the effects of menopause.

———•·•·———

I had selected Dave because he and Buck showed the greatest maturing among the men from 17 to their 60s. His initial PSQ score was the lowest of the men and women. His Rorschach responses as a sophomore also confirmed his immaturity.

To the first Rorschach card, he said, "Unsympathetic watchdogs who populate a decapitated Salem witch's environment. Curiously there is a little imperfection in here. Gives the impression of a Slavic spy who is uncommitted to any cause at all." Because of the symmetrical nature of the ink

158

blots, people commonly see two interacting people or animals or bats and butterflies. Dave's bizarre elaborations of the watchdogs are atypical.

To the second card, he saw, "Central content as a phallic possibility that is defensified [sic] or dealt with ironically by the two dancing hussies, who grapple for it."

To the third card, "Wholly surrealistic. Distinct movement of cannibals around a brazier of affection which oughtn't to belong to these cannibals. These are horrible specters. They suggest complete chaos of form."

What is troubling about Dave's responses is not their form but their autistic emotional elaboration, e.g., unsympathetic watch dogs, decapitated Salem witch, horrible specters.

Evaluation by Roy Schafer, a diagnostic expert, to Dave's responses to the first three Rorschach cards: "As sick a record of any in the total group. Deals with inner and outer reality by intellectualization which has become bizarre in form and content, severe limitations of usable affect for real relationships."

Fifty years later when he reviewed this chapter, Dave rationalized the pathology of his responses by claiming that he had consciously given "sick" responses. I doubted at the time that he had just been playfully perverse. However, comparison of his other Rorschachs given when a freshman and later when middle aged, showed no bizarre or similar responses. Robert Holt, a premier researcher of the Rorschach, wrote me that very bright persons comfortable in their relation with an examiner can, as Dave insisted, playfully relax their controls to show what are seemingly bizarre, unconscious ideas. So Dave may well have been right.

Comment by Dave's departmental chairman:

> He is a bright, perceptive young man, whose confidence in his own intellect leads him to make few concessions to the need to make himself intelligible to others. As a result, his work, while often highly original, fails to communicate. He has a tendency, moreover, to trade on his charm and intelligence in order to bypass the drudgery of mastering classics that he insisted on majoring in.

He rated Dave's determination, emotional stability, and personality to be poor, his intelligence and originality to be excellent.

Five years of work in mental hospitals and clinics helped me to accept and enjoy Dave's delightful "craziness," as he called his abstract unintelligibility.

Though Dave is not like Barbara, both improved similarly on the PSQ. But they differed radically. Barbara scored 30 to 40 points higher on the PSQ. She is a model of self-disciplined rationality. She is in command of her high intelligence which she successfully applied to be remarkably productive. Dave is a model of an undisciplined pleasure-seeker. As bright as Barbara, he was unable to consistently apply his talents to fulfill their potential. He lived very close to his unconscious, its irrational imaginativeness, its egocentrism, its unpredictability.

I have always been fond of Dave. If he had been one of my students, he would have frustrated my professorial expectations and angered me. His flashes of imaginative brilliance would not lead to their realization. Though scoring at the ninety-ninth percentile on every intelligence and scholastic aptitude test on record in his file, he was a B-minus student who worked only in those courses he enjoyed. But not having him as one of my students, I could enjoy him without feeling responsible and so guilty for failing him. With me, he was always open, not defensive or stubborn. I felt his needs for the respect and affection which he never had had from his parents but which I have always had for him. I have always sensed his promise.

Dave's Family Background

About his family, Dave said, "I was just parked there; I didn't have much function in my family." Although an only child, he felt rejected by both parents. His father, a top student for his Harvard undergraduate and law school years, became ill and was bedridden during Dave's early growing-up years. He later became the lawyer for a national service organization. Dave said, however, he never fulfilled his talents. Nor did he have the paternal strengths that the study's competent fathers had. (Heath, 1994b) He withdrew from family conflicts, wasn't accessible when Dave needed him, did not encourage Dave to participate in physical activities like athletics, never expressed the importance of loving others, was not self-disclosing or socially outgoing; and did not stand up to his wife to protect Dave from her. Dave did not have the type of father he wished he had had and needed.

His mother was an artist who had her own shows. Dave describes her as a tense, conflicted, and authoritarian person with poor mental health. She was hostile to males, resented her own father, and "tried to pull the same act on me." In his sixties, Dave recalled that his mother had been very anti-Jewish, though having been raised as a Jew herself. His father deferred to her atheistic beliefs. Dave said she "went to almost any lengths to destroy me." He had been very scared of her. His mother told him one time to get lost when he asked for advice, to get out of the apartment when he was sixteen, and later, when he was visiting his parents, threw him out because she got too anxious around him. To the question about how willing he would be to take care of his mother in her old age, he said, "I wouldn't want her in the house here. She'd be a deadly influence on the kids." She seldom visited her grandchildren. Recall that the participants completed the Developmental History Questionnaire (DHQ) about their childhood, family climate, and parental traits that contributed to a child's maturity and success. Dave scored lowest of any of the men in his maturity as a child. Barbara scored at the sixty-eighth percentile among her peers.

Dave left Haverford after his junior year to go to Italy where he taught himself to speak Italian in three weeks to be able to make a living by selling encyclopedias. He made enough money to survive and wander around Europe. Eventually he returned to the states to go to Columbia for a semester and then to the University of California to get his BA, majoring in geography. He met Elise and asked her to marry him. "When he told me he would like me to be the mother of his children, that sold me. A year later I was pregnant and he was terrified." He insisted Elise get an abortion, the first of six. "We were both going to school, both broke. He was very frightened about earning money."

Elise's Family Background

Elise's parents were born in central Europe. Her father came from a family of weavers and her mother from a landowner family. They farmed their fields in France which Elise worked on when young. She remembered her early reactions to nature as a "farm girl" when in 1942 she said, "I opened my eyes to see the beautiful fields, forest, and butterflies and thought what a wonderful world I'm in and I am going to have fun."

She felt her father taught her to see the good side of people. Though very strict with her she knew he cared for her. He insisted on exposing her to life right away. At the age of ten she took bags of money from the sale of their cows to the bank by herself; she wrote business letters for him because he couldn't write. He encouraged her to go to college, which she did and eventually earned a BA in science as well as the equivalent of an MA in French. Her father, like Dave, was easygoing, preferred visiting people, and would have liked "spending his whole life playing, like a big kid." He "adored Dave." They were good friends and worked together, like when making wine.

Elise's mother was more complicated. From her, she inherited her energy and learned to work hard. She modeled to Elise a love of and care for babies and small animals. But she abused Elise, terrorizing and beating her for no reason, and rejecting her. She nagged Elise's father to work harder, just as Elise does Dave. Several times she called her mother "neurotic," an alcoholic, a drunk, nuts, and a schizophrenic who had been hospitalized twice.

Elise ranked fifth from the bottom in her maturity in her 40s and scored lowest in maturity by her 50s, largely due, I believe, to her prolonged severe menopause. She had recovered her former level by her mid 60s.

Dave and Elise's Work

Dave has been Elise's cross, one she has not infrequently wished she didn't have to bear. Dave had an unreliable, checkered job history that made their early years economically uncertain. Though they assisted each other in their work, differences in their working styles as well as tenacity led them to create their own businesses. Dave eventually created a business to lubricate trucks, which he didn't like doing. He soon found it to be boring. A severe recession undermined the business, which he tried for years to sell. A confrontation with his workers further sapped his interest in his business. There was an "awful racist turmoil in the company," Dave said.

> I had hired a number of blacks in positions of responsibility. One bad apple soured the business. They became a conspiracy to destroy me. I utterly thwarted and defeated them, but it took me down. What was left of the business and enthusiasm for it? It certainly turned me into what I would have to say objectively was an outspoken racist. A case of good will squandered.

Elise's view was that

> he became completely demoralized. He had trained the men for nine years, taught them how to read and write, and made men of them. Then because of one bad apple he was in shock for six months. Main thing I had to do

was get my husband more together, to give him some
strength and hope. So I went with him to a negotiating
meeting. I started screaming left and right. Then this guy
started insulting me. I screamed back; I was feeling my
way of how to get out of this. When there is an emergency
I know somehow what to do. Like a second wind, but
there is a force coming from somewhere, a real strength.
I get very clear, like a super power. When Dave said we
couldn't keep sending kids to private school, I got to
work to create a new business to keep the kids in school.
I didn't want to be an employee and the only thing to do
was to begin a business.

I asked, "How did this conflict get resolved?"

There were eight men against one woman. They all got
fired and now he doesn't have a single black working with
him. He has this humanitarian soul trying to educate them
and give them jobs. They didn't want any of that. And the
union is Italian and they don't want any blacks. The union
is the most racist union in a 75% black community.

"Why not fire them when it first began?"
"They were protected under the union umbrella."

For decades, Dave stewed about what he might like to do. In the
meantime he considered other possibilities. His three passions—jazz,
windsurfing in San Francisco's bay, and reading—were scarcely reliable
money-generating possibilities. Dave had organized and led a jazz group,
which eventually specialized in playing music for Jewish weddings. But
gigs were few, because, as he explained, audiences didn't appreciate his
type of jazz. "I'm too flaky a character" to make music a mainstay. As he
became increasingly absorbed in Judaism, he dabbled in futile dreams such
as learning Hebrew so he could go to rabbinical school, though nominally
Catholic, and minister to a congregation. "I'd be fired too damn quick.
I'm too private for that type of thing." Or becoming a staff manager "for
which I have no affinity or enjoyment." Or selling computers which he had
done twenty years earlier but the technical side now is "so staggering to be
complete smoke" for him.

Although Dave had always worked to provide for the family and their children's private schooling, he had never found a vocation that fitted his talents and which he consistently enjoyed. Why could he not find his calling? One clue was his answer to the question, "Which period would you want to live over again?" Most answer, "None." Dave said the years between nine and twelve. Of the few who would relive their lives, none cited their years prior to puberty.

I asked, "Why?"

> My sense is from what I have learned that that is really the time when your genuine capabilities and tendencies can really be developed in later life and are really brought out and exercised. I'm not in touch with that period. I don't think I developed at that time. My life would have been different if I had succeeded or been encouraged to reach beyond anything during that period. It was a scattered period. How would I live differently? I haven't the foggiest idea. The biggest thing would not have been put off and pulled down by all of the hassles with my mother. She's always been an oppressive drag, and I knew it already at that age and was wallowing in it rather than kicking it aside and being an energetic kid.

Another clue came from the SVIT which had suggested that Barbara might find a more fulfilling administrative vocation. Dave was similar to successful people in only three occupations: lawyers, marketing executives, and photographers. Law was not a possibility; he was not up to competing with his father. Besides, he consciously refused to consider any work that utilized his intelligence and which might be called "academic." He was already a business manager and didn't like it. Nor did photography sound appealing to him.

On the other hand, Elise was similar to twenty-eight different successful types of people ranging across every major type of occupation, e.g., from engineers, dentists, commercial artists, to YMCA directors, managers, and IRS agents! She settled very early in the marriage into consistently making some money by drawing upon her expertise working with stained glass, for which she had sought expert supervision. She developed her own business repairing and tinting windshields and later buffing out scratches on buses.

She made enough money to keep their four children in a private elementary Hebrew school, though raised as a Catholic, when Dave's business limped through a severe recession.

Elise had worked their entire married life and had become tired and resigned that she always would.

Dave continued to dream about finding a "pot of gold" that would solve his problem of raising money to maintain his company's overhead until he sold it. But where to look? Wall Street's futures market. With continuing guidance from a shrewd broker, he had become rich. When I visited him in his late 50s he claimed his ship had reached port. It had brought him millions. Had he managed to keep them when his ship sank in Wall Street's financial collapse in 2001? Yes. They sold their businesses, bought a house near a lake, and took a three-month vacation in Kauai, Hawaii, the winter of 2003. Ironically, Dave became one of the wealthier men of the group.

Elise and Dave's Married Life

How else might Dave have succeeded? As a marital partner and father? I now pick up the couple's story from Elise's point of view.

Their Marital Relationship

Elise has consistently rated her marriage to be a "little unhappy," ranking in the bottom quarter of the women in the study. Over the years, Dave has consistently rated his marriage to be a "very happy" one, a typical gender difference. Of the 55% of the couples who have divorced, with very few exceptions, the wives initiated it, sometimes much to the surprise of their husbands. Since she had married, Elise has occasionally regretted she married Dave and thought of divorce. Since my first interview with Dave and Elise I have known both were unhappy with each other. Dave's first words were,

> She has always been very dissatisfied with me in practically every way and I think I've been kind of dissatisfied with marriage. Resembles enslavement. She's very fearful and that transfixed itself into fierce jealousy that makes me very miserable.

He bemoaned his lack of sexual freedom. Forty-five years later his third most important wish was to "keep wife entertained" but "off his case." Elise's second most important wish was "to appreciate my partner better" which she felt would very likely happen in their remaining years together.

Elise had bitterly complained to him for decades about their marriage: his inability to communicate how he feels, instability, unreliability, aloofness, lack of pep, and especially self-centeredness. In their rare discussions about their relationship,

> Dave denies something is wrong with him. I am the shit
> disturber. He never calls me names; he's been very polite.
> He is so damn cold at times I'd rather he'd yell at me. I
> guess men are like that.

Ironically, they have almost always agreed about their philosophy of life, most important goals, major decisions, and that things are going well between them; they confide in each other more often than not. They feel quite comfortable sharing their feelings about their parents, bodily illnesses, accomplishments of their children, and their happy times. Like most others of the group, they both are uncomfortable sharing their socially unacceptable wishes, especially their sexual desires and insecurities. Dave is more uncomfortable than Elise talking about his failures, discouragements, and death.

Parenting

When their children were home, Elise was most unhappy with Dave as a father. He had told her when they married, "I am not going to help you care for the children; the children are your bag." He not only kept his word; he remained distant and uninvolved with them. This disturbed Elise who felt he made fun of and humiliated them, a principal reason for her wish to divorce him. She did not trust him to take care of their children if she wasn't there. Her distrust became alive for me when eating dinner with them in their 50s. Their son, who had been windsurfing, called to ask Dave to come get him. He had become becalmed and paddled several miles to call for help. Dave refused to go, saying the wind surfer would not fit in the car. Elise said she would go; I volunteered to go to help but she said she could handle it. She did.

We now must confront some illustrative seeming contradictions. Recall that the PAS, modeled on the VAS, measured satisfaction with 28 attributes of one's parenthood. Dave made no pretense of being a perfect father. While he usually enjoyed being a parent, he often wished he were not a father. Unlike Rich who enjoyed being a "Jewish father," Dave did not. And for twenty years he consistently held to his position, scoring similarly in satisfaction with the lowest third of the study's fathers.

If Elise means by "involved" with the children, physical affection and contact—e.g., she wrestled with the children on the floor and was demonstratively affectionate—then she is correct. Dave seldom played games with or hugged his kids except when they were in trouble. He did teach their children how to windsurf and play tennis; he was not a "cold fish' around his children. But she is incorrect if by "involved" she means participating in making decisions about them. To measure amount of parental involvement in making decisions about each of thirty typical child activities, e.g., refusing to go to bed, each of them identified one's self, spouse, or both as the decision-maker. They agreed on 60% of the identifications. Elise agreed that either Dave or both made the decision about 57% of the activities. She also rated Dave as the decision-maker in 40% of the activities. They flatly disagreed which of them made decisions about only 10% of their children's activities.

Elise's satisfaction about parenting is a perplexing problem. Like her mother she enjoyed having and rearing babies usually. She consistently claimed over the years that she never wished to be free of the responsibility of rearing children. But in her 30s, she was the group's most dissatisfied mother; in her late 40s she was the fourth most dissatisfied. She was "somewhat dissatisfied" on twenty(!) of the PAS's 28 sources of possible satisfaction. She was more dissatisfied than Dave. Given his remoteness from his kids and the pressures of buying and preparing the food and cleaning up after a meal, it is understandable why she was not satisfied with the "job"-related attributes of being a mother.

But most telling, she was not satisfied with motherhood as a calling; it did not utilize her best potentials; it was not compatible with her temperament and personality. She did not even answer how self-fulfilling parenting was for her. Why? Effects of menopause? No, she felt similarly in her early 30s. Her mother provided no model of being a fulfilled parent? Possibly. Too high expectations of an ambitious woman over-committed to being a mother? Probably. Since eighteen she always wanted to have a baby. She married Dave for that reason. Lingering resentment against Dave who forced her to abort her first child? Yes. "A lot of good feelings just went with that. I distrusted him from then on." Especially since he persuaded her to marry him to be a "mother to his children." Perhaps her children caused problems she never anticipated, giving her a feeling of maternal inadequacy. In her 50s, her eldest son got a girl pregnant and started taking LSD; her eldest daughter had run away from home for three days. Elise put her in a boarding school for her senior year. From the perspective of their 60s when their children were no longer at home, both agreed that they still did not wish they could be free of their responsibility for their kids. However, they both were "vexed," in Elise's words, by the disregard and disrespect for them of their eldest son, with whom both felt their relationship was tense and strained. Elise felt closer to the remaining children than Dave felt.

Their Views of Marriage

Halfway through her menopause, Elise had an affair which she broke off when she realized she might have to take care of another man. She impetuously filed for divorce, "shocking Dave" and herself. Dave thought some of her feminist friends had influenced her. They both agreed to continue living with each other while Elise worked with a "shrink" for more than a year. She said of these years:

> I realized the divorce is not working out. I really love Dave. It was very painful; it was right in my stomach. I felt I'm making a terrible mistake. The children are falling apart. The reason I married is to have children. I get hyper around kids. My oldest son was particularly hurt by the separation; we have a tight nest here.

She also learned that, like her mother, she saw only Dave's worst parts. "Why do you remain with Dave?"
Without hesitation, Elise said,

> The affection we have for each other. That is what got us together, and probably is a solid base. I have to be candid. When he is not around I miss him. When I'm not around, he says he misses me. I believe him. We have a sense of humor; somehow we share a lot of ideas that we discuss. We share similar values about beauty, art. He is loyal, intelligent; that is the number one thing.

To the question, "What are the best things about your marriage?" Dave answered:

> We laugh; physical comfort with each other, just warmth of being affectionate, smooching, love-making, relaxing. We come together as a machine for reducing external stresses. We share a lot of the same feelings about being abused by the world; we built a kind of fortress together.

Twelve years later he added:

> She finds neat ways to describe things; very sensitive to delicious incongruities; she is much quicker than I, a real mind-opener, very entertaining person. We come together in what we want for the kids, on guarding them against hostile influences and evil ideas, nasty people.

Had they created a mutually satisfying marital relationship sexually? No. They both rated their sexual satisfaction to be "very low." But sex remained important to each. Though Elise had not mentioned it as a reason for staying with Dave, she had sought out her first affair in her 50s. Dave listed "love-making" as a reason for staying together, although they had made love only four to five times in the three months during their 50s. Both would have preferred to have sex eight to ten times a month in the preceding three years. Also Dave had had an affair during their year-long trial separation which reassured him he could still perform. An insurance exam discovered he had non-symptomatic diabetes, the medicine for which diminished his sexual responsiveness. His recent heart repair has not helped his potency. By their 60s, like most other couples in the study, they had little sex but still wished they could have sex four to six times more a month.

Such brief comments are not intended to minimize the importance of sexual fulfillment to a happy marital relationship. Immersion in the men and women's lives over many years told me how critical sexual fulfillment is to marital happiness and health, a theme to which I return in the commentary.

Dave's Growing Psychological Health

Dave had gradually become healthier emotionally. The signs in his tests were clear. I reported in my analysis to him that his thought was less privatized, more socialized; it was not so dominated by emotionally charged dream-like images, such as his two hussies grappling for a defensified phallic possibility. His worst enemy is his own interiority, his own turning inwards, for there are not enough internal controls or checks for him to speak clearly to himself and hence to others. But when he must respond to external stimuli or deal with facts in his external world, he can function very well. There does not seem to have been a deeply internalized "sociality," the presence of the objective other, which can then be held up in mind to monitor his own inner dialogue and so force the communicative clarity necessary to make effective use of his intellectual potentials.

I also thought he had developed a more positive, though still fragile, self-esteem. I then suggested he has shown the most growth in his relations with women.

He is much less overtly aggressive (no longer sees in the Rorschach decapitated witches or grappling hussies) but intriguingly is more passively stubborn or negativistic. It is as if the development of a strong self requires an identity based on opposition, so he is not overwhelmed by ambivalence. Though he still reacts to women as sex objects, there has been such improvement that I would have to say his relations with women provide a real source of support to him, even though the tenor of the relationship may be one of opposition.

Finally, there is an emerging tone of warm and affectionate bonding relationships; they are more lively, delightful, and freer. These benign changes are harbingers of a healthier self-concept as a possible loving, giving, and compassionate person if he will encourage this growth in action.

His reaching out to teach his black crew how to read and write and become "men," in Elise's words, was just such a step. Tragically, this "case of good will was squandered"; he might not risk another step. At times, Dave is like a little hurt boy who has never really understood the meaning of responsibility.

Causes of Dave's Growth

Personality of Partner

Dave identified a rich variety of influences that contributed to his maturing. Elise had taught him to value the good in many different types of people [Other-centered values] as well as how to get along with people he didn't care for [Other-centered and Autonomous relations]. Her ceaseless critical comments told him that "as freaky as I was, I was not a special asshole but to go ahead and do what needs to be done" [Other-centered self]. That is, to be responsible in the here and now, not to drift off into cerebral abstractions which did not demand action [Integration values]. Her earthy manner, feet firmly planted on the ground, and no nonsense attitudes kept bringing him back to earth and responsibility.

Religious and Philosophic Experiences

Dave, as well as Elise, was drawn to religious philosophical beliefs and sought insight and meaning for his life from Sufism and Judaism. It was workshops on Gurdjieff, however, that were most influential. Their impact was to strengthen the value of effort, to not be so afraid to try what he might not like, which is a cop-out. One has reservoirs of energy to keep on persisting. Both Dave and Elise were tenacious despite frustrations [Stability and autonomy values].

Counseling—Group Therapy

Dave never profited from erratic attempts at individual therapy but he did respond to group therapy in his 40s. It "took the edge off of my hostilities, probably less obnoxious" [Other-centered self and relations]. Made me aware of gratitude and brought me more in contact with people who share that" [Awareness and Other-centered values].

Elise's Questionable Health

Elise wasn't selected as an exemplar because she was Dave's wife. She was selected in her own right. She described herself as less mature when in her 50s than she had described herself in her mid 40s. The decline in her PSQ score was so great I worried that she might be suicidal, a thought that had indeed crossed her mind she said, when I later asked. I was relieved when I checked her MMPI score for depression; it was within the normal range and had shown no change over twelve years. The Rorschach signaled some depressive signs but nothing too severe to worry about. Her Personality Trait Survey (PTS) showed that the only two traits that had changed most since Time 4 were greater moodiness and less cheerfulness, which she subsequently confirmed again in a letter to me. By her mid 60s, Elise had bounced back in her maturity to her mid 40 level, suggesting that the dramatic decline may have been a transitional reaction rather than a major personality change. Her resilience is a sign of her fundamental healthiness. That she continued to function effectively, though lethargically, during her 50s was another sign of her basic healthiness. Elise is a good example of the limitation of personality research that does not study persons over long periods of time. How shall we understand what I view to be a transitional reaction rather than a more permanent change in her character?

Her precipitous decline in maturity during her middle age was generalized across every dimension of healthy growth and personality sector, except for a noticeable increase in maturing in her relationships with women and decrease in her relationships with men. She had become more autonomous of formerly unfulfilled childish needs to depend upon women, which she confirmed in the interview when she said she no longer needed close women friends. She had been gradually freeing herself from her emotional ties to her mother. At Time 4, she had completed the Incomplete Sentence test's stem, *My mother and I* by "shared some very crazy years" but at Time 5, "were not too close." Or in her 40s to the stem *When she thought of her mother,* she wrote "cried" but to it at Time 5, "became sad." However, Elise had become more of a stranger to herself, disagreeing now with the PSQ item, "My ideas about myself are reasonably stable and don't differ too much from what they were several months ago." She could not understand, for example, why she "shocked herself" by filing for divorce or why she had become more moody. These changes were affected by her ambivalent relationship with Dave, about which she now was less certain.

Could Elise still be having a depressive reaction to some after-effects of her menopause during which four events had occurred, any one of which could unsettle her ideas about herself: psychotherapy, affair, impetuous decision to divorce Dave, and father's death? She was troubled by her loss of enthusiasm and will which

> used to fuel me all of the time. I took estrogen for three
> months and felt my head was in a vise. I thought I was
> going crazy. It made me feel like a horse. It is made out
> of horse piss and I don't want to feel like a horse. I don't
> feel as sexy as I used to. It bothers me. Dave is not as

> potent as he had been. In the middle of the night I would feel his penis and it would excite me. I don't feel that any more. I know he feels distressed about that too and I have not been able to talk with him about it. When he used to touch me I used to break into a sheet of water from the hot flashes. We were very close body-wise so hot flashes pushed me apart from him and he probably felt that too.

Though Time 5 began about a year after the end of Elise's menopause, she had not freed herself from the memory of its effects which kept intruding throughout the interview. When I asked what surprised her about middle age, she said:

> What hit me were the hot flashes. I never expected them to be like that. And the emotional roller coaster every day. I was screaming, next minute I'd be depressed, next time I would find injustice all over the place. I would be very unstable, emotion was taking over the brain; I was in a great turmoil. It was a stop in everyday functions. Every woman should be warned about these possibilities. I wasn't.

Men should be warned also. Dave wasn't.

Elise recalled in her 60s that as "horrible" as menopause had been, when her emotions had so "engulfed" her, it had been the period of her greatest creativity. The route to new ideas and their combination was through her intensified emotional life.

Dave joined us when Elise and I began to interpret her test results. Among other changes, I suggested she was in the emotional trough of a major shift from an overly externalized masculine or yang way of life to a still unfulfilled feminine or yin one. For the financial stability of her family she had been forced to draw upon stereotypic masculine yang strengths that had pulled her away from her more intuitive yin self. Her loss of enthusiasm and will to continue her two businesses were signs it was time to take another path. I said nothing she hadn't already thought about herself in other words. "Basically I am a yang type. At this point I feel I am very balanced with my yin and yang." (Chinese symbols of femininity and masculinity.)

Causes of Elise's Changes

Though much of her waking life was devoted to creating and managing her business, she chose no occupational attribute to have influenced her, a curious result because every man and most working woman I studied did. Instead she selected most frequently her parental role, children, and daughter.

Parental Role

Elise's parental role created negative effects.

> I have less time, more demands, more energy being taken to care for children and their well-being; I cannot take care of my mind. I just go dormant. I get frustrated about 100 times a day. I can take just so much [Immature Integration cognitive]. Before, I was looking to be a parent and now I am. That was when the work started. There is where a lot of illusions and delusions were put into a proper place [Awareness and Integration values]. I have no image of myself. I have no time for an image [Immature Stability self]. I had to learn to be a parent [Autonomy value]. It is to be a mother and friend to my children [Awareness self]. Seventy-five percent of my time is occupied by that tie; not much left for being a spouse [Immature Autonomy self]. A lot of satisfaction to see children grow year after year [Awareness relations].

Children

Elise's children were great teachers as they were for most parents.

> My children bring my intellect to research about children; I watch their behavior at different times. I have to go to psychology books and find out what is going on [Integration cognitive]. What to do with them, how to channel them. I sit in school to watch teachers and use my judgment about how to make choices [Awareness and autonomy cognitive].

Daughter

Elise's oldest daughter had a transforming and confirming effect.

> She taught me how to be a woman. She touched the woman part in me, the feminine part [Integration self]. She is very feminine. She is very delicate, pretty. She likes to dress up. She is aware of her female friends. She is pretty dandy. I stopped to watch her and it touched, it woke me up. It made me want to get in touch with it [Awareness of self]. I was thinking of myself as a little girl afterwards. In other words I was nurturing the little girl in me, taking care of her was like taking care of me [Other-centered and Stability self]. So I have found much more me.

Several months later Elise wrote to thank me for my visit. Several sentences made me feel good. Research, despite its stresses, can be personally rewarding.

> Dear Doug,
>
> I do not know if your interviews, or my decisions or both but I have experienced "joi de vivre" and a return of optimism I thought long forgotten and gone. So I thank you from the deepest of my soul for rescuing me. I have been quite morose for a few years and did not like it.
>
> Love, Elise

A seed does not sprout unless the ground is fertile and watered.

Visit During Dave and Elise's 60s

I revisited Dave and Elise and others about whom I had written when they were in their mid 60s and whom I felt might be upset by their chapters. Dave and Elise met my plane late at night to drive me to their new expensive home in the mountains. Almost apologetically they said they lived in an upper class and conservative community (certainly by San Francisco standards) whose neighbors lived on a different planet than the one they felt comfortable on. They had not yet found any like-minded friends. They had kept their San Francisco Bay home for their eldest son to use while managing Elise's old business.

Their large home fit them. It had large rooms behind other rooms, paintings and masks on the walls, innumerable objects of art aesthetically placed throughout by Elise. Their library had hundreds of art folios and books reflecting their similar intellectual interests; their music room had Dave's instruments; his office had the necessary computer technology to keep him in touch with the outside world. Their rooms looked out to Elise's two lovely gardens with a patch of van Gogh's blue-purple irises.

I met with each as they read a draft of this chapter. Dave's mood was somber; Elise's more upbeat and acceptant. I sensed Dave felt hurt [I hope not betrayed]. He retreated to the garden to reflect about the chapter. He said I had failed to capture the essence of his growth. He gave me a copy of Yitta Mandelbaum's book, *Holy Brother,* a collection of anecdotes about Rabbi Shlomo Carlebach's mission to bring young lost Jews back to Judaism. I read the book on the flight home. I called Dave several days later to learn more about his Yiddishkeit, the importance to him of being, as he explained, a "continuing witness to what happened at Sinai" and its effects upon him.

I have not yet begun to read Dave's long, suggested reading list to teach me about Judaism and another Rabbi Zalman Schachter, a colleague of Shlomo, whose influence Dave believes has been most important. But intuitively I feel Dave is correct, though I remain vague about how he has specifically changed not just in his beliefs but in his behavior. Like Rabbi Carlebach, however, Dave finds his fulfillment increasingly with his guitar, playing Jewish music for wedding parties. Dave and Elise have asked me to return. When I do, I will ask Dave to play the music most meaningful to him.

For the fifty years I have known Dave, he has been silently crafting his own calling. It is a calling that integrates two foundations of his life now emerging more visibly: his decades-long, self-educating search for meaning to his life and his growing certainty about his Jewish heritage that had been denied him by his oppressive mother.

Dave had maintained his level of maturity by his mid 60s with one exception. He reported, "I would have difficulty accurately recalling the thoughts I had several years ago about various intellectual issues" and the feelings he had had about himself when younger. I believe he is correct. In our discussion about the chapter, I had noted how, like many of us, he had tried to rewrite parts of his earlier history for which I had his earlier verbatim account.

Though Elise had taken workshops with and been involved in Gurdjieff's philosophy for more than fifteen years, she had never spontaneously elaborated its effects. Dave insisted that I had misunderstood Elise also and urged me to call her, which I did. Yes, she said, Gurdjieff had been important to her own growth. She had become more aware of herself and tranquil. Elise had not accepted the Catholicism of her parents when young, but as a result of her workshops had been drawn to Judaism because it integrated "the bad and the good."

My hunch was correct that Elise's generalized decline in her PSQ scores for maturity during her 50s was a transitional reaction to her prolonged menopause. Eight years later she had resiliently recovered to describe herself to be more mature than she had reported when in her 40s. Her greatest growth was in her relations with Dave and her concept of herself. She felt she now understood him better and had a closer, less defensive relation with him. She also now felt much more certain of who she was. Her "joi de vivre" during my visit was the visible sign of her growing interpersonal and self-integration. Is it not a sign of Elise's and Dave's maturity that they agreed to share their lives with readers?

Dave and Elise Contributed These Lessons to the Book

A hostile and intimidating mother can destroy a youth's self-confidence in his or her ability to cope unless there are powerful compensating supports available, usually a caring father.

The cultural isolation of a couple marginal to the surrounding society reinforces each person's need for the other's confirmation and support of their worth.

For a couple whose partners so need each other, the pains of their relationships can become goads to maturing. A shared intellectual commitment to search for meaning in one's religious or similar heritage provides stability to a couple.

A vocational identity and calling provide a generalized stability to daily life. So does a fulfilling sexual life.

Commentary

Dave's reticence to talk about his sexual needs was not atypical of most of the men. Like Elise, most of the study's women were more at home with their bodies and their rhythms and more articulate about them, hence were much more forthright. The statistical analyses of the men's descriptions of their sexuality had alerted me to how contributory sex was to their marital happiness. But not until I immersed myself for the first time in all of the men's and women's sequential interviews did my perspective deepen. I now appreciate more the centrality of sex to healthy development and happiness. As animals, our biological sexual heritage affects our health and marital happiness more than we may be aware, or even value.

The centrality of sexuality to well-being is shown in the study's results, most persuasively in the men's and women's sexual compatibility with their partners when they were in their 40s. If you haven't yet assessed your marital sexual compatibility, you might wish to do so now by completing Appendix D-5.

Partners' Sexual Compatibility

My index of partners' sexual compatibility combined scores for their beliefs about their own and partner's enjoyment of sex, their partner's consideration of their sexual needs, degree of how well-mated sexually they are, similarity of their sexual standards, and mutual sexual faithfulness. Dave ranked within the lowest third of the men in marital sexual compatibility. (Elise ranked lowest among the women.) Men of high rather than low sexual compatibility with their partners were judged by their partners to be better sexual partners and lovers. The most astounding result was that the men's sexual compatibility reliably predicted 39% of more than 400 other very diverse measures of the men's personality. It predicted every different measure of the men's mental health or maturity, the men's interpersonal maturity and mutuality, vocational and other adult role competencies, and, not surprisingly, marital happiness. (Heath, 1978a)

That the original simple seven-item index about sexuality predicted so many other personality qualities was so stunning as to be almost unbelievable. But after excluding every factor that might account for the findings, I came to this conclusion: It is not just the acquisition of new sexual techniques but the enhancement of the maturing of the marital partners themselves that is the route through which mutually considerate, enjoyable, and faithful marital sexual relationships will grow.

Effects of Menopause on Marriage

Menopause is no exception to the general rule that sexual needs and activity vary greatly from one person to the next and between women and men. Some women did not know that they had completed menopause until affirmed by their doctors; others like Susan found menopause to be un-eventful; and a few like Elise found it prolonged and painful. Menopause's hormonal changes can produce precipitous declines in a woman's desire for sex. A recent Australian study found that, after separating out the effects of aging, menopause produced progressive declines in women's sexual desire, and adversely affected their feelings about their partners, sexual enjoyment, and therefore the frequency of intercourse. Increased vaginal dryness and frequent unpredictable hot flashes, as Elise experienced, impaired women's well-being and caused pain during intercourse. (Schorr, 2001) A large global study of sexual behavior in 40- to 80-year-old men and women found that a declining majority continued to have sex. About twice as many women than men reported lack of interest in sex and at least one or more sexual problems, such as experiencing no sexual pleasure. However, the researchers did not seek information about the menopausal status of the women. (Nicholson, et al, 2004)

On the other hand, testosterone's more gradual decline contributes only partially to men's declining libido and sexual frequency. Men need increasing erotic stimulation to maintain their potency into their later years, one reason the pornographic industry is supported by many more men than women.

Menopause aggravates the growing disjunction between men and women's libidinal desires that creates severe strains or mismatches in many marriages. When sexual release is a strong need for men and strong inhibitions about different ways to provide such release are present in women, severe strain may occur. But there is no room for blame, recrimination, or guilt about basic biological facts. Strong marriages, like Jim and Barbara's, based on trust, open, and honest discussion can weather these facts' effects. Barbara, familiar by virtue of her position as co-chair of the Women's Health study, agreed.

Sexuality is indeed central to many adult's continuing marital well-being.

Chapter 10

———≫·○·≪———

HEALTHY GROWTH: STABILITY AND CHANGE
I: THE PERSONALITY YOU ARE STUCK WITH

What have our exemplars of change told us about becoming psychologically healthier? Have they spoken for others as bright, highly educated, and
achieving persons? For you? I now step back from the vivid and moving
lives of Barbara, Charlie, Mary, Josh, and the six others to compare their
truths with those of the entire group of men and women that I interviewed.
I discipline my clinical portrayals and hunches by relying on statistical
methods to sort out from the rich and diverse measures of change those
results most likely to be true for others. Appendix E describes the statistical
conventions that guided this and the following chapters.

Their lives provoke questions like these: How stable is an adult's personality? Are there critical periods in a person's life which alter the rate of
maturing? Is maturing continuous or episodic? Does maturing occur more
readily in some personality sectors than others at different periods of life?
Can we continue to grow psychologically throughout our adult years? Do
men and women differ in the stability, timing, continuity, and focus of their
maturing? I do not have as complete information from the women as I have
from the men. I have little about their growth in their late adolescence and
early adult years before entering the study. Regretfully, too few women
participated when in their 60s to give reliable information.[1] So I had to rely
on information secured in their late 30s to early 40s and 50s as I examine
the above questions.

How Stable Is an Adult's Personality?

Three impressions remind me we do not easily escape our adolescent, even our childhood, personalities, much as we ourselves, moralists such as ministers, idealists such as educators and societal reformers assume that we could. My first enduring impression is how resistant my personality has been to efforts to "improve" it ever since I, as a sixteen year old, tried to take charge of it. I tried to inhibit my tactlessness for years; later I defined it as a mellowed frankness; and even later yet I rationalized it as a guiding Quaker principle of a commitment to "speak to truth." My wife, Harriet, still feels I am too outspoken and, worse, resistant to subduing it. Barbara also discovered how resistant Jim's personality was to her devious efforts to reform his procrastination. Perhaps you are more successful in fulfilling your New Year's resolutions to change your more annoying habits and traits.

A second more objective impression about how stable our personalities are comes from a widely-used personality test, the Myers-Briggs Type Indicator (MBTI) which measures Jung's types like introversion and extroversion. It had initially been validated on my high school class by Isabel Briggs-Myers, the mother of two of our classmates. Despite graduating into and surviving World War II, Vietnam, and the 60s' assassinations, when we retook it at our 50th class reunion, we discovered these and other traumas had barely nudged our adolescent types for the majority of us. This past spring my surviving high school classmates celebrated their 60th reunion. Though some of us were rickety, dumpy, and forgetful, I was surprised to recognize the essential personality of most. I have not used the MBTI because it assumes that the personality types it measures have nothing to do with healthy growth, an assumption I have urged one of MBTI's current owners to test on larger samples than I had access to.

My third impression began to form during the study's third wave. Recall I selected Charlie, Buck, and the others as examples of the greatest personality change among my group of 105. I kept exclaiming to Harriet how similar they were to what I remembered about them decades ago. By their 40s, and more by their 50s, they began to tell me they didn't think they'd learn anything new about themselves from participating. By their 60s, some wrote me long letters about what they had been doing rather than complete the tedious ratings about how they had changed, which they said they hadn't.

The question of how stable is our personality is much too broad to answer with a definite "yes," or "moderately," or "not at all." We must specify what attribute of personality and its stability we are most interested in. My central concern has been healthy psychological growth as defined by the model of maturing, its associated attributes, and competencies. I define "stability" by reliable similarities in measures assessing health, preferably over three time periods.

Since I have insisted studies over time should be as comprehensive as possible, I rely on repeated personality tests like the PSQ and SIQ which measure the model of maturity, the Minnesota Multiphasic Personality Inventory (MMPI) which measures changes in behaviors symptomatic of lack of psychological health, the Rorschach test which measures less conscious psychic attributes of health, and direct self- and judge-ratings of the change in personality traits, as well as interviews on change in the model of maturity's sectors scored for dimensional maturing.

I postpone to the next chapter what type of New Year's resolutions I might more successfully fulfill. Or my children might try to change to make me a better father and easier to live with.

How Stable is Adult Health During the Middle Years?

By "health" I include both psychological and physical health. Physical and psychological health generally went along with each other for the group as a whole during the middle years.

Overall, the men's health had remained about the same for at least three decades and possibly five.[2] The women's remained about the same between their late 30s and early 50s. The men and women's evaluation of their health was supported by their three most knowledgeable judges. Confirming other studies, men tend to report better health than women report, though the men believed their physical health had gone downhill more noticeably during their 20s. Both men and women report that their physical health tends to decline from their 30s, though slowly, until their 60s.

I like to crosscheck the results of one test with a different one measuring a similar attribute to confirm the reliability of a result. Each man and woman rated the frequency/severity of 33 physical and psychological symptoms, e.g., stiffness in joints, irritability, and headaches. Only the 40-year-old women reliably reported suffering poorer symptomatic health than the men. Among other symptoms, they cried more, worried more about their bodies, had more nipple pain, and reduced sexual desires. (Neugarten & Kraines, 1965)

The men reported better health in their 40s than in their 50s and 60s, between which there were no reliable differences in overall health. However, men in their 40s did smoke more frequently and had more gastrointestinal upsets than when in their 50s. By that age they began to report they suffered stiffness and pain in their joints, had reduced sexual desire, and increased impotence; their pre-viagra drug use had also increased.

These self-reports generally confirm the stability of adults' health during their middle years. Not unexpectedly, men like Buck who had major health problems in their 20s and 30s had continuing health problems in later middle age.

Are There Critical Periods that Alter the Rate of Maturing?

Though our measures of overall health, psychological maturity, and self-esteem were so consistently highly correlated, the PSQ and SIQ provide more specific information about sector and dimensional maturity over the course of adulthood.

Barbara, Rich, and the others have told us that individuals vary in their rate of maturing. Moreover, when we step back from their individual lives to those of the entire group of men and women, the answer to the question about critical periods in healthy growth is an unequivocal "Yes. There are critical periods." Figure 10.1 portrays the course of maturing and self-esteem from the late teens and early 20s to the mid 50s for the men. Both the PSQ and SIQ average scores show that the men matured most in the decade following their graduation[3] and then their growth stabilized from their 30s to their 50s. The men did not mature more or increase in their self-worth from their 40s to their 50s. (Nor did the women for these years.) Their ratings of their health reflect this continuity. The results confirm the findings of the few studies that have assessed health or adjustment over the early and middle adult years. (Block J. & Haan, 1971)

That the same rate of growth was found by two different measures like the PSQ and SIQ is important. Too often in personality studies, researchers rely on single measures of a trait not confirmed by a somewhat different method. Recall that the SIQ consisted of 26 self-rated traits, e.g., adventurous, gentle, realistic, which had been drawn from others' research and were associated with varied positive outcomes like mental health, achievement, and self-esteem. Equally as important, the judges agreed with the men in rating the SIQ's measure of self-esteem or maturity. Though different

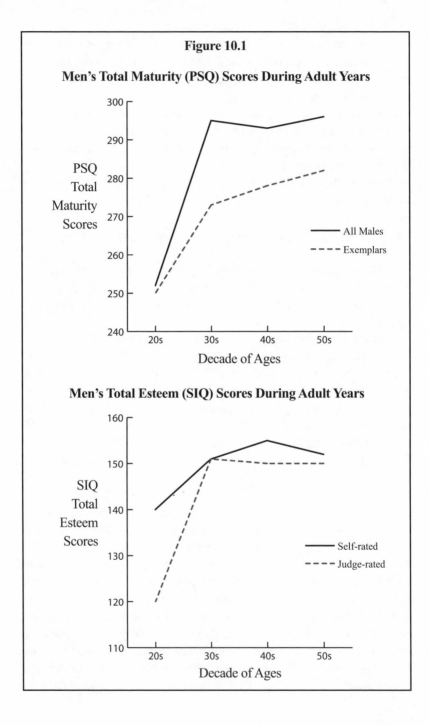

Figure 10.1

Men's Total Maturity (PSQ) Scores During Adult Years

Men's Total Esteem (SIQ) Scores During Adult Years

judges rated the men from one time to the next, they agreed that the men were least mature when in college but had stabilized their level of maturity from their mid 30s to their 50s.

Directly measuring the dimensional maturity of the self-concept also confirms that the rate of maturing for every dimension is greatest during the 20s and begins to slow down and stabilize from the 30s to the 40s. To appreciate the significance of Figure 10.2, which portrays this change in rate, you need to know that each dimension of the self was measured *differently* and *directly*. Figure 10.2's lower scores indicate greater dimensional maturity For example, accurate awareness of the self was measured by minimal differences between a self- and judges'-ratings of the SIQ about the participant. An other-centered self-concept was measured by minimal differences between the social self, i.e., participant's predicted ratings of the judges, and the actual ratings of the judges. An integrated self-concept was indexed by a low difference score between a private self- and social self-rating. Stability of the self-concept was measured by minimal differences

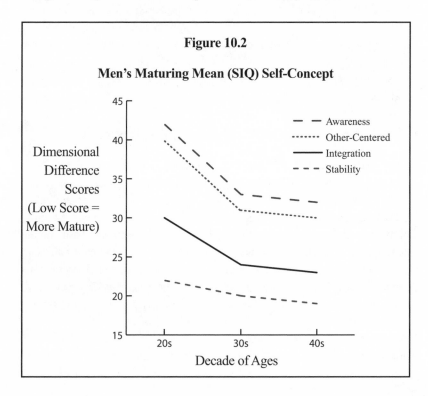

Figure 10.2

Men's Maturing Mean (SIQ) Self-Concept

between two administrations of the SIQ separated by varying amounts of time. (Heath, 1965) Change in the autonomy of the self-concept is not portrayed since it was measured by falsified reports about how a judge had rated a participant, after which I told him about the deception, which I could do only once.. Thirty-one years later one man spontaneously recalled I had lied to him. I had. I felt uncomfortable at the time violating the men's trust; I have never used deceptive experimental procedures since.

Why the difference between the rate of maturing in the early 20s and late 30s and later adult years? The post-college years confront most youths with three realistic problems whose solutions may have fateful long-term consequences for their health and happiness: First, how to survive independently but with work that is fulfilling and a calling. Dave never found his calling which left him restless and dissatisfied.

Second, to whom to make a commitment as a long-term partner? One man had made three transitional commitments, each of which ended in "failure" and eroded his feelings of competence and self-esteem.

And third, if and when to assume the responsibility for caring for one's children? Elise accepted caring for her daughter during her childhood but had only a grudging commitment to parent her daughter during her teenage years.

Solving these problems contributes to a person's eventual stabilization and freeing of energy for other growth.

Is Maturing Continuous or Episodic?

Figures 10.1 and 10.2 confirm other researchers' findings, summarized by McCrae and Costa (1990), that after 30 years of growth personality becomes relatively stable. However, Dave, Buck, and Susan tell us that individual growth can continue, all be it more slowly, during the adult years. Continuity of the personality implies that a general theory of development based on the assumption of continuous growth—maturity, health, well-being—through adults' middle years may have limited validity. Growth can slow; plateaus can occur, as Barbara reported. Regression can be temporary, as occurred for Rich, or continue much longer, as another man experienced until he retired.

Maturing is not just a progressive unfolding of an intrinsic biological program dictated by our genes. It also occurs largely as a response to the events of one's interpersonal environment, whose timing is much less predictable. So

I believe maturing is not continuous throughout adulthood but is episodic, initiated by changing external demands for new adaptations.

Does Maturing Occur More Readily in Some Sectors and Dimensions of Personality Than Others?

Lowell Kelly, whom the Preface quoted, relied on earlier research and his own limited variety of measures to hazard the generalization that our intelligence is most stable, next our values and vocational interests, followed by our ideas about ourselves, and then by more variable specific attitudes, (1955). An implication of his ordering is if your New Year's resolution is to change your personality, begin first with your attitudes, then your self-concept, but don't expect it will be easy to go much further.

Changes in Psychological Maturity and Self-Esteem

Figure 10.3 shows that the pattern of the changes in the model of maturity's sectors and dimensions over four decades for the men and two decades for the women was remarkably consistent. However, comparing the averaged five sector and the five dimensional scores to each other showed that maturing in one sector or one dimension can lag behind or move ahead of other sectors and dimensions. For example, the maturation of the men's relationships with other men had undergone major growth when in college. Their friendships with other men persisted into their 20s, but gradually receded in importance, except for Josh, as they matured in their relationships with women.

The growth of the men's minds from their 20s reliably outpaced that of their values, self-concepts, and interpersonal relationships. Not surprisingly, the men's continued graduate and professional training during much of their 20s and their demanding intellectual occupations in their 30s enhanced their minds' continued growth. Might such growth temporarily have stretched the men beyond a healthy balance in their lives and contributed to their wives' observations about their husbands' inability to talk about their feelings?

Figure 10.3 shows that the men grew most in their awareness and stability from their 20s into their adult years. However, the pattern of their dimensional growth remained relatively constant through their adult years. Dave matured least in other-centeredness.

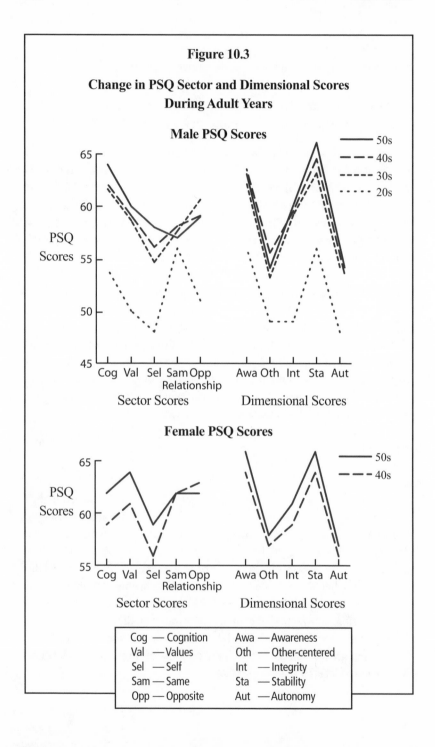

Figure 10.3

Change in PSQ Sector and Dimensional Scores
During Adult Years

Too great gaps among personality's sectors and dimensions can cause strain, as Rich's story told us. His commitment to his professional growth may have interfered with maturing in his relationships with his wife.

I have been pursuing evidence for the stability of our psychological health, which the data so far confirm. But I increasingly encountered signs that other attributes of the personality are not so "fixed" or stable throughout an adult's middle years. Changes over the years in two of psychology's more widely used methods to assess psychological health, the MMPI and Rorschach, suggest some personality attributes are more open to continued change than others.

Changes in Psychological Adjustment

The MMPI, given four times, beginning with the entrance to college, supports the two principal findings found to date. The men's greatest change in their overall maladjustment score was between their late teens and their early 30s.[4] Their overall maladjustment did not reliably change for the next several decades, which again confirms that stability in psychological health into the 50s is more the rule than the exception.

The trend for maladjustment to increase after entering college is due to changes in four of the MMPI's component scores, changes that continued to occur until the men's 50s. Compared to when they were freshmen, the men had reliably become increasingly less inhibited in their emotionality, a not uncommon effect of a liberal education that shakes up overly intellectualized youths (Heath, 1968) and, as chapter 3's commentary argued, the effects of becoming a father. The men experienced two other consistently increasing changes beginning in their college years: increasing predisposition to depression and decreasing energetic activity for every age period. Rich's growth reversed these changes. He had extraordinarily high energy, which he had learned how to channel productively. But why did he have a severe depression in his 40s? Of the men, he had had the ninth highest MMPI score for energetic activity and efficiency (84%) but lowest (2%) score for depression. In accordance with the equilibrating principle, the discrepancy was much too great psychologically, and under the stresses he was experiencing at the time a temporary depression erupted. As I suggested in chapter 3, clinicians have noted that excessive activity can be a defensive reaction to an underlying but repressed depressive potential in a temperamentally inclined, possibly bipolar, personality.

The fourth consistently rising MMPI score was increasing hyper-alertness, if not suspiciousness, and sensitivity to other people's reactions. Remember Rich's excessive sensitivity to others' approval of him? Only three other men of the group, one being Buck, scored higher than he in this potential hyper-alertness. Buck provides other examples of some of these changes. Among his peers, he scored at the ninety-first percentile for depression and ninety-sixth percentile for suspicious sensitivity. His actual scores, like Rich's, however, were within the MMPI's normal ranges. His suspicious monitoring of his maid's cleaning is consistent with his hyper-alertness; his immobilizing withdrawal into his factory for three years would be consistent with an elevated depressive potential.

Though these trends, all within MMPI's normal limits, may sound pathological, they may be, in fact, signs of healthy growth. Inhibited intellectually achieving and not very interpersonally mature young males need to re-equilibrate (establish a healthier balance within) their emotional-interpersonal selves.

Cognitive Stability and Change in Controls

The Rorschach is used more by clinically oriented than research psychologists to assess psychological health. Clinicians rely on it for clues to unconscious cognitive and character attributes. Researchers believe exploring a person's less conscious inner life is too subjective and unreliable. I gave the Rorschach four times from the men's college years through their adult years and have reported some of its clinical interpretations. They were administered similarly and scored for Robert Holt's scoring system by two Holt-trained psychologists. Holt's scoring system has two impressive strengths: it measures what clinicians who are sensitive to deviant thinking and their control actually rely on when interpreting imaginative responses, and the scoring categories have been carefully defined to produce objectively reliable results. Changes in scores over the years were, therefore, more likely due to developmental than to extraneous administrative and scoring factors. (Holt, 2005)

Freud had identified numerous attributes of dream-like or unconscious modes of thinking, called primary processes, as opposed to conscious, every-day logical types of thinking, called secondary processes, which we ordinarily call "thinking." Holt refined and extended Freud's analysis of primary process thinking, as well as of the defenses and types of controls that people use to defuse or defend against potentially disruptive primary processes associated with unconscious mental activity. He scores a response's degree of realistic fit with the blot and the effectiveness of the defenses used to control its primary processes. More mature persons give more realistic and accurate images to the Rorschach. I had used Holt's primary process scores to check if cognitive immaturity declined over time.

To illustrate some sample scores, I interpret one of Dave's imaginative responses. Compared to the group, he gave the highest percentage of primary process (pripro) responses. Consider Dave's response, "Central content as a phallic possibility, which is defensified or dealt with ironically by the two dancing hussies who grapple for it." Many persons see the two persons or animals benignly interacting with each other. Dave's response would be scored for both content and formal components of pripro thinking: libidinal and aggressive content and an unsocialized formal mode of verbalization, e.g., "defensified." Dave scored at the eleventh percentile of the group in realistic accuracy with which his images fit the structure of the blot and at the forty-sixth percentile for the adequacy of his defenses of the potential pathology of his pripro. What distinguishes highly imaginative persons from the rest of us is the ability to abandon every day conventional and logical modes of thought to permit the controlled emergence of primary modes of thought, which is what an adaptive regression score measures. What saved Dave from being engulfed by the potential pathology of his pripro was his adaptive regression percentile of 95. Dave may have been right 45 years later to claim in retrospect that he perhaps was just being playfully imaginative. However, his unrealistic drive-dominated images and other low scores on other measures of health at the time suggest he, like many of us, may have been defensively reinventing his past.

The results of the repeated Rorschachs are unequivocal; their meaning for understanding personality stability is puzzling. The percent of primary process, and every other Holt score measuring immaturity or unhealthiness, did not vary reliably from one decade to the next. Unconscious modes of thinking apparently persist for decades. Clear so far; Holt's scores confirm the stability of our dynamic unconscious.

The puzzling result, for which I have no convincing hypothesis, is that the men became progressively and reliably less adept at giving realistic or accurate images that precisely fit the structures of the blots. They also became less able to defend themselves against their libidinal and aggressive content, two of the main components of the adaptive regression score. Holt has suggested the men might have become increasingly comfortable with me and more self-acceptant, not feeling it necessary to be more realistic and guarded in communicating what they saw in the blots. Or the reliable negative association between their perceptual accuracy and MMPI depression scores may suggest that increasingly depressed people may not have the aggressive energy or will to maintain realistic and conventional contact with their environment.

Value Maturation

The stability of our personality is also seen in other attributes than those directly related to our psychological health. For example, 50 years ago Kelly had suggested that our orienting values, such as our economic, political, and religious ones, were quite stable. I too found that the order of the freshmen's same value commitments reported by Kelly generally heralded their preferences for the next 40 years (1955). By their early 30s the rank-order of their value preferences had stabilized; it persisted until their 60s. The degree of their commitment varied, though not enough to radically change their ranking. Aesthetic values consistently increased. Traditional religious ones consistently decreased. The relative order of their values' importance remained similar from one decade to the next, however.

A few of the men and women, like Mary, grounded their identity on an intrinsic religious commitment. For others, like Buck who went to church to please his wife, religious practices were extrinsic to their daily lives. Curious about the relation of intrinsic and extrinsic religious values to healthy growth through the adult years, I found neither was related to how healthily a person grew. It was a person's ethical commitment or virtue, which the commentary on Buck discussed, that made a difference to one's well-being. Though other studies suggest people become more religious as they age, I found no reliable differences in overall religiosity for four decades. I have no plausible explanation why the men reliably rated themselves to be somewhat religiously-minded when they were 50 but less so when they were 60, though they occasionally attended church then but had not in their 50s.

I also created a second, more extended, self-report measure of the dimensional maturing of values which I gave only in the men's 30s and 40s. The men's values matured from their 30s to their 40s due primarily to the reliable increase in their awareness of their values. They did not mature on a value's other dimensions.

Changes in Personality Traits

Within the past several decades more researchers have studied how adults develop through their middle years. They have focused on changes in specific personality traits, frequently those for which existing measures were conveniently available such as for masculinity, femininity, and dominance.[5] I too explored similar traits including androgyny—the sum of both masculinity and femininity scores. While not direct indices of maturity or psychological health, they are reliably related to maturity. Personality traits may also indirectly facilitate or limit the effective contribution that maturity can make to adaptation.

I have two ways to understand how personality traits change over time. I converted the list of adjectives that the men had checked about themselves when in college and in their early 30s (ACL), asking them to rate on a five-point scale (PTS) how much of each trait they had. The difference in their two ratings identified how much they had actually changed from their 30s to their 40s. I also asked them to rate how much they believed they had changed on each trait during the previous ten to twelve years, the years since my previous visit. Then the three people—partner, closest friend, and colleague—who had known them most intimately for the same period completed the same two ratings.

Self- and judge-rated traits and their changes.   Regardless which of the above two ways of getting personality ratings I analyzed, the results consistently confirmed that, after a period of great change in the 20s, increasing stability of the personality is the norm for both men and women until at least the early 60s.

By their 30s, the men had changed on 32% of their collegiate descriptions of themselves (ACL). Between their 30s and 40s, they did not materially change their descriptions of themselves (PTS). In their 50s, the men described themselves similarly on 94% and the women on 95% of the traits they had rated in their 40s. By their 60s, the men rated themselves exactly as they had in their 50s except that by now they reliably rated themselves to have become less aggressive. This impressive consistency in their ratings over three decades bolsters once more the evidence for personality stability.

The knowledgeable judges selected by the men and women generally agreed with the trends I have described. The men's friends who rated them in college and their partners, friends, and colleagues who rated them in their

30s disagreed on 73% of the men's traits. However, the men's judges in their 30s disagreed with the men's new judges in their 40s on only 3% of their traits. I know of no other more persuasive evidence for the stability of some attributes of personality during an adult's middle years.

Masculinity-Femininity.   For both men and women, their androgyny, especially its masculinity component, is reliably associated with their maturity. Men's femininity is not related to maturity; women's is, but not as firmly as their masculinity is. Charlie illustrates the importance of the contribution of their androgyny, to adaptation. Of all of the men, he was the most unbalanced in his high masculinity score of 94 (out of a possible 100) and low femininity score of 44. His masculinity and its dominance component contributed to his effective leadership as a Vietnam officer and surgeon. His much lower femininity score, which includes interpersonal traits like sympathy and sensitivity to another's needs, severely limited his effectiveness as a marital partner and parent, as also happened to Dave. Both scored lowest on maturity's other-centeredness dimension, of which empathy is a cardinal attribute and also contributes to marital happiness. Though Charlie's masculinity had mellowed slightly over the years, his femininity had not changed one reliable iota.

Apparently our masculinity and femininity are quite stable. The men did not change reliably in either from their 40s to their 60s, neither did the women. Nor did their judges rate them as changing over their adult years. Before we draw any conclusions about the stability of masculinity and femininity, we must see if any of the specific traits making up each pattern did in fact change.[6] Would we confirm other researchers' claims that as men move out of middle age they become less masculine and women more so? (Gutmann, 1987)

Before turning now to the issue of what aspects of our personality do change during our middle years, I summarize what the results suggest to date. We have confirmed that psychological healthiness (as measured by the PSQ), its component self-esteem (SIQ), adjustment (MMPI), cognitive maturity (Rorschach), dimensional value maturation (except for awareness), and personality traits, including our masculinity and femininity, are quite stable during the adult years. These results unequivocally confirm again that the 20s are a time of great change which are followed by at least three decades of little personality growth, except for some consistent changes in the men's and women's androgeny and masculinity. Do men really become softer and women tougher?

Chapter 11

———⟫∙◦∙⟪———

HEALTHY GROWTH: STABILITY AND CHANGE

II. THE PERSONALITY YOU CAN CHANGE

Obviously, we not only remain the same for many years, but we also can change more at certain times than others. I recall biblical wisdom that promises adults the possibility of transformation, salvation, and entrance to the Kingdom by accepting Christ wherever they are on their journey. The stories of the twelve disciples, and most dramatically Paul's conversion on the road to Damascus, assert the possibility of personality change in adults. Whatever language we use to describe the Bible's message, I believe one is its testament to our potentiality for continued growth.

Now I am not a doubting Thomas about the possibility of continued growth. I know its truth as certainly as I know the sun will rise tomorrow. Not just from my own past 60 years of adult living but from the men and women I have journeyed with. I am aware that some readers may find the exemplars' lives depressing: many marital and parental conflicts, unappealing and destructive mothers and absent fathers, affairs, divorces, even deaths. But the exemplars show us what it means to be human not just in these days but in every day since Adam's expulsion from the garden. We sometimes confuse the rockiness of the road to maturity with immaturity itself. So let the lives of the book's models of growth speak for themselves about how they changed during their adult years. Barbara and Jim remain happily married and productive. Rich also, even more so. Susan became happily married and proud of her sons. Mary died her own person. Josh, still in a loving relationship of 13 years, died with "great dignity." As I said goodbye to Dave and Elise, I impetuously told them, "I am so very proud of you both and how you have grown over the years." Every month I call Buck and Charlie's wife. Buck's physical illness has stabilized; his recent eye operations have restored his ability to read; he knows his devoted wife is there to care for him, just in case. Charlie accepted his death without further struggle.

Growing into Adulthood

How do the personality measures of all of the men and women of the study answer how we can grow during our adult years?

Though the women's total masculinity and femininity scores had not changed reliably, the women had changed on a number of their associated traits in the ways I described in the commentary on Mary; Susan demonstrated them also. By their early 40s, during the heyday of the women's liberation movement, some of the women's latent strengths became more visible. They saw themselves more than before as self-reliant, independent, self-confident, and masculine persons. They described themselves to have become stronger personalities: less receptive to flattery, functioning better under stress, and more honest, not trying to please men by telling them what they thought men might want to hear? (Heath, 1994b)

Generally, the men and women's actual differences in their ratings of themselves in their 40s and a decade later in their 50s approximated their beliefs about how they had changed since their 40s. The women believed they had become stereotypically more masculine; the men more feminine.

By their 50s, the women believed they had changed more than the men believed they themselves had changed. The women reliably thought they had become, even more than they had thought ten years earlier, more self-reliant, assertive, willing to take risks, aggressive, competitive, purposeful, and enthusiastic. The men did not change in these traits, perhaps because they already thought of themselves as assertive, competitive and purposeful. On the other hand, the men believed they had become more eager to soothe hurt feelings of others, sensitive to others' needs, loving of children, and yielding.

Each spouse had rated his/her partner and their amount of change. The spouses' views of each other generally confirmed their partners' own self-ratings. By their 40s, the women believed their husbands had become more "feminine" in these respects: yielding, eager to soothe hurt feelings, tender, gentle, soft-spoken, child-like, but also more analytical. The men believed their wives had become more "masculine" in being more independent, assertive, forceful, dominant, acting like a leader, and having deeper interests.

How else can we test Kelly's idea that there is "a basis of fact for those who dare to hope for continued psychological growth during the adult years"? (1955, p. 681)

The strongest evidence for continued growth comes from intensive interviews with the men and women, first from statements about their felt change, and second, from their reports about the effects of different significant events in their lives.

Interview Indices of Change

To assess each person's impetus to continue growing, I asked of everyone, "Do you feel set, stable, on a plateau? Or do you feel you are moving, on the verge of a new spurt ahead or moving backward, retreating, regressing?" In his 40s, Buck replied,

> Until this foundry proposition came up, I felt I was going backwards, withdrawing from people. Seems like things had turned downhill, really not going any place. I felt I had moved forward and now was losing the gains I had made. Based on a telephone call I just got maybe I'll be able to do things that will improve the lot.

Despite Barbara's success, remember she had felt stuck on a plateau until she had been confronted with brighter possibilities.

I scored each person's replies on a five-point scale ranging from strong to moderate and steady growth to slowing down or retreating. I also scored their emotions about their anticipated future ranging from very positively excited through no emotional reactions and few plans to very negative anticipations and no plans for the future. While 53% of the men in their 40s and also in their 50s felt they were strongly or moderately still growing, 38% and 45% respectively felt they were stuck on a plateau. The women's pattern of anticipated growth was generally similar.

However, the men's more than the women's futures were emotionally "graying." Forty-two percent of the 40-year-old men and 49% of the 50 year olds had no positive or negative feelings about their futures.

Maturing Effects of Life Events

A second reason to question the validity of the idea that the rate of maturing ceases in the adult years are the men's and women's descriptions of maturing in the interviews identifying the causes of their changes. (INTD) In their early 30s, the men cited 2737 examples of maturing and 332 of regressing, which agrees with the self-reported results showing great growth into their early 30s. But how shall we explain these data from a decade later? The men cited 2281 examples of maturing and 277 of regressive changes since their early 30s when the tests showed no or little change from their 30s to their 40s.[1] Enough men and women continued to describe maturing from their 40s to their 60s to be chary about researchers who firmly conclude no or little personality change occurs after 30. Failure to assess personality change comprehensively risks distorting our understanding of significant maturing changes. Clearly, the course of maturing is murkier than Figure 10.1 suggested. Chapter 13 traces the typical maturing changes from the age of 15 to the mid 50s.

Do Men and Women Differ in the Stability, Timing, Continuity, and Focus of Their Maturing?

So far the study shows that the continuity or stability of men has been firmly established with few exceptions. Men and women seem to be much more alike than our stereotypes of each other have persuaded us to not believe. Their differences have been selective but not disruptive of the principal findings. If I had had more complete information their differences might have emerged more saliently. Chapter 10 noted men's and women's most important differences between specific health symptoms and their changing ratio of stereotypically masculine to feminine traits. Their differences become more prominent as I focus on their motivations and needs as well as on their changes in their sexuality.

Did the men and women differ in the strengths of their wishes and needs? If so, did they become increasingly similar during their adult years? Did they become less conflicted and guilty, even less passionate and more serene, about their needs as they aged? Surely it is easier for people in their 60s to be more faithful sexually than randy young adults cruising the malls and bars every night. Aging does increase our chances of becoming a saint.

Differences in the Strengths of Men's and Women's Needs

In their 40s, 50s, and 60s the men and women rated the strength of their needs for emotionally depending on the same and opposite sex, being their own boss, seeking risky adventures and excitement, and fourteen other needs. They also rated how much the intensity of their needs had changed in the past decade as well as how much anxiety and guilt they felt when each need was aroused. It doesn't take much imagination to understand why married couples stumble when the strength of their more important needs is or becomes severely mismatched. Think of Dave and Elise's changing sexual needs as the result of her disturbing menopause.

In our quest to understand maturity, we now begin to reach a surprising limit of its effects upon and relations to our impulses and needs. I remember Henry Murray, the grandfather of studies of personality, asserting in a graduate seminar that healthy people have intense passions, an abundance of vital energy, and strong commitments and enthusiasms. In psychoanalytic terms, they have clamorous ids not squelched by tyrannical superegos; they are lively people whose impulses are guided by resolute egos. The study clearly showed, however, that the strength of the men's and women's needs and drives was irrelevant to their maturity. It may not have been the strength of Casanova's sexual drive itself, but how well he controlled it that probably would have marked his health. But Murray was correct, nevertheless, to assume that healthy people have conscious access to vigorous ids without anxiety or guilt. The study's mature men and women were comfortable with and accepted the strengths of their needs.

The men and women did differ reliably in the strength of most of their needs. In their 40s, the men had much stronger urges for seven and women for six other of the eighteen needs they rated. Both had stronger needs to depend on and be sexually attracted to the opposite sex, as well as to compete aggressively with their own sex. But the men had stronger needs than the women to be well-known, recognized, and in the limelight as well as to have power and be their own "boss," though they did not differ from the women in their needs to achieve and create. The women were much more needy for hugs from men than the men were for hugs from women. Confirming sex role stereotypes, the women needed more cooperative and harmonious relations with everyone and the opportunity to cry when depressed or emotionally moved.

By their 50s, the gulf between the strength of the men and women's needs had narrowed by more than half of the 13 motives they had differed in earlier. Only their respective sexual needs and emotional dependence for each other and the men's need to compete aggressively with other males reliably differed.

Principal Changes in Men and Women's Needs

The men reported changing more between their 40s and 50s than the women did, though their changes were similar. In some respects, the men believed they had become less typically masculine and vital. They had become somewhat more dependent on women to whom they had become less sexually attracted and needy for sensuous bodily pleasures. They believed they accepted their need to cry somewhat more than they had in their 40s. The decline in the intensity of the men's sexual-emotional needs was matched by the decline in their needs for power and influence as well as to achieve and succeed in their work. Their maturity played no role in these changes.

On the other hand, the women believed they had become more needy for affectionate and loving relationships with other women with whom they had also become more angry, though not necessarily competitively so.

Changes in anxiety and guilt about the arousal of needs.   In their 40s, both sexes consistently reported being more anxious and guilty about 30% of their needs than they reported being in their 50s, which seems to be a quieter time. Both became less conflicted about their sexual needs for and anger towards the opposite sex. The men now had less conflict about being affectionate with and dependent upon men for care. The women also felt more at home with their competitive feelings toward both men and women and needs to achieve and be successful. As you might expect, more mature persons reliably accepted the arousal of their needs without feelings of anxiety or guilt.

Changes in sexual needs and behavior.   When reviewing all the interviews of the summer and fall of 2002, I was constantly taken aback by how disruptive almost every one's sexual needs and their frustration had been. With the exception of Barbara, all of the exemplars of change had at one time or another struggled with their sexual needs and their effects on their relationships. Recall Mary's desperate effort to rely on her Christian faith to protect her from her attraction to a church organist. Buck's precipitous emotional decline was aggravated by his wife's "messing around." Josh's compulsive search for sexually loving friendships must have contributed to his death. Dave and Elise's physical connectedness in bed was broken by her menopausal sweating. Charlie's wife insisted he had to "earn" the right to bed her. Other untold stories testify to the imperious grip of sex and love's transcendence. Because Carol naively thought men wanted a lot of sex, she demanded sex two and three times a day, which exhausted her husband who was unable to say no because of a compulsion to prove his manhood. Howard had sex with his sales clerk every night before going home to his unsuspecting wife. And Tom wrote me a month after the death of his wife to explain why he could not complete the last survey's questions about sex. Though they had not had sex for sixteen years, "We were always faithful to the end. She had ulcerative colitis and it would have been cruel for me to insist and very destructive to find sex elsewhere." He ended with a quote from George Eliot, "The delight there is in frank kindness and companionship between a man and a woman who have no passion to hide or confess."

What does the study tell us about sex throughout the middle years? More than I anticipated.

First, and most important, what I said in the commentary on Dave and Elise told us how pervasively marital sexual compatibility is associated with a host of measures of personality and competence, most prominently with the men's and women's maturity. Men's maturity reliably predicted 30% of the measures of sexuality; women's predicted only 10%. The only sexual behavior reliably associated with maturity for *both* men and women was that the more mature persons talked openly about their feelings about their sexual relationship. In addition, the more mature woman felt she was well-mated sexually and was satisfied with how frequently her partner initiated sex.

In contrast to a less mature man, a more mature man was more sexually attracted to his partner, believed that she was considerate in fulfilling his different sexual needs, that he and she should have the same standard of sexual morality, that is, each should be sexually faithful to each other 100% of the time. Finally the mature man believed his partner felt the same way.

Second, the great variability in sexual intensity and expression among both men and women makes generalizations suspect. I found that the frequency of intercourse in the study's marital beds declined about 40% from early middle to late middle age. Kinsey had told us in 1948 this would happen, especially for highly educated persons. In their 40s, the men reported an average of four plus couplings a month, though dreaming of more than nine; their wives claimed a full five sexual encounters a month though preferring seven. The much younger second wife of Peter, a creative entrepreneur, wanted fifteen relations a month when in her 30s. She upped her desired stakes to twenty-five a month when in her 40s; by then she had a lover on the side who may have been making up the difference. In their 50s, the men recalled having had about three lovings a month, though desiring more than twice that number. These gender differences are not significant, statistically that is. By their 60s, 30% of the men no longer had any sex with their partners.

Third, the women changed during their 40s and 50s reliably more than the men in other attitudes and desires, possibly, as related in the commentary on Elise, as a result of menopause. Their sexual interest and needs seem to have been damped down. They felt they were not as well-mated sexually, wished their husbands were not as spontaneously interested in initiating sex, needed less intense and varied stimulation sexually, less freely shared their feelings about sex with their husbands, but paradoxically indicated that they felt more sexually attracted to them.

The men's changes in their sexual attitudes took place more slowly in their middle years. Not until I compared their changes between their 40s and 60s did significant changes emerge. (Unfortunately, too few replies from the women in their 60s prevented making any reliable comparisons.) Compared to their 40s, in their 60s the men needed much more varied and intense sexual stimulation to be as responsive; they also had sexual desires not being fulfilled by their partners. In their 40s about half of the men had found occasional sexual solace in other persons' beds rather than their own marital ones. But in their 60s, only 23% reported they had been unfaithful the previous decade. By their 50s, 27% of the women, including Elise, had also sought sexual satisfaction from men other than their partners.

I am not certain how to interpret these figures about sexual unfaithfulness primarily because of the Clinton artifact: I do not know how the men and women had defined "sexual" and also "unfaithful." The few men who had wandered sexually when younger but had remarried since claimed they had been faithful (most likely answering with respect to faithfulness to their second wife?).

Fourth, what surprised me was that the men and women did not reliably differ in as many sexual attitudes as they did, though the women's scores were consistently lower. In their 40s, the men were more sexually attracted to their wives than their wives were to them. Some wives reported talking about their sexual feelings more freely than the men reported, which I had also observed in the interviews. In their 50s, the men wished their wives would initiate sex spontaneously more than their wives wished their husbands would. The men's sexual enjoyment depended more reliably than their wives' on their partner's sexual enjoyment.

I cannot escape two impressions. First, sex is more than just its frequency and degree of enjoyment. It is its centrality to the mutuality of the partners' relationship. Because of its centrality, disturbance or disruption of the sexual relationship has widening effects on the marital relationship that extend far beyond just sex itself. Second, the effects may be more disruptive for men than for their partners.

Changes in Concerns and Confidence to Cope

Another impetus to change are our anticipations about future events that are likely to demand new adaptations and our confidence we can respond effectively. While taxes and death are inescapable, other events vary in their likelihood of occurrence from our 30s to our 60s: declining sexual needs, increasing signs of aging, sickness and death of a parent or a child, falling in love with someone other than our partner. Might not frequently thinking about a future event index our degree of concern about adapting to it? I assumed that the degree of anticipated coping with each event indexes a generalized confidence in the ability to adapt to a variety of events.

As for most of the previous measures of change, large proportions, i.e., 75% to 80%, of the men and women did not reliably disagree about how frequently they thought about each event in their 40s and 50s. In each decade, both were preoccupied most frequently about signs of aging; next, creating a notable achievement; and then having the opportunity for extensive recreational travel. Reaching their highest level of competence and responsibility was one of the men's five most frequent preoccupations for every decade. Death of their last surviving parent was one of the women's most frequent concerns in their 40s and 50s.

The men and women agreed even more about the events they felt most confident they could adapt to, not surprisingly all positive events. They agreed for each time period that they could actively cope with their grandchildren, adapt to their last child becoming financially independent, and adapt to the opportunity for more leisure travel.

The men and women's concerns changed reliably but not similarly over the decades for a few events. In their 50s, the men began to think about retirement, increased leisure time, arrival of grandchildren, cessation of sexual desire, and the possible long incapacitating illness of their spouses. Approaching their 60s, the men's thoughts reliably turned to, among other themes, their parents' dependence on them and future death, premature loss of their job and security, work becoming repetitive and tedious, and the severe illness and death of a child.

As the women moved through their 50s, they began to think more frequently about their children becoming financially independent, retiring from their work, and, among other events, their children having a severe marital or career crisis. Their growing concerns did not overlap with any of the men's, a potential source of marital misunderstanding and conflict for couples who had not developed empathic communication skills.

The men's and women's confidence about coping did not change from their 40s into their 50s for 83% of the 30 events I assessed. Dave was the least confident person that he would cope overall.

The men and women were reliably more confident about adapting in their 40s than 50s but to different events. The men became less confident from their 40s to their 50s that they could cope with the death of their last parent, retirement, their reduced level of power and responsibility, and signs of aging. The women became reliably less confident from their 40s to their 50s that they could cope with a child's serious illness, anticipated reduced stamina, increased attraction to another than their husband, and closer friendships with another woman. I am not clear why confidence may ebb about these events as one moves into the 50s. Might the increased probability of the events' occurrence challenge a man's ability to control them? After all, "real" men control and dominate, not yield and submit. Might the occurrence of menopause in the late 40s and 50s make some women, like Elise, feel they are powerless prisoners of their hormones? However, Neugarten has shown that there is no *consistent* relation between menopause and any of the personality effects she assessed. (1968)

Summary

The study used a large variety of methods to identify the stability and change of important core adaptive attributes of personality over four decades.

I have not discussed other methods and attributes, reported in Appendix C, that affect adaptation to our principal adult roles such as our vocations and marriages. Not because they contradict the tenor of the results to date, but because of my growing concern that the chapter's density may be making it less assimilable. What have bright, highly educated, and achieving men and women told us about their healthy psychological growth or maturing from their early adulthood to their retirement?

1. The early adult years until the 30s are a critical, educable period after which healthy growth stabilizes and continues as such at least to retirement.

2. Personality stability is clearly the rule, not the exception, during adult development. Kelly may have overstated the evidence for "significant change" during the middle adult years, though it may occur for some, as it did for the exemplars who were selected because of the magnitude of their changes. Psychological health and its associated attributes, traits, and motives remain relatively stable during the middle adult years. Changes in masculinity and femininity and in our sexuality are two of the areas in which significant change occurs.

3. Maturing is not uniform. Its dimensional leading edges are increasing awareness and stabilization. Its lagging one is autonomy. Its sectors' leading edges are cognitive skills, values, and interpersonal relationships with the opposite sex. Sectors' growth lags in the maturation of the self and, most consistently, personal relationships with one's own sex.

4. Maturing is not continuous but episodic; the episodes can vary in timing and pattern. Slowed rate of growth and plateaus are more common than researchers have reported. Individuals vary greatly in the rate and pattern of their maturing over their middle years.

5. Males and females mature similarly. Gender differences in maturing may become less as we age, especially as bio-sexual initiators of change become more mute.

6. While the contributors to or causes of maturing are numerous and vary over an individual's adult years, a common limited core, such as familial interpersonal relationships, persist throughout the adult years to produce maturing effects. But any single maturing effect may be produced by a variety of causes. No one royal road to maturity exists.

7. Societal patterning and timing of events requiring new adaptations seem to prevail over some inevitable universal, sequential schedule of adaptations—except those grounded on commonly shared hormonal biological events like puberty, beginning and ending of pregnancy possibilities, menopause, and reduction of hormonal support of libidinal strength.

Chapter 12

———≫◦◦◦≪———

DISCOVERING MID-LIFE CRISES AND
OTHER MYTHS ABOUT ADULT GROWTH

I have been asked: What have I learned that surprised me about healthy growth in adulthood? What has surprised me is how many of my expectations have been confirmed. A few key expectations were:

- Growth must be viewed in person or systemic terms: It is the person as a whole person that affects whether a specific type of growth is judged as healthy or not.
- Growth is episodic, not continuous.
- Growth can continue far into adulthood if the conditions are favorable.

I have also been surprised by how little evidence I uncovered that confirmed some of the most popular ideas about healthy growth. I now call them myths.

Myth Number One

There is an invariant, universal, bio-psychosocial sequence of stages to maturing during an adult's middle years.

When I call this widely held idea a myth I may upset most researchers and those who write about adult growth. Yes, there are more or less invariant sequential stages in early cognitive development associated with the maturation of the brain. Yes, hormonal changes at puberty initiate profound changes in our minds, relationships, and ideas about our selves.

Yes, other bio-hormonal changes, including men's declining testosterone, women's recurring menstruation, pregnancy, hormonally-based nursing capability, and menopause may affect healthy growth. And yes, our bodily programming we call "aging" in the later years provides the foundation for possibly invariant, sequential, developmental effects, like failing short-term memories and declining stamina, vision, and hearing.

But post-adolescent biological changes become quite silent for decades as societal and cultural events take precedence. Harvard's Robert W. White, observer of adolescent development, expressed great reservations to me about applying the idea of children's invariant stages to adults. I had a similar conversation with Bernice Neugarten, University of Chicago's researcher and interpreter of adult development, about Daniel Levinson's ideas that an adult grew through several fixed stages, his most famous being a mid-life crisis. Like me, Neugarten was not persuaded by Levinson's detailed invariant sequential stages that so influenced Sheehy's populariza- tion of age-specific mid-life stages. (1976) Neugarten did not deny that widely shared changes occurred during middle age. After all, she had noted a number, including increased introspection, judgment, and measuring time no longer by how many years lived but by how many years left to live. What may seem to be an invariant sequence of stages in middle age is more likely due to a society's social clock. She believed each society had consensual expectations about the appropriate timing of acceptable behaviors.[1] Society has been resetting the social clock over the past decades quite radically in fact.

I have been puzzled why I have not discovered sequential age-linked stages when studying men and women for so many decades. Was I just not perceptive enough? Was I too wedded to empirical testing and were my methods just not sensitive enough to identify possible emergent stages?

Levinson visited me to learn what I had found from my Time 3 stud- ies. To his questions I said I could not replicate his ideas that men had a "big dream" that motivated their lives, that mentors were an influential determinant of men's growth, that they seemed to be unduly worried about dying, which he and some others have proposed triggers a mid-life crisis. (D. Levinson, Darrow, Klein, M.H. Levinson, & McKee, 1978) I had reservations about stage theories, but said I would test his ideas, including a universal mid-life crisis which I did for Times 4 and 5.

Men Have "Big Dreams" that Are Central to Their Motivation

Believing the stereotype that college students are idealists with "big dreams" to change the world, I asked the men and women to recall the "big" dreams they had had in college, in their 30s and in their current 40s. I scored them on a five-point scale from no dream at all to an atypical "big" dream of high ambition and distinction. Forty-eight percent of the men denied that they had had any dream at all for their future when they graduated from college. By their 30s, 19%, and by their 40s, 29% claimed they had some distinctive or novel dream or goal motivating them. A minority rejected the idea one should work for long-term goals. Living day-by-day appealed to a few. A future dean of a medical school claimed he was "not the type of person who has big dreams. I don't think about the world in that way." Charlie was one of the few motivated much of his active life by a dream of improving society. However, to the question, "How central or important is your dream to your life now?" 53% of the men in their 40s claimed it was very important, even though only 60% had admitted to even having a dream, let alone a "big" one, about their future.

Men's Growth is Influenced by Mentors

Few of the highly achieving men I studied identified a mentor to have been important to their growth at any post-college time to their 40s when Levinson expected their effect to be most pronounced. As chapter 1's commentary showed, other events were far more influential. When I asked in Time's 4 and 5 interviews if they had had a mentor only a few agreed that they had.

Anticipation of Death

Not just Levinson but others suggest that in their 40s men and women begin to measure time in terms of years left to live and that the prospect of death becomes more real. (Neugarten, 1968) I asked my men and women to rate their reactions if told they had one more year to live. Forty-four percent of the men and 62% of the women would feel dread. However, when asked how imminent did they feel death was, 82% of both rated it to be "very" to "quite" remote. Other results suggested the men and women had to first come to terms with the anticipated deaths of their parents, which in turn made their own future death less remote.

Men's Universal Mid-Life Crisis?

I included in Times 4 and 5 four different ways to identify such a crisis stage during the men's and women's 40s.

First, if a mid-life crisis is as disruptive as it is described should we not expect the measures of psychological health and maturing, like the PSQ and SIQ, to reflect the upset? Or at least some variation in their graphical representations? As chapter 10 showed us, no evidence indicates that such disruption occurred; if it did, my methods could not detect its effects.

Second, a clue to the presence of a mid-life crisis might be the tenor of the five associations every person gave to different periods of their lives, one of which was the early 40s, the critical period for its alleged occurrence. Each association was scored for its degree of positive and negative affect. Examples of the least positive associations given by a journalist to "early 40s" were "gray hair, paunch, failing powers, rigidity, fear." An English professor gave one of the most positive sets of five associations to the "early 40s": "vital, productive, exhilarating, happy and other positive words." Billie Leighton, the lead in *Lives of Hope*, subsequently associate director of a NIH institute, replied, "I consider myself middle age now: productive, interesting, settled, fun, exciting." When I compared the total affective scores of the men and women to each period of the life cycle, I found no reliable differences in affect for them between their 30s, 40s, and 50s.

My written impressions of the tenor of the associations given to the early 40s when I scored them two decades later were non-conflictual; self-acceptance; lacking in intense words; much quieter life with absence of words about striving and tension; sense of being "over the hump." The tenor of the women's associations was similar: quieter time; calmer; "not as much struggle as in my 30s"; settled; clearer emergence in awareness of physical signs of aging; stabilizing.

Third, I asked in their early 50s if they had had a mid-life crisis. Only 18% of the men agreed; 69% disagreed. One man pithily replied, "No. My whole life has been a crisis." Another replied, "Have been looking for this and haven't found it yet." "My 20s and 30s were one long crisis." Those who agreed linked the "crisis" to some circumstance, such as a divorce, rather than to a particular age. Rich said, "I'm not convinced there is a mid-life crisis. It could come at various times."

The women agreed and disagreed about equally: 37% agreed and 43% disagreed that they had had a mid-life crisis. A woman living in an isolated fishing village said, "I remember having some misgivings about going downhill when I reached the halfway point and was now going downhill and at the bottom of the hill was death, but that doesn't frighten me any more." A librarian replied with brief sentences: "Menopause was definitely a mid-life crisis. Constant hot flashes every hour. Victimized by your chemistry. Husband not very understanding."

The fourth way assessed if adult development could be understood in terms of stages. For every five-year period since their early 20s, the men and women rated on a nine-point scale a global index of their well-being. The index was composed of four components: energy from low to high; mood from unhappy to happy; productive from stagnant to high; and self from empty to fulfilled.

This task was not as daunting for my type of men and women as it sounds. I had asked them to first record for each five-year period the significant events of their lives which made the task personally concrete. I assumed that the ages bracketing a mid-life crisis would be rated lower in well-being. Such was *not* the case for the men. Most varied widely in their rated well-being scores for the five-year periods. As a group, their ratings of their well-being did not differ for every five-year period since graduation through their late 30s. But, they reliably rated their well-being *more favorably* from their late 30s to their early 40s—just the period for Levinson's mid-life crisis! Their elevated well-being at that phase continued through the 40s. The women also did not differ in their well-being for every five-year comparison. I got the same results from the judgments about their well-being made at Time 5 which confirms the reliability of the Time 4 ratings.

Moral? Check out one's hunches by testing them. Maybe Levinson's own mid-life crisis, so Vaillant reports, was his evidence for its existence. (Vaillant, 2002) I had had no mid-life crisis. Is that why I am skeptical? Other researchers have also not found evidence to support Levinson's idea. (Helson, Soto, & Cate, 2003)

My conclusion? If you want to have a "mid-life crisis" to justify leaving your spouse and fleeing to Tahiti or go home to mother, fine but don't blame it on reaching 40 or some other nearby age. Above all, don't go searching for a mid-life crisis; you might learn what a self-fulfilling prophecy means.

Myth Number Two

Erikson's developmental model, as expounded by George Vaillant, a psychiatrist, researcher, and the most recent articulate interpreter of Erikson's ideas, includes what I think is another myth: vocational consolidation depends upon mastering an earlier intimacy stage.

Vaillant defines "intimacy" to mean having lived with another person in "an interdependent, reciprocal, committed, and contented fashion for a decade or more." (1980) The kicker is "for a decade or more." Peter, the entrepreneur, didn't marry until he was 30; yet he had consolidated his vocation in his 20s by Vaillant's definition, essentially a calling. Until his downfall, he was very content with his vocation, was paid very handsomely, was highly competent as an entrepreneur, and was certainly committed—Vaillant's criteria for vocational consolidation. Barbara and Jim had long settled into their careers before their early marriage had reached the criterion of a decade. One of my men, a distinguished international executive, had been called to exemplary service to his adopted country that honored him with its most prestigious award. He had a miserable intimate relationship with his wife from the earliest years of his 20-plus year marriage before he divorced her for his mistress.

Let's ignore the "kicker" qualification. Positing the dependency of one stage upon the mastery of a previous stage during adulthood is risky theoretically, given the fluidity of today's social clocks. Neugarten's social clock for marriage of professionals has slowed down since the Grant Study of men's typical early marital age in the 1920s. More contemporary youth now live with each other as unmarried partners, but what then does "commitment" mean? How dependent is continued mastery of one stage upon the continued stability of its antecedent stages? The trauma of his divorce did not slow down Rich's vocational commitment one whit. Vaillant does waver, however, when stating that mastery of antecedent stages is necessary for healthy growth. He admits that the last stage of integrity may be reached without full mastery of its antecedents. We should not rigidly hold ourselves to some preordained sequence, in other words. I think Vaillant would agree. (2002)

More than anyone else, Vaillant[2] has searched for evidence of the predictive efficacy of his ideas about stages and mental health throughout the adult years. (1974, 1979, 1993, 2002) That competence in our adult roles is associated with mental health stands. I remain uncertain, however, that his work on marriage, fatherhood (1978), and work (1981) necessarily convert the myth into a reality. His results stand on their own two feet and don't need the idea of "stage" for their explanation.

Myth Number Three

Even if the idea of stage appeals to you, identifying several age-defined sub-stages within the 40s and 50s cuts the cake too fine to be believable for me.

Three researchers and commentators about growth during the 40s propose different ways of slicing the decade into distinct, and for Sheehy, very precisely aged sub-stages. (1982) As wise and perceptive as are their descriptions of growth during middle age, independent confirming empirical evidence of sub-stages remains weak.[3]

If the idea of stage is to be useful as a sign post of greater maturity, should it not be identifiable by some measure of well-being and fulfillment? The men and women rated their well-being no differently from any other period, beginning with their college years and ending with their early to late 50s. Another nail (even if misshapen and not of the quality a defender of stages would accept) in the coffin of stage models?

Perhaps they and you could find more common regularities within the lives of the book's exemplars at each age period than I have been able to intuit. An individual's growth seems much messier, more complicated, and not so time-bound or age-linked when studied over 40 to 50 years. It is more vulnerable to intervening accidents or events than theorists want to believe. After all, Barbara's growth spurted as a result of Jim's and her decision to return to Washington and her appointment as president of her research group by the fortuitous departure of its former leader.

Neugarten's warning to researchers more than 30 years ago speaks for me about applying a stage model to development in middle age. Psychologists "should proceed cautiously in assuming the same intimate relationships between biological and psychological phenomena in adulthood that hold true in childhood." (1968, p.142)

Chapter 13

———=»-0-«=———

GROWING FROM ADOLESCENCE INTO THE 60S

I have assumed that the model of maturing's generic dimensions evolve throughout the life span. They are dimensions of adaptational efficacy for mastering varying developmental tasks or problems such as creating one's identity or an intimate relation, and are universally applicable. Type, order, and timing of developmental tasks may vary for individuals and society's consensual expectations, within the bounds set by humans' innate biological possibilities. Because the adaptational dimensions define the most effective way to solve a problem, no wonder they predict a wide range of adult competencies and successes. The generality, validity, and utility of the model have not been found wanting. It has comprehensively mapped the effects of growing healthily.

At least three questions remain unanswered about the model of maturing as a means of studying growth across the life span. How adequate is it for describing what psychoanalysts call the "ego's executive strengths" across the portion of the life span that has been studied to date? I postpone to the next chapters a discussion of the remaining two questions: What are the principal individual predictors of an adult's healthy growth? What principles can be implemented to further dimensional maturing in the personality's sectors?

The Person's Adaptive Strengths

Table 2.1 mapped some of the generic adaptive strengths associated with each dimension and their visible outcomes. I drew the dimensions from Piaget's model of the growth of intelligence—really a model of adaptation

214

(1947) and John Dewey's similar model of problem-solving. (1922) The implication of each is that there is a dimensional sequence to how we adapt. Whatever the problem is, we must first become aware of it, which is why Dewey valued the development of reflection as a cardinal outcome of education. When consulting with faculties, I recommended Margaret Mead's most wise prescription: Clear understanding of a problem prefigures its lines of solution. The search for a solution next requires what Piaget calls associativity or skill in identifying alternative lines of solution. For both Piaget and Dewey, possible part-solutions need to be tentatively combined and integrated with a view of the whole problem. The next phase in the sequence is to repeatedly test and apply the provisional solution until it is so stable that it becomes freely mobile and transferable to varied situations. The consequence of such autonomy is increased mastery and competence.

This ideal model of the process of adaptation becomes blurred, messy, frustrating, redundant, and inefficient as soon as we apply it to a person's growth. Chapter 11's summary told us growth is systemic, but some sectors mature at different rates. Might there be an analogous metaphoric dependency between the development of personality's sectors as there is between the adaptive dimensions? Development of mind's competence enables growth of interaction skills, as Piaget showed us in his analysis of the development of the coordination between the sucking and grasping reflexes. Out of mind-interpersonal schemata emerge our values which guide the self's maturation and stabilization. I don't press these playfully speculative dependencies, but to me they suggest that maturing moves expansively from Table 2.1's upper left quadrant to its lower right one.

Since I organized the study by different decades of study, e.g., Time 3 is the early 30s, Time 4 the 40s, I trace aging in terms of developmental tasks. The tasks are typically encountered during the different ages, without assuming they are specific to an age-linked stage.

Adolescent Healthy Growth (Time 1)

The developmental task of adolescents is their own healthy growth as Table 2.1 described. That is, they continue to develop their mind's competence; their characters' humanization, such as empathy; and their self's autonomy, such as mastery of their impulses and independence of their parental dependencies.

Schools are society's playing field, so to speak, on which to further students' growth. Recall that the men and women associated five words or short phrases to different age periods, one being their high school years. Their words illuminate the inner meaning to them of high schools as a place for them to grow. In their 40s, only 26% of the men and 23% of the women used words like stimulating, exciting, growth, learning, expanding, and self-development to describe their high school years, despite being high achievers presumably ready to learn what schools had to contribute. In their associations, 29% of the men and 23% of the women mentioned loneliness and friendship. The high school years reliably garnered the least number of positive words of any age period; that and the early 30s were for many the most stressful periods of their lives.

Michigan's Bloomfield Hills school district created its Model High School (MHS) to keep the growth of its students *as persons* in the forefront, not just the growth of their minds, which is now the singular focus of national educational policy. As the school's consultant in the early years of the MHS, I worked with the faculty to create ways to evaluate the effectiveness of the school. Chapter 2 describes how individual students' written comments about how they had changed at their former high school and then at MHS were scored for the model's generic maturing categories. One sobering result was that not one student of several hundred reported that they had changed in any of the traditional curricular subjects, like French or algebra. Table 13.1 compares the ranks of the seven most important student-identified maturing effects of MHS to the effects of their previous high school. (1999b)

Table 13.1 tells us that, regardless of which school they were in, the students believed they became more tolerant and caring of others who differed from them. Moreover, they believed that MHS taught them how to become more independent, self-educating students, an effect much less discernible in their more traditional high school.

I draw three significant conclusions from this school-evaluation exercise. First, the model of maturity may provide a generic set of categories that can be used to describe maturing throughout the life-span. To test the model's usefulness for elementary school students, one of my students developed a questionnaire for their teachers to rate the maturity of their students, which he then proceeded to validate. (Lowry, 1967) Measures designed to assess Erikson's stages are age-limited, so comparisons cannot be made across the life-span that a dimensional model of growth makes possible.

Second, schools can be created to educate for maturity of which the mind's maturation is of course a priority. I have described in detail MHS's innovative educational steps to achieve its goals, which Table 13.1's entries summarize. (Heath, 1999b) Might not Margaret Mead say that lack of clarity about a school's educational goals is a harbinger of its failure in implementation?

Third, current methods of holding a student and school accountable, such as achievement test scores, are too narrow, violate the equilibrating principle, and eventually are self-defeating. As Table 13.1 dramatizes, students recognize the growths that are most important to them and their future. Some lose motivation to work for the tests when they don't feel they are growing in ways most important to them.

Table 13.1

Principal Maturing Effects of Students' Former High School Compared to Effects of Model High School

Maturing Effects	Rank of MHS Students' Ratings	
	Previous School	MHS
Developed more other-centered, caring, tolerant, and understanding relationships (Other-centered relations)	1	1
Became more in control of self to make talents work for them (Autonomy self)	12	2
Developed more autonomous values, such as forming own values (Autonomy values)	9	3
Increased reflective and communication skills (Awareness mind)	8	4.5
Became more aware of their own values, beliefs, and assumptions (Awareness values)	4	4.5
Became more aware of own personalities (Awareness self-concept)	2.5	6.5
Developed strong sense of self, self-confidence (Stability self-concept)	12	6.5

Young Adult Healthy Growth (Time 2)

The developmental task of the college years is to develop the strengths of awareness, (symbolization), other-centeredness, and integration, which prepare them to adapt successfully to an adult's responsibilities.

The college years were the most favorable ones for the men. Their word associations to these years were reliably more positive than to their high school years. They were also reliably more favorable than their associations to their early 30s. Perhaps because the women came from many colleges, they did not associate their college years to be more favorable than any other period of their lives. Fifty percent of the men gave associations to "college years" such as exciting and stimulating. Predictably, Dave's associations were the most atypical: "Silliness; opportunity for something if one could ever guess what diversion that ought to be; been cheery but made me to be too serious and solemn; an external influence; something that really came from outside the main stream of life's experience; a side-ways acceleration." Josh's were much more typical: "happy, active, worried, hard work, lots of rewards." Bryn Mawr Barbara's reflected her pre-achievement focus: "carefree, relaxed, exciting, stimulating, immature from this point of view; I didn't think I was at the time."

Growing Up in College (Heath, 1968) reports a much more intensive study of Haverford College's principal effects with three different groups of young adults, none of whom appear in this book. Many of this book's basic methods were used to assess the college's effects over the students' four years. Table 13.2 describes in declining order the impact of ten of the college's 20 most important maturing effects

How did I understand what the important determinants or causes were of these maturing effects? I created the same procedure used in this book to identify the order of the most influential determinants of adult maturing listed in chapter 1's commentary. Judges identified for me what they believed to be the college's 50 most influential determinants. The procedure made it possible to identify for each personality sector the most important collegiate determinants of its maturation, e.g., value maturation was most influenced by the college's intellectual atmosphere, social and academic honor systems, and close friends.

In addition to confirming the three lessons of the Bloomfield Hills study, the Haverford study produced three additional significant insights.

First, it demonstrated that the model of maturity's generic categories could be used to compare the effects of different institutional settings. For example, note that growth in other- centered relations ranked first for Model High School's students but fifth for Haverfordian students.

Second, studying change over the four-year period made it possible to identify how maturing proceeds from freshman to senior year. The freshman pattern of change was a harbinger of change for the remaining college years. Early adaptation to the college's demands was critical to a student's subsequent maturing. A faculty, located in and isolated by the Appalachian mountains, despaired about its students' lack of interest in their courses and its top students' transfers out of the college. The faculty became aware of the significance of the freshmen's first months in college for their subsequent growth. It insisted that fraternity rushing and partying with its expectations and support of alcoholic binge drinking be delayed until the second semester. The dean told me two years later the college's climate had changed noticeably. Students came to class more clear-headed and awake; the college no longer lost its academically top students at the end of their freshman year. (Heath, 1999b)

Third, learning how to link a college's environmental determinants with different maturing effects provided a model of how one might understand

Table 13.2

**Comparative Importance of
Personality Change in Haverford College**

Type of Change

Integration of intellectual skills

Awareness of self

Integration in interpersonal relations

Awareness of interpersonal relations

Other-centered interpersonal relations

Stabilization of self-concept

Other-centered intellectual skills

Integration of values

Other-centered values

the causes of change. More clarifying questions could then be asked about how to produce maturing. For example, the results of the Haverford study bolstered those who intuited that the students' social honor code, i.e., be respectful of others and confront those who showed disrespect, was a major contributor to its students' value maturation. The code's ambiguity demanded that students reflect about and develop more other-centered values. Too precise definition of "respect" might actually reduce the maturational effect of the social honor code.

Healthy Growth from Early 20s to Early 30s (Time 3)

An important developmental task typically encountered between the 20s and 30s is accepting the responsibility for one's adaptive strengths and applying and testing them in one's adult roles.

Confirming chapter 10's finding that the 20s and early 30s were stressful, the men's but not the women's associations to their "early 30s" were reliably less favorable than those given to the college years. Only 17% of the men, though 33% of the women, gave growth-related associations. Thirty-eight percent of the words produced by men were like "bloom off the rose," confusion, uninspired, unrest, stress. A lost alcoholic minister thought his early 30s were "chaotic, unsettled, job-hunting, scared, unable to handle." A favorable exception to the tone of the group was a San Francisco bay area psychiatrist who had explored the hippie way of life. His early 30s were "fun, friendly, happy, confusing, anxiety-provoking."

Though struggling to establish their careers, especially physicians just completing their specialties like surgery, only 28% of the men gave words relevant to their careers. Moreover, I had not anticipated that only 11% of the men and 15% of the women would associate any word about marriage to the "early 30s," given theorists' emphasis on the vocational and intimacy stages during these years. Only 30% percent of the women thought of children.

The principal maturing changes recalled about the 20s were almost identical to those the men described about their changes during their early 30s to their mid 40s. So I mention now only the four most frequently cited ones for the 20s: increased self-awareness, self-integration, stabilization of self, and caring for others. The effects of the principal determinant, their wives' personality, is delightfully described by this man:

> She has helped me to learn what I don't have to be. I
> don't have to be a perfectionist. I don't have to be deadly
> serious about everything I do. She has helped me to have
> fun, to laugh at myself. She has challenged me when I've
> been pompous or pedantic or petty. She really made me
> feel that no matter what happens she will stand with me
> and by me and that gives me a great sense of security and
> confidence in what I do.

One potentially new insight this period provoked was troubling. If
tasks like intimacy and work were so central as organizing foci for adults,
why did such few associations spontaneously come to mind about them?
Inadequate methods for detecting them is probably the explanation, but an
additional possible reason keeps haunting me. Are those of us who study
adults unconsciously imposing a received ideology on our data?

Healthy Growth from 30s to 50s (Times 4 and 5)

The typical developmental task met during the 30s to the early 50s is the
stabilization of commitment to one's vocational, marital, and parental
responsibilities.

As I described when examining the mythical mid-life crisis, I had found
no reliable difference in the emotional tone of the 30s and 40s. Yet, the
recurring associations suggested the 40s were a quieter, less conflicted
and pressured time for the men and women. The less stressful tone was
confirmed by the men's reliably increased well-being in their 40s which
persisted into their 50s. Chapter 10 and its graphs of personality change
from adolescence and the 20s through the 40s and 50s also consistently
confirmed that growth had been settling down from the 30s to the 50s.
(Bergquist, Greenberg, & Klaum, 1993)

Vocational Commitment and Maturity

Was increasing personality stabilization shown in the men's vocational
adaptation? Yes, for some but not for others. Of Vaillant's criteria for vocational consolidation, I have specific measures of the men's satisfaction,
commitment or considering their work a calling, and competence. From
what you know of Barbara's husband, Jim the hospital administrator, Rich

the wordsmith, Josh the lawyer, Buck the engineer, and Charlie the surgeon, whom would you select as having mastered the vocational consolidation task? Jim and Charlie had progressively improved in their satisfaction, competence, and commitment. With the exception of Rich's depression, he also had increased his mastery. The three were the best of the study's five most vocationally well adapted men in both their 40s and 50s. Dave and Buck hovered together near the bottom of the group at each time.

What is the relation between psychological health or maturity and vocational adaptation? For every age period, the men's maturity reliably predicted their vocational adaptation. (Heath, 1976, 1977b)

Marital Commitment and Maturity

The developmental task of creating a stable heterosexual marital commitment has become much more daunting than it was for the men of Harvard's Grant Study. And much more daunting for a researcher to study *commitment* given that the social clock no longer prescribes when marriage should occur. Do cohabiting years count toward "commitment?"

For Vaillant, four criteria, other than length of the relation, define mastery of the intimacy stage: interdependence, reciprocity, commitment, and contentment for at least ten years. How he precisely defined "interdependence" and "reciprocity" in his study to measure them is not clear to me. So I searched my data for possible indices of "interdependence," but discovered only the men's and women's ratings of their emotional dependence on the opposite sex. In their 40s, the men and women reliably depended on the other; but instructively, their need for emotional dependence on the other had become negligible by their 50s. Why? Could it be that the intervening women's movement had taken hold, and women did not believe they had to depend on a man?

The study's signs of having created a stable mutual marital relationship were understanding of each other's ideas and feelings, feeling comfortable sharing with each other the 20 troubling issues I have told you about (IC), meeting research-based criteria of marital adjustment (Spanier, 1976), and being maritally sexually compatible. (Heath, 1978) I discussed the latter in the commentary on Dave and Elise. Remarkably, and reassuringly, the four measures agreed with each other so well that any one could be an index of marital commitment between the late 20s and mid 50s, the period during which all but one of the divorces occurred.

These criteria proved to be too stringent. I estimate that about 15% and no more than 20% of the men had created a stable, mutually intimate marriage by their 40s and 50s. Fifty-seven percent of the men had either been divorced or one of the partners had rated the marriage to be "extremely" to "fairly unhappy"; the prospects were poor at the time that it might survive. However, the compromises the couples subsequently made had resulted in less unhappiness but not enough for the men and especially women to rate their marriages as happy. Barbara's marriage met my criteria for a mutually intimate marriage. Susan, while still married to her aviator husband, was the unhappiest of the exemplars. Compared to the entire group, she scored lowest on the marital adjustment test, mutuality of understanding, and comfort in sharing her intimate feelings. After her divorce and remarriage, she zoomed to the top of the group on these signs of a fulfilling marriage.

As I expected, the psychological maturity of both the men and women predicted at high levels of confidence the four indices of their marital adaptation for their early 40s. Though my expectation was correct for the men in their 50s, it was wrong for the women. At that age, the women's maturity made no contribution to any of the four strengths of a marriage of mutuality.

Parental Satisfaction and Maturity

Before exploring how the course of maturing during their middle years may differ for men and women to account for their marital differences, we must learn about the relation of maturity to parenting. It is the last of the principal developmental tasks to master between the 30s and 50s. Rich's and Susan's commentaries illustrated how parenthood can nurture the development of other-centered interpersonal skills such as caring and empathy. These are the necessary skills for mastering the subsequent generativity stage for Erikson and Vaillant. Generativity assumes that caring and empathy are transmuted into altruistic concern for the welfare of increasingly different others. As the commentaries implied, growing out of egocentrism may take years and years of many adults' lives.

Satisfaction with the 28 attributes of parenting (PAS), which had been modeled on the VAS, was reliably stable from both the men's and women's early 40s to their mid 50s. That is, the men and women retained their relative rank-order of satisfaction with being parents over the years. They did not change in their overall satisfaction from their 30s on, but they did begin to separate in their specific parental satisfactions. The woman's role as a mother reliably became less central to her identity as her children's demands on her energy slowly decreased, as did her day-to-day involvement with them. Being a mother no longer provided as many new interests and friendships as earlier. It also no longer satisfied as many of her needs or provided opportunities to create new ways to raise her children. Now, with her children's increasing involvement with their friends and activities away from home, she began to secure more control of her own time, as Elise told us. With time's perspective, she became more satisfied with being a mother and with how good a job she had done. She was becoming free of her maternal responsibilities to chart new directions for herself. The results confirm Neugarten's earlier finding that mothers didn't typically get depressed about how empty their nests had become. Only Barbara wished she could have had another child. The mothers now looked forward to becoming grandmothers. Barbara and Susan emerged out of their 40s as the most satisfied mothers.

The fathers changed also, but not as much. Their 40s had been marked by greater satisfaction with the centrality of being a father to their identity, fatherhood's contribution to developing new interests and friends with other fathers, and to meeting more of their important needs. But they, like their wives, also became reliably more content with the lessening time that parenting required. Jim was by far the most satisfied father, an exemplar of generativity. Rich remained more satisfied as a father than Buck, or even Charlie.

The men's and women's maturity continued to reliably predict their parental satisfaction in their 40s and 50s.

Gender Differences in Maturing

Vaillant acknowledges that the weakness of his work was its unavoidable lack of adequate information on women comparable to that of Harvard men to compare whether their maturation followed similar paths. I have found the maturing paths of men and women are similar, but not identical. Time 4's interview identified the principal determinants of the men and women's changes which are reported in chapter 1's commentary. Quite remarkably, the determinants of their growth from the 20s to their 50s were as similar as they are. The commentary lists each gender's determinants in order of the frequency of their cited maturing effects in their interviews. In their 40s, the men and women differed from each other in two of their principal determinants. Major changes in work and approaching middle age were more important to the men than the women. Important causes of women's growth, but not men's, were children and the women's liberation movement.

Though the magnitude of the determinants' effects varied, the ordered pattern of the men's and women's maturing was quite similar.

- They became more aware of themselves (Awareness self).
- Their thought became more relational and integrative (Integration cognitive skills).
- They became more other-centered in their relationships (Other-centered relationships).
- They developed a stronger sense of themselves (Stabilization self).
- They became more aware of their values (Awareness values).
- Their values became stronger and more certain (Stabilization values).
- Their selves became more autonomous (Autonomy self).

The men reported their selves to be much more together (Integration self); the women grew to like themselves better (Other-centered self) and to develop a clearer sense of priorities (Integration values).

To illustrate that a variety of different events may contribute to any specific maturing effect, I summarize the principal causes of the men's and women's increased sense of self and self-confidence. The men's vocational and marital uncertainties in their 20s were reflected in the sparse number of causes of their more stable selves at that time: their wives as persons, type of occupation, and atmosphere of their home. By their early 40s, however, seven events had contributed to stabilizing their identities since their early 30s: major change in work's responsibility, spouse as a partner, physical-emotional health, type of occupation, and demands of their paternal role, among others.

For the women, their husbands' personalities and their own role as a partner had contributed to their stronger sense of themselves. Barbara is a good example of how Jim's support and model of the personal professional relationships she needed contributed to her growth. Next in order of their contribution were the women's physical-emotional health, maternal role, and type of occupation.

The women's liberation movement profoundly affected 25% of the women and to a lesser extent all but 15%, including Mary, of the remainder. As Jim said, until the role of women entered into his and the national consciousness, he had never thought of Barbara committing herself to a career.

The two most formative causes of the women's maturation of their values and selves were the feminist movement and its disruptive effects on the women's role as a marital partner. The study's older women—like Barbara and Elise—felt most provoked by their teenage children, especially their daughters, who demanded the freedoms and opportunities the movement promised women. One unsettled mother said, "I feel like my adolescent daughter, trying to figure out what I want to do the rest of my life, particularly now as I see her leaving home in a few years. We're dealing with the same issues. It's scary."

It is indeed scary to wrestle as a middle-aged adult with an adolescent developmental task of creating one's identity. So when women began to wrest control of their identities from men, who still tell women how to act and what to become in the Afghanistans and Irans of the world, they had to experiment, sometimes at the expense of their traditional marriages. Disruptive though their explorations were, the outcomes for reasonably mature women were the liberation of energy, enhanced self-confidence, a more mature assertive autonomy, and heightened creativity.

Two insights dominate what I learned about healthy growth during middle age. The first is how rapidly societal and cultural changes in "natural" gender-based definitions of our roles as males and females can unsettle us, our marriages, and families. I remember when men would never be seen in a grocery store or a girl would not ask a boy for a date and pay her own way. Social historians will tell me how egocentric is my limited view of historic realities. Such changes in our relationships and values are historic moments of personal vulnerability that can have enduring maturing and, yes, to the conservatives among us, (temporary?) unhealthy effects.

The second insight is how consistently our maturity in our adult years is associated with how well we have adapted vocationally, maritally, sexually, and parentally to give us a greater sense of fulfillment. An unanswered question is whether maturity's adaptive strengths contributed to our efficacy, whether they are the outcomes of succeeding in our roles, or whether the association is both a cause and an outcome.

Chapters 14 and 15 examine two other principal issues for understanding healthy growth. What does a longitudinal study contribute to understanding the antecedents of later maturation? What principles can be applied to further healthy growth?

Chapter 14

————≫•●•≪————

PREDICTING ADOLESCENT AND
ADULT HEALTHY GROWTH

Chapters 10 and 11 showed that our personalities are both stable and changeable over many decades. We are most educable for change in our youthful years. We experiment with long hair and ear rings, how low on our hips to wear our jeans, whether and what to smoke. We test our ability in tennis and track. We discover we are a "natural" guitar player but not a vocalist. Our jokes crack up our friends but antagonize our teachers. We search for the friend we can trust. We are in the "sorting stage" discovering what fits us. We are creating our identities. Of course, some discover their identity when much younger. Franklin Chang-Diaz discovered he was to be an astronaut at the age of seven when inspired by Sputnik. His identity as a future astronaut determined every course of his subsequent life until he flew into space. Mary knew her identity from her earliest years. Then there are those who do not discover what they are to be until middle age, like Barbara, or even older, like Dave who struggled for decades to sort himself out.

So I anticipated that the men's adolescent and early adult personalities might not predict their adult selves as consistently as their 30-year-old ones might predict their 40-year-old selves.

I first searched for clues from the early lives of the men and women that predicted how well they turn out as adults.[1] Next I briefly summarized what strengths, as adults, contribute to our future effectiveness and happiness. Not surprisingly, adolescent and adult maturity are the keys that open the door to future effectiveness.

Familial and Adolescent Antecedents of Adult Maturity

Maturity of Participants' Parents

The evidence consistently identifies the maturity of the men and women's mothers and fathers and of their relationship with their children as contributing to some adult outcomes. Elise, Dave, and Charlie struggled for much of their adult lives with their dominating mothers. Even Susan suffered, so she claimed, from a too-permissive mother, who gave her more freedom than she could handle wisely when an adolescent. The sons of the more mature fathers with whom they had healthy relationships adapted more successfully to their vocations, as they and their colleagues rated it. The tenor of the results agrees with the Kauai (Werne & Smith, 2001) and Grant studies' (Vaillant, 1974) longitudinal findings about the positive effects of favorable family environments.

The men's and women's mothers and the quality of their relationships with their children reliably contributed to the children's subsequent marital adjustment and intimacy. Moreover, the maturity of the women's mothers most consistently predicted their daughters' satisfaction and fulfillment as mothers. Elise's relationship with her rebellious daughter mirrored her own mother's relationship with her.

The other consistent finding, for which I have no persuasive explanation, is that the men and women seem to have been most affected by their parents in their 40s, rather than in their 30s. Perhaps the stresses when in their 20s overshadowed the effects of their parents. Might parental effects on their children diminish the older their children become? The children become freer, so to speak, of their earlier parental influences.

High School Involvement

Admission to Haverford College required a description of an applicant's extra-curricular, athletic, and other non-academic involvement. My other studies of high school students have shown that involved students use drugs less frequently, do better academically, have higher morale, and are better school and community citizens. (Heath, 1999b) I compared those who had and had not extended themselves into their immediate school and local religious, political, and community activities. Those who had extended themselves during high school had greater self-esteem when in college.

They were more purposeful, enthusiastic, energetic, and adventurous, among other traits of maturity. When they were graduating college seniors, their departmental chairmen rated the more highly involved high school students to be more determined, emotionally stable, intelligent and to have more favorable personalities than they rated those non-involved high school students.[2] But what does high school involvement predict about an adult's future? In his 30s he will be more mature, more accurately understand himself, feel more together, and be more satisfied with his vocation's social value. He also will reliably believe his work fulfills his strongest needs, fits his temperament, and is a source of new interests. These and other vocational satisfactions persist into his 40s. The involved, but not the non-involved, high school student also believes 30-to-40 years later that he has had a fulfilling life.

Moral to parents: encourage your children "to give themselves away," to use Vaillant's apt phrase, and serve others, even if their involvement does take time and energy away from doing their homework perfectly—up to a reasonable point!

Intellectual and Academic Grade Predictors

Much research has been done to discover what intelligence and academic grades predict about a person. Intellectual level has been intensively studied to determine its contribution to academic achievement, which is substantial, even for highly homogeneous and very bright 17-year-old Haverfordians. What intellectual level predicts later in life has intrigued many, beginning with Terman who devoted his life to studying gifted youngsters as they grew through adulthood. (Terman & Oden, 1959) The commentary on Rich summarized some of my findings about what SATs predict later in life. One result provides a warning. While men with high quantitative aptitude may not fare as well as more ordinary men in their future interpersonal relations, by their 50s they have become more mature and are judged by those who know them well to be more fulfilled adults. Only comprehensive longitudinal studies can fairly assess if any singular talent may emerge as having a positive sleeper effect long after its initial assessment. Josh did not exploit his intellectual giftedness as Rich did; instead, he concentrated on overcoming its potential to isolate him from others to develop close friendships with men who Greg, his lover, claimed were "below" him in talent.

Academic achievement is popularly dismissed as being irrelevant to living. This opinion is not quite true, at least with respect to what professional men's academic grades predict about them. The more academically achieving men, and their most knowledgeable colleagues, were reliably satisfied with their vocational adaptation for every decade to their 60s. The opinion does carry some truth if by "living" is meant being a good marital and sexual partner, parent, community member, or happy and mature.

I inadvertently stumbled upon a possible intellectual-academic predictor that contributes more to later adult effectiveness than either intelligence or academic achievement. Recall I had created three types of problem-solving tasks, i.e., logical conceptual ability, analytic and synthetic skill, and judgment, with personally threatening and non-threatening content (COG). I verified Freud's suggestion that a strong ego does not let disturbing information interfere with adaptation, and if it does, it can resiliently recover its intellectual efficiency.[3] It is the dispassionate analysis and judgment a judge needs to prevent his personal biases or anxieties from unduly coloring or influencing his decisions. Or a politician needs to prevent making decisions that support his biases or wishes without carefully weighing all of the evidence or lack thereof—like justifying invading Iraq to find weapons of mass destruction on the basis of flimsy and unverifiable evidence to produce "regime change."

Stability of cognitive efficiency powerfully predicts a host of adult personality strengths and competencies in addition to those that traditional intellectual and academic measures predict. It predicts in one's 30s a person's psychological maturity, physical and psychological health, competence as a spouse, vocational competence, and other traits. In one's 40s and 50s, a youth's cognitive efficiency predicts colleagues' ratings of the quality of his work achieved, competence, and level of responsibility, among other work-related traits.

Personality Predictors from Teenage Years

Contrary to my expectation that the potentially unsettling adolescent years might not predict adult outcomes very well, an early teenager's maturity persists for more than 30 years. Retrospective ratings by the men of 50 on signs of maturity as an early teenager predicted their maturity as an upperclassmen when independently rated by their peers and faculty. These judges' ratings of the seniors' maturity in turn predicted their PSQ scores for maturity when the men were in their 30s. Given how many adult outcomes the PSQ predicts at different ages, those responsible for raising psychologically healthy children and teenagers may find help from the principles that chapter 15 describes for encouraging maturity.

The two most powerful predictors of adult outcomes secured during the college years, prior to adapting to vocational and marital tasks, were the MMPI measure of maladjustment and the SIQ measure of self-esteem.

MMPI measure of maladjustment as a predictor. Entering college freshmen whose total MMPI maladjustment scores were high, scored significantly higher on 50% of the 52 measures of **negative** adult outcomes that I explored.[4] Fifteen years after entering college, the more maladjusted freshmen when compared to well-adjusted ones were still more immature, unhealthy, and rated by their colleagues to be poorly adapted vocationally. Twenty-five years after entering college, these differences still persisted. Maladjustment as a freshman continued to be consistently associated with other measures of immaturity and poor psychological health, including judge-ratings of immature self-concepts, femininity, and his beliefs others would rate him to be immature, which was in fact how others rated him.

Self-esteem as a predictor. The evidence that maturity is a meaningful contributing antecedent to adult adaptation is solidly buttressed by a youth's SIQ-measured positive self-evaluation. To distinguish between the PSQ and SIQ measures of maturity I have called the latter "self-esteem." It tells us how favorably a youth thinks of himself in terms of 26 attributes of maturity.

Favorably describing one's self when a junior or senior in college significantly predicts twelve to fifteen years later, every measure of his maturity, health, and competence, except his fulfillment as a father. He and his colleague agree that he is vocationally well adapted. (Heath, 1976) They agree about how much his vocation has contributed to his opportunity to grow, which in fact he has fulfilled, to the quality of his work, and as a source of new interests and friends. An upperclassman's self-esteem also contributes to his later competence in fulfilling his marital roles, greater frequency of sexual relations, and closeness in his personal relationships as rated by his closest friend.

In his 40s, an upperclassman's self-esteem reliably predicts an impressive 75% of the 52 adult outcomes I measured at that time, including now his involvement and leadership in his community.

By his 50s, his self-esteem when an upperclassman has diminished as a predictor, as I had also discovered for the men's parental influence and other adolescent measures of competence.

Summary of Adolescent Antecedents of Adult Outcomes

What conclusions and insights has the longitudinal study of the antecedents of the principal adult outcomes generated?

First, the evidence convinces me that maturity is both a cause of and an outcome of adapting effectively to an adult's developmental tasks.

Second, early developmental antecedents such as parental maturity (and other similar personality attributes I have not reported here), involvement in high school and community activities, academic achievement, and possibly adolescent SAT and other intelligence measures become, over time, less useful as predictors of adult adaptation. With increased maturing, the past becomes less a prologue to how well we adapt in the future.[5] We ourselves become our own causes. Might increased freedom from our past contribute to increased freedom of will enabling us to live more fully in the present not encumbered by our pasts?

Third, unpredictable "sleeper" effects may occur when early excessive growth of one sector of the personality has suppressed the development of other types of growth. When conflicting inhibitions are removed we now can grow on our own terms. Again, think of Barbara's metamorphosis into an outstanding administrator; Dave's eventual reclamation of his Jewish heritage that had long been suppressed by his hostile mother.

Adult Predictors of Adult Outcomes

I briefly summarize the adult predictors of the mastery of adult tasks like marital and vocational adjustment. (I had reliable information for women only from Times 4 and 5.)

1. Maturity in the men's 30s reliably predicts their maturity in their 40s which in turn predicts their maturity in their 50s.
2. Maturity in the men's 30s reliably predicts more than 60% of 40 key adult personality attributes and competencies in the men's 40s, including physical and psychological health, happiness and satisfaction, self-esteem, masculinity, vocational adaptation, marital

adjustment and sexual compatibility, parental fulfillment, and community involvement.

3. In the men's 30s, their health (combined physical and mental) predicts 75% of the same adult traits and competencies I just listed in numbers 1 and 2.

4. Also, in their 30s, men's self-rated happiness and fulfillment and ratings of their well-being for every five year period predict the same outcomes as listed in 1 and 2.

5. In the men's 40s, maturity, self-esteem, health, and happiness predict similar outcomes in their 50s. However, self- rather than judge-rated health and happiness in their 40s predict far more outcomes in the 50s.

6. In their 40s, the women's maturity, self-esteem, health, and happiness predicted the same outcomes both in their 40s and 50s, but less consistently than they did for the men.

The evidence is convincing. Maturity consistently contributes to later personality strengths and competencies. The model of maturity is impressively validated as a predictor of adult success and fulfillment.

Chapter 15

GROWING INTO MATURITY
HOW?

I have completed describing individuals who changed the most during their early and middle adult years and the principal statistical findings from the entire group about the course of adult healthy growth and its causes. Some readers of the book's early drafts asked me to tell them how they could become more mature. I cannot prescribe one route; there are many ways to grow up healthily. But from this work have emerged generic guidelines, principles, strategies which, if implemented wisely, can contribute to maturing. (Heath, 1968) I illustrate each by applying it to raising a child of any age to become more mature. I also suggest how adults could become more mature by applying the same principles. The principles may be obvious and seem simple. When we don't keep them in mind, however, raising a child or assisting ourselves or another can be frustrating and self-defeating.

Encouraging Growth of Awareness

1. Teach skills of labeling one's feelings and reflecting about them

Parents do a lot of labeling for their children about the external world; much less about their children's inner world of feelings and how to manage them. To a nine-year-old boy, a father might say, "When you stamped off of the field, Ben, you gave me the feeling that you were very angry. How else could you have expressed your feelings? How else could we have dealt with your losing the game?"

Psychotherapists similarly help adults to become more conscious of their feelings by labeling them. "Michael, does your restlessness mean you are becoming angry?"

2. Model how to ask questions to understand interpersonal strains, conflicts and motivational differences

"Ben, do you get angry when you feel I am expecting too much of you?"

"I am wondering, Michael, if my silence may be so upsetting that you can only tell me by moving your foot up and down so fast?"

3. Encourage planning and anticipating consequences

Learning to plan and schedule our time and anticipating the consequences of our plans is an important adaptive skill to become an effective adult.

"Ben, let's make a list of what's most important to us to get done by tomorrow night and check off each as we finish it. We'll try to figure out tomorrow night why we couldn't check everything off."

"Michael, if you want to visit northern India and see the Dalai Lama, what kind of questions are you asking yourself? Have you looked into the problem of traveling at different seasons to that part of the world?"

4. Be clear about growths you are expecting by describing specific step-by-steps to achieve

Too frequently, we tell our children "Be nice to grandmother" but don't describe what nice, polite, or kind mean specifically. So a child is left without knowing what he could do.

"Ben, your grandmother is staying with us this weekend. I hope you will listen to her, even if she forgets what she started to say and wanders. What else can we do to make her feel welcome? "

"Michael, if you want to go that soon, what is your timetable to get ready? Getting a visa to India takes at least ten days. It takes a lot longer to make an appointment with the Dalai Lama's secretary. So what is your schedule of steps you have to take?"

Nurturing Other-Centered Growth

5. Create trusting relationships to reduce defensiveness and increase educability

No principle will be effective in furthering maturing, especially of interpersonal relationships, unless we are vulnerable to change. The study identified three parental cardinal attitudes necessary to create the trust to allow children to become vulnerable: Love for them, respect for their individuality, and firm expectations of how they are to grow. Children must feel all three. Two are not enough. Adults also need such a relationship. The premier contributor to the men and women's growth was their personal relationships with their partners. A loving relationship with a caring person who respects us but who has expectations of us can release us from the inhibitions and defensive maneuvers that mark more typical socially conventional relationships.

6. Teach the skill of how to take another's point of view with empathy and feel compassion for the other

Believe that children, even boys, have the capacity to feel empathy and let them know your belief. When six years old, Ben and I went to Burger King to get our hamburger treat; we found a long line. He asked me if he could go to the counter to see the store's bribe, some toys. When he had been there for a few minutes, he said loudly in his pre-testosterone voice, "Granddad, are you lonely? Do you want me to come back?" Is his mother's training to help him care for Luke, his younger brother, paying off?

Our more challenging task is how to keep that empathy alive as Ben enters into his cool peer relationships that put down such emotional sensitivity.

With Pat and Duncan on the verge of a divorce, I asked each to describe a pencil I held up in front of them. Each had a different view of it. I asked who was right. They got the point; bought a dozen pencils and pasted them up in different parts of their apartment where they had had searing arguments. As they began to argue the next day, Pat said to Duncan, "Remember what Doug showed us." Several days later she told me she had withdrawn her suit for a divorce. They are still married eleven years later. They had learned that perceptions are reality and to respect the differences they create between people.

7. Encourage skills of listening and rephrasing what is heard

Ben and his best friend, Adam, were arguing about what movie to see, and why each separate choice was the best. Neither was listening to the other. I broke in and asked Ben to tell me why Adam wanted to see *Spider Man* so badly.

Pat and Duncan self-consciously worked to improve listening to each other when they felt the other hadn't "heard" what they were saying. They created a hand signal to use to inform the other that they felt they hadn't been heard. Accurately rephrasing what was just said tells the other that they were understood.

8. Expect caring and responsibility for growth of another

Luke now has a large, aggressively affectionate dog that demands her stomach be ceaselessly rubbed. She jumps into Luke's bed at night and snuggles up to him expecting to be held. Luke has full responsibility for his dog, including satisfying her affectionate demands, feeding her, and taking her out for a walk.

For adults, volunteer to become a big brother or sister or grandparent to children who have no parent. Remember the maturing effects that taking care of a child had on the men and Susan.

Encourage Integrations

9. Create ways to be actively engaged

Passively absorbed information seldom sticks. It must be actively used.

Ben is teaching Luke, his five-year-old brother, how different chess pieces move. He holds up a black knight and white bishop and asks Luke to show him how they move on the board.

Just watching my son use my computer to move files around, create a template for the book's headings, convert my files in WordStar into Word just don't wash. I must insist that he slow down, model a few steps, and then let me repeat the moves—more than just once.

10. Learn how to combine several steps to achieve a goal

Ben teaches Luke how to move the queen's pawn, bishop, and queen to checkmate his dad in four moves.

Write a book like this!

11. Rely on reflected-upon experiential learning

Take Ben and Luke to the zoo. On the way home play a game of recalling all the ways the animals they saw differ from each other. Then ask each to describe which animals belong to the same family.

I want to learn how to play golf. I have read about the different clubs, bought a set, and created a practice area in my basement with large mats. My neighbor is advising me how to figure out why my balls keep veering to the right.

12. Present complex problems that require combinations of different ideas and methods

When planning or initiating change, it is wise to take small steps appropriate to the developmental readiness of a child or adult and begin to take bigger ones with more complex problems. Otherwise, failure is risked and disappointment, reduced confidence, and unwillingness to risk again may occur.

"Ben, the Smiths next door have invited Daddy and me to meet our new neighbors. We will be gone from 5:00 to about 7:00. Luke will be happier with you than with a baby sitter. Do you think you can take care of him? What will you plan to do with him to keep him happy?"

Microsoft's Word program frustrates me. I have skipped too many basic steps necessary to master its complexities. I am here in Acapulco trying to finish this book. Something has gone wrong again. What does the message, "Program has performed an illegal operation and will be shut down" mean? It shuts down; I lose what I have written. What is an illegal operation? How does one correct it? I've retreated back to the security of my WordStar program. The real problem? My impatience and taking steps that are too big.

Building Strong Foundations (Stabilization)

13. Encourage anticipatory rehearsal

The power of our minds is that they enable us to anticipate, plan, and reflect not constrained by the immediate "here and now."

Ben's older sister, Joan, joined her school's drama club which gave her the opportunity to try out different roles to discover characters she felt comfortable portraying. Frequent rehearsals of her lines for an upcoming play before acting on the boards taught her how rehearsal stabilized her role and freed her from over-preoccupation with her lines. She then could attend more fully to her acting.

The next time I move my office so far away from Harriet, I will have to bring the user-unfriendly computer manual with me to at least read and then reread again. Better yet, read the sections about the error messages it has been giving me before I move my office away from her nearby assistance.

14. Do not protect from consequences of decisions and acts

Luke is impulsive and doesn't think before he moves his chess pieces. Ben plays for "keeps," but because Luke is just learning, Ben gives him only two warnings when he is in danger of losing a piece. If Luke just guesses or has no idea of where to look on the board, Ben tells him which piece is in danger and asks if he can figure out why. Luke loses the piece if he is not correct.

I have relied on Harriet's greater experience with computers and willingness to help me when my computer misbehaves. It arbitrarily takes over my monitor with incomprehensible messages or just balks or threatens me it is going to close down. Might her ready availability and caring character be protecting me from experiencing the consequences of my passivity and impatience? Is this why I am having so much difficulty mastering Word?

15. Demand constant externalization and practice

"Ben, Jean Brown needs someone to care for her child after school while she gives a piano lesson. She has seen how well you take care of Danny. Would you want to?"

I still am embarrassed by my first kiss. I was a tense inexperienced 15 year old. Janice's front porch was dark. I lunged, lost my balance, and missed her lips. The next day everyone at school knew. I then did not leave my kisses in my imagination and dreams; I practiced them on my next date with better light and even dared to try a French kiss that didn't taste very good.

16. Appreciate and affirm varied strengths

At the dinner table that night, Ben proudly said that Mrs. Brown had paid him five dollars because he had done such a good job. She could tell by the sounds she heard coming from the playroom. It was the first time that Ben had been paid for working for someone other than his parents.

When seventeen, I met my first real girl-friend. As I slipped my silver football and chain around her neck and then wrapped my arms around her and effortlessly kissed her, she spontaneously said, "I can tell you've had a lot of practice." Practice, practice!

Educate for Self-Command (Autonomy)

17. Express realistic faith in capacity to be responsible

Ben announced at the dinner table, "Mrs. Brown wants me take care of her child every week on Thursday afternoons."

When visiting Luke's Montessori first-grade class, I was impressed by how the children took their own snack dishes to the nearby sink, washed, dried, and stacked them in a cupboard under the sink without being told to do so by the teacher. I congratulated the teacher for so effectively implementing the principle.

18. Encourage assumption of responsibility for growth early and consistently

"Mother, do you think Mrs. Brown's baby would enjoy coming over here to play? She could play with Steve. It is time he has a friend!"

In the pre-internet days I asked each freshman the first day of class to prepare an oral report about the meaning of alienation without using a dictionary or encyclopedia and to tell us how he had educated himself—the principal goal of the course. On the basis of their reports, the students organized themselves into small working groups for the next few weeks. More entrepreneurial students had interviewed the college dean, members of the philosophy department, the college's psychologist, and one, me.

19. Educate to create own standards of excellence

"I think I am good at taking care of babies. I can tell when babies need to be changed. And when they're tired. Today, Mrs. Brown's baby got fussy. I rocked her and she went to sleep."

When I was in a Pasadena third-grade class I was given a list of behaviors and attitudes to rate myself on as one part of the evaluation of my growth during the year. I've always remembered this exercise as a self-reflective opportunity to be my own teacher of excellence.

20. Educate to self-affirm what one does well and self-reward for approaching one's own goals.

"I goofed today. I got involved in listening to music and didn't catch Sally before she dumped all the Legos. I had to stay and pick them up after Mrs. Brown finished teaching. I mustn't turn on music when I am responsible for a child."

My nine-year-old daughter was practicing a new piano piece. Suddenly I heard a slap and "Don't do that." She had slapped her left hand and told it to stop straying to a nearby key. She no longer depended upon us to tell her when she made a mistake. Later I heard her tell her left hand, "That's right. Good."

Adult Reflections about Continuing to Grow Healthily

When I asked Erich Fromm what his therapeutic goal was, he simply replied, "Help a person become more and more alive." To resume your growth, become more alive. But how?

Read what some of the men and women wrote in response to my offer to share with you their "words of wisdom about growing healthily through adulthood."

———•◦•———

Elise wrote,

Since I was very young, I have disciplined myself to be a
better person, to know who I am and what I am able to do
and be kind to myself. To continue to learn new materials
through reading, traveling and talking, to constantly look
at nature and admire her beauties to the very minute
details. To be upbeat and joyous and laugh. To reject
the negative thoughts and anxieties. I have taught my
children to listen to their own voices and be aware of the
pitfalls created by ambitious, envious, and poor friends.
Optimism and energy have been my friends.

Dave wrote,

Keep in mind at all times, we are the "greatest of the
apes," never more nor less. Act accordingly. Optimism,
however false, trumps awareness of the inevitability of
our demise, a uniquely human handicap (Lionel Tiger).
Optimism is also a socially acquired convention for success and it works.

———•◦•———

Phil and Martha are one of the few couples who had met my criteria of a
mutually intimate marriage for decades. He is a prominent legal negotiator
who has lived with diabetes for many years, she is a productive artist who
has survived breast cancer, also for several decades.

Phil wrote,

I have tried to live with the understanding that I am spending my life hour-by-hour and that I don't want to spend it
being angry or resentful even if bad things are happening
to me or around me. I have learned to accept my feelings
as facts and to understand that what I wanted was okay
even if my parents looked down on my choices.

I have been blessed with a wonderful wife, children, and grandchildren who have supported me and contributed to my growth and well-being and are a great source of pride in their accomplishments and, most of all, their goodness and compassion. I have progressed from an identity as my father's offspring to an accomplished professional, to being known as the father of two enormously talented religious leaders. I feel I have grown over the years and hope never to stop growing.

Martha says

Phil is her compatible mate and best friend who has made the "journey" so much more enjoyable. I have learned how important it is to listen, especially to one's own voice. A healthy and honest communication with self can be very rewarding. And always take time to listen to those you love.

Find your passion and work at it passionately even if only for your own satisfaction and enjoyment. Ideally, make a living at it.

I believe in the possibility of change at any time. Never too late to change though it gets harder to do as we age.

My life is filled with a loving and lovable husband and children whom I adore. I am very blessed with several precious friendships. I cannot wish for more. But I do. More of the same!

Wonderful framed quote in my oncologist's office. "In the midst of winter, I finally learned that there was in me an invincible summer," Albert Camus.

———

You have met Jim and Barbara, another one of my scarce mutually intimate couples.

Jim feels he has been blessed

having had loving and selfless parents. I have received and been able to develop my intelligence and leadership skills. I've been the recipient of one of the finest educations available. I have enjoyed a very challenging and fulfilling professional life with concomitant financial success. But most importantly, I have truly been blessed with a wonderful, loving, intelligent, and successful wife and my true wealth is in my children and grandchildren. I try to enjoy every day.

Barbara gives us five prescriptions:
1. Don't give up; persist in your job, and if you do a good job you will move forward.
2. Try to have self-confidence.
3. Stay fit.
4. Accept adversity.
5. Be thankful for what you have.

Marty, featured in *Lives of Hope*, a leader of the feminist movement, recovered alcoholic, and divorced by her soul-mate, Andy, because of her lesbianism, reveals her vitality and aliveness in her words of wisdom.

In some cultures older persons are revered for their wisdom and experience. As we age we will do well to honor our intuition and our deeper knowing. Intuition is honored by nurturing and sharpening it with right brain activities like yoga, meditation, massage, acupuncture, friendship, and, for me, continuous political activism.

I love knowing, deep in my heart, that I am a wise woman due to my years of experience. It feels good to know that I know. I believe that mentoring is a way to honor wisdom, to stay vibrant, and to pass it on. For me, the use of holistic health modalities gives me energy and zest. I work at staying in a frame of mind that sees the glass half to almost completely full. There is abundance and it is mine.

Andy, a distinguished creative medical researcher, regrets he had not secured counseling.

My life would have been more satisfying and certainly easier if I could have made a healthy/loving marital choice (of his wife before Marty) during my 20s. At the same time I realize life doesn't always deal you a "straight flush" and playing the hand you are dealt is what life is all about. I feel I have made the best of it, but it means I put more energy and time into my calling than my personal life. While I have had enormous satisfaction and growth from both, they weren't as balanced as I would have wished.

———

Rich listed a number of insights, some of which were:
1. Some of us are put on this planet for a purpose. Try to discover that purpose and make it a center of your life.
2. One of the great opportunities in life is to be publicly humiliated.
3. Education is a life-long adventure.
4. Love is the truest spice of life.
5. Life is an incredible gift.

———

Other themes from
1. A college professor committed to environmental issues: "A sense of commitment to something larger than self. A cause, a campaign that others are engaged in also, ideally for social justice and an end to violence."
2. World's largest private collector of historic books: "Seek responsibilities, help others, accept self somehow, no matter what."
3. An accountant for an island's fishermen: "Find something that really INTERESTS you. This is where to find contentment."
4. A social worker: "A shedding of 'shoulds' and perceived prohibitions around self-expression has freed me to become more of myself."
5. A professor of linguistics: "I feel like Hamlet. He said it about death; I mean it about both life and death. 'The readiness is all.' I still feel eager, expectant, hopeful."

———

Did you note their recurring themes about how to stay alive?
- Fully accept your self, which releases energy from inhibition and conflict.
- Create a strong foundation of interpersonal blessings.
- Have a strong commitment to continued growth.
- Live "out of the mainstream" to increase the feeling of aliveness.
- Have a consuming and organizing passion and commitment to external causes.
- Seek out and fulfill responsibilities.
- Balance work and family so neither usurps energy from the other.
- Keep optimism and hope alive.
- Develop a self-concept of being an adventurous, confident person who can make your future work for you.
- Value disruptions, even distressing humiliations, which may open freshets of new growth.
- Find friends who themselves are alive, growing people.
- Create your own ways to stay alive, keep your self overflowing with hope, and become a mentor of that hope to others.

One reader of an earlier draft of this book wanted to know what I had learned from my long journey with my extended family. I spontaneously replied:
- Behind the facade of power, singular achievement, great prestige and wealth is a human being with whom I share the same needs, apprehensions, troubles, pleasures, and joys. I no longer stand in awe of such people.
- How lovable individuals are once I shed my expectations and judgments about them and respect them for the persons they are.
- How responsive and open people can be to explore themselves with another when they feel respected, treasured, and loved.

My long, arduous, but illuminating journey with so many highly achieving and articulate men and women has also taught me a great deal about psychological maturity or healthy growth. Rather than now review the numerous specific findings I have previously summarized, I step back from their details to reflect in the next chapter about some of the leading themes that have deepened my understanding of maturing.

Chapter 16

———»·•·«———

REFLECTING ABOUT HEALTHY GROWTH

For many years I asked hundreds of college-educated parents throughout the USA and abroad to rank the importance of twelve values for themselves and their children. Most ranked self-fulfillment and happiness first, psychological maturity and healthy growth second, physical health third, and a happy marital relationship fourth. Men ranked sexual fulfillment and a high income to be more important than women ranked them. Women ranked having a close friend of the same gender and contributing to their community to be more important than men did. Most ranked high income and leadership-power to be least important, probably because they were financially well-off professionals and executives. (Heath, 1991)

I measured each of these values, and so could explore the personality traits associated with them as well as the relation of the values to each other. Chapter 1's commentary reported that happy persons shared core character traits: maturity, mental health, optimism, confidence in one's ability to direct their lives, and willingness to take risks. The commentary also identified the traits of happily married persons: maturity, androgyny, marital and parental competence, and a history of being happy persons since adolescence.

Was I too hasty to equate mental health or healthy growth with maturing? No. They go together in reality, just as the other highly rated values generally go together. Of course there are exceptions, but the study's men and women who, like Jim and eventually Barbara, were physically healthy were also more mentally healthy and happier than those who, like Buck, were unhealthy and unhappy for most of their adult years. Happy and healthy persons are happily married and fulfilled parentally. While vocationally satisfied men are healthier and happier than vocationally dissatisfied ones, the same truism did not hold for women 30 years ago. The mothers I studied in the early days of the feminist movement were conflicted, like Susan, about working full-time. More young women today may not be so.

These valued qualities tend to persist together through adulthood. Mature adolescents who are happy and healthy, living fully and productively, will continue to be so when middle-aged. For me, the consistent pattern for maturity, health, and happiness to co-vary together and predict similar traits justifies equating healthy growth with maturity.

For me, the lives of the men and women raise two significant questions. What is the relation between maturity, competence, and achievement? What have their lives told us about the causes of and blocks to maturing?

What is the Relation of Maturity to Competence and Achievement?

The book's subtitle, *Insights from the Lives of Highly Achieving Men and Women,* may have misled you when I described the participants' occupational achievements. There are many varied types of "achievements," such as remaining happily married for 50 years, raising healthy children, living a virtuous life. So I consider here the relation of maturity to more varied types of achievements than only vocational ones.

Chapter 2's commentary briefly summarized the consistent evidence from different groups that maturity contributes to a variety of competencies and achievements. Compared to PSQ-defined immature high school students, more PSQ-defined mature ones rated themselves to be more independent, adventurous, and self-acceptant, among other positive traits. Their teachers rated them to be more mature. They participated more frequently in extra-curricular and community activities. They also felt more comfortable with people who differed from them. American, Italian, and Turkish college professors and student leaders selected their most and least well-functioning students. They reliably differed, as predicted in their PSQ-defined maturity. Finally, PSQ-identified mature, in contrast to immature, adult men and women are happier, understand themselves and predict others' ratings about them more accurately, have more integrated self-concepts, have stronger marriages, are more competent in fulfilling their varied adult roles, such as being a good parent or lover. Mature men, but not women, are more vocationally satisfied. The mature women had closer, more intimate friendships than the immature ones. A man's maturity was not related to the quality of his friendships—the sector of the men's personalities in which they had matured least.

Why has the PSQ measure of maturity so consistently predicted so many more positive outcomes than the other numerous methods listed in the glossary? You might argue that because mature persons describe themselves very favorably (which is true), their positive self-concepts influenced their ratings about themselves on other similar measures that also rely on self-reports—the well-known halo effect. But the PSQ predicts other types of measures not directly affected by favorable self-evaluations, such as judge-ratings of personality traits, vocational and marital adjustment, and quality of interpersonal relationships.

A more persuasive explanation for the consistent PSQ predictions is that it was constructed to measure directly the implied personality dimensions that Piaget had identified to define the process of adaptation (1947) and Dewey of problem-solving. (1922) The network of predictions based on the PSQ tends to confirm the validity of the model of maturity. It identifies the core strengths to adapt successfully to life's developmental tasks.

However, maturity is not equivalent to competence, achievement, or success. The study's vocationally achieving persons varied widely in their maturity as well as in their marital, sexual, and parental success. There are competencies and achievements to which maturity may or may not make a major contribution—e.g., in mathematics and chess. Besides, some achievements may depend upon a host of factors, even luck, over which a person may have little control. Most of the men's divorces had been initi-ated by their wives, such as Susan and Mary. Susan's sexual needs were squashed by an oppressive, insensitive Alan. Barbara's and Jim's parental fulfillment eluded them for years as they struggled with a high-spirited and assertive Helen.

However, most adults hopefully seek to achieve some commonly shared goals: creating enduring marriages, raising healthy children, fashioning a fulfilling vocational life. Achieving such goals requires many of the same core competencies.

To demonstrate further that maturity contributes to such adult goals, I asked the men and women to identify the six principal strengths they had discovered are necessary to succeed in each of their commonly shared roles as citizens, marital and sexual partners, parents, friends, and workers. I then combined their cited strengths for their six adult roles. The following lists the declining importance of the most frequently cited strengths.

First: Caring, honesty, integrity and sense of humor.
Second: Openness, lack of defensiveness, tolerance, and acceptance of others.
Third: Dedication, commitment.
Fourth: Understanding of, respect and empathy for others, adaptability, and self-confidence.

The model of maturity, sketched in Table 2.1, includes these and other less frequently cited competencies.

The participants' partner, most knowledgeable colleague, and closest friend then rated them on these core traits of maturity. Those who scored highest, like Jim, compared to those who scored lowest, like Dave, were more happily married, interpersonally intimate, vocationally fulfilled, ethical, idealistic, and PSQ-defined mature.

What are the Causes of and Barriers to Healthy Adult Maturing?

The causes and barriers to an adult's healthy growth are much too numerous, varied, and complex to offer more than the few insights that the participants' lives suggest. I briefly examine the effects of the participants' families, adult roles, and the emergent adolescent growths themselves to identify some underlying generic conditions that contribute to maturing.

Parental Effects on Maturing

I reviewed what each participant taught us as well as the group's statistical results about the principal influences on the course of maturing. Susan taught us that the most favorable parental attitudes for encouraging maturing were to love and respect the individuality of each child but hold him/her to firm expectations of how to grow up. The group's results confirmed that such attitudes contribute to numerous favorable adult outcomes. (Heath, 1994b) The voices of such parents became increasingly more silent as their children matured and became their own autonomous and competent adults.

But the voices of rejecting, manipulative, and authoritarian parents, especially of mothers, continued to distort healthy growth far into the adult years, especially of Dave and Elise. Charlie's maturing was hindered and distorted for years by his parental programming that trampled on his individuality.

On the other hand, fathers tended to be either more emotionally absent or, as Buck's and Elise's, benignly supportive.

Interpersonal Role Relationships as Primary Causes of Maturing

Chapter 1's commentary told us that the primary persistent contributors to maturing through the adult years are direct, sustained, and contemporary interpersonal roles. Each creates its own expectations and associated responsibilities. Assuming sustained roles as a partner, parent, lover, wage earner/home-maker, and friend creates multiple responsibilities and opportunities for new growths. Each can also become a source of conflicting problems that can spur maturing, denial, or regression.

A partner's personality can have decisive effects because where there is love there is vulnerability to influence and expectations. Parenthood challenges one's emotional self-sufficiency and narcissism. When sex is primarily a stress-reducer and not integrated with friendship and caring, as Susan felt was the case for Alan, sex loses its power to strengthen intimacy.

Emergent Adolescent Growths as Causes of Maturing

Reflective awareness in mid adolescence
The emergence of reflection initiates conscious efforts to direct, control, and change one's self. Billie Leighton, one of the study's most mature adults, illustrates this distinctive maturational leap. She is featured in *Lives of Hope* as the study's most all-round successful and fulfilled woman. Her parental home had been chaotic. Her mother had divorced her abusive husband and subsequently remarried three times; she was later killed by her first husband. Billie's father had remarried twice. She was shuffled back and forth between her parents and step-parents. To survive such emotional turmoil, she learned as an adolescent to take control of her own life. Introspective by nature, she "kept a log in which I wrote about what was troubling me and how to change myself by consciously developing a 'problem-solving' approach to living."

When sixteen, I began a daily journal. Its first entry revealed the new advance in my mental life. "This year I have developed maturity. I have developed mentally from a non-entity to a person who can think and correct it. I still have many faults but the main point is that at least I am aware of them and I am trying to do something about them."

Not until 63 years later when I reread this first journal entry did I realize how momentous the emergence of such reflective awareness had been for my subsequent growth.

Delays in maturation of reflective awareness. Buck's arduous growth to understand himself took years. Even with psychiatric help, he never understood why his high school roommate so irritated him to the point that he impulsively locked him out on their room's snowy balcony. Nor did he fully wake up to his wife's "messing around" until long after he had begun to become vaguely aware of her infidelity. Nor could he acknowledge the reasons for his low vocational satisfaction as a president of his engineering firm. Not until his remarkably self-revealing story to the blank TAT card, when in his 50s, had he become more maturely aware of himself. "Perhaps for the first time ever in his life he is enjoying doing this. I guess I am looking at myself. I seem to find it more and more intriguing what I want to find out about myself. In some ways I was afraid to find out."

He taught us how reflection about one's self and relationships contributes to continued healthy growth. Avoiding the pain of what one might be "afraid to find out" blocks learning more adaptive ways of coping with the sources of pain.

Maturation in other-centeredness in late adolescence
The late adolescent and early adult years are critical times for becoming more other-centered. Not just increasing awareness of and sensitivity to how others view one self but emotionally empathizing with how others feel and view themselves signal maturing changes that persist into adulthood. Acceptance and tolerance of others become more deeply rooted during adolescence.

Our parents are the first and most important persons to draw us out of our childish egocentrism by teaching us how to adapt to our surrounding world's expectations of what we are to become. Dave's rejecting and suppressive mother and psychologically absent father left him mired in his own narcissism for decades. Not until his 50s, when he found his way back to his Jewish identity that his mother had suppressed, did he, with the assistance of his wife and group therapy, become a more "loving, giving, and compassionate" person.

Adolescent friendships and marital relationships provide the playing field on which to learn and then test one's other-centered maturation. When seventeen, one of my close friends ruthlessly taught me to look at myself from others' viewpoints—most critically from his own. Mary's reciprocally close and caring friendship with Paula led to a deeper religious commitment bolstering her will-power to resist temptation. Friendships can teach us vulnerability and the educability it can open us to.

Contemporary marriage, the intimacy it now requires, and parenting are two of the more contributing but also demanding tests of two people's mature other-centeredness. Over half of the study's couples failed their marital test. Though Barbara rued she had married too young, she and Jim succeeded in consciously creating a strong marriage that contributed to their continued growth. For every decade of adult growth, a partner's personality produced more maturing effects than any other of the 49 possible causes.

Parenting is a high risk role that not only demands other-centered maturity but also can spur even greater other-centered growth. Two mothers spoke for most about the effects of being a mother. One said, "I have become less self-centered." The other, "I have had to think of others as opposed to just of myself." Other-centered growth in a nut shell! The statistical results were impressively convincing. Fathers are more healthy and mature than men who are not fathers, though they did not differ in either health or maturity when in college. Rich taught us that dedication to the growth of others, as in teaching and parenting, is both a cause and result of maturity.

Maturation in integration in early adulthood
Growth in other-centeredness sets the stage for creating a responsible and valued way of life that integrates one's talents, interests, and emerging identity. For males, to settle for a job to survive rather than for an integrative vocation to be called to can have long-term fateful consequences for their future health. Dave successfully worked to survive though never found a fulfilling vocation that had maturing effects. Buck eventually grew beyond his vocational discontent to fashion a more integrative and stable identity as a creative technical engineer. He became happier and more mature by his late 50s. Rich's ambitious vocational commitment provided a strong, almost unassailable, bulwark against his temporary dark depression.

Though world-wide most men barely survive in jobs that contain few growth incentives, I have known a few, like Spencer, my lobsterman friend, and Bahdur, one of my trekking guides, whose dedication and pride spoke of their calling. Not to have a job, let alone a calling, can devastate a male youth who has no societal recognition of or support for his worth. Alienation from his society or attacks against the cause of his hopelessness become inevitable alternatives especially during his 20s, the formative years of greatest hope for the future.

Marriage and parenthood may not be as valued alternative paths to maturity and health for males as they historically have been for females. Men cited more maturing effects of their work than they did of their role as fathers; women cited more for their role as mothers. As was true for almost all of the study's men, Buck, Charlie, and Rich devoted much less time to their marriages and children than to their work. The seeds of many couples' future divorce were sewn in their early marital years when cooperative mutuality, especially marital sexual compatibility, was not present.

Women's biology can make the challenge of creating a valued way of life that furthers their growth easier to come by. Historically, marriage, creating, and raising children could confirm a woman's worth and provide potential maturing effects. For modern women, these roles may not be enough. The feminist movement shook the majority of the study's women for whom a greatly expanded sense of self became a real option. They entered into the men's preserve. They quickly developed the strengths necessary to survive and flourish there; they, like Susan and Mary, became more mature, healthier, and happier as a consequence.

Societal sanctions blocking male's self- and interpersonal integration. Cultures vary greatly in their expectations of how males and females should act. The commentary on Josh described how restrictively the American culture sanctions the expression of affection and sexuality, especially for males, when compared to Italian and Turkish cultures. Or when compared to many Asian countries like Nepal, India, and China. Ohio seventh-grade boys cracked up and lost their cool when I off-handedly mentioned how my Nepalese Himalayan guide reached out to take my hand while we walked Kathmandu's streets. American males' homophobic confusion of affection with sexuality and devaluation of stereotypic feminine interpersonal strengths such as gentleness and emotional sensitivity lead to compensatory aggressive macho behaviors. The growth of mature, integrative personal relations is thereby handicapped, not only with males but also females. Charlie's large discrepancy between his masculinity and femininity scores blocked becoming more interpersonally mature and androgynous.

Maturation in stability and autonomy from their 30s to their 60s
The study has provided scientific support for the view that the high rate of maturing during adolescence and early adulthood is typically followed by

stability in the adult years, in which little measurable change in maturity may occur for decades. Recall that I had selected exemplars of the greatest change during their adult years to learn about maturing. The majority of the men and women showed little change in their maturing or mental health during their adult years.

The exemplars' lives provide numerous other insights about the course of maturing during adulthood. Jim and Barbara confirm that two very highly achieving persons can succeed in creating a happy married life and be parentally fulfilled. Mary's life illustrates that one's identity can develop very early and provide a strong foundation for later mature autonomy. Buck and Dave tell us healthy growth can consistently improve through the adult years. Susan and Barbara show how rapidly growth can resume in mid life after securing freedom from an oppressive marriage or the discovery of more fulfilling paths for one's talents. Rich illustrates that high achievers are not immune to severe regressions that can be overcome and lead to greater maturity if they have a strong vocational identity and are resilient. Josh's life reveals the depth of humans' need for love and to love. Elise and Dave show us that a shared commitment to search for meaning in one's religious heritage provides the stability to endure a relationship's pain that can become a goad to maturing. Charlie tells us that when life's idealistic commitments and passions have died, death itself becomes acceptable.

Summary of Generic Conditions that Cause and Bar Maturing

Acts Likely to Increase Maturing

Chapter 15 listed a number of ways to keep growing and so become more alive. I summarize eight of the more important ones that further maturing and seven others that may retard it.

1. Accept a new role and its responsibilities.
2. Endure the pain of frustration while experimenting with other ways to cope.
3. Deliberately abandon or disrupt even an on-going effective way of living.
4. Form a close, loving, non-defensive relationship with a companion not hesitant to confront or challenge an act or thought.
5. Associate with others who are models of growing persons.

6. Commit one's self to a transcendent faith or calling that expects continuous growth.
7. Develop a concept of one's self as a continuously self-educating, growing person.
8. Take judicious risks by seeking novel adventures.

Acts Likely to Retard Maturing

1. Repress or deny what causes pain.
2. Unreflectively accept and conform to society's values not truly congruent with one's self.
3. Be compulsively single-minded and focused.
4. Overdevelop an ambition or talent that limits growth in other valued roles.
5. Lack clarity about and fail to order priorities.
6. Fail to accept responsibility for one's talents in order to seek immediate pleasure or solutions.
7. Rigidly reject contra-sexual character traits.

If you are free to choose your own goals for living and choose happiness and health, the men's and women's lives suggest you have no other choice but to seek to become more mature.

How can we keep growing into maturity, to keep waking up until aging's inevitable sleep of non-existence becomes permanent? We must create our own ways. When sixteen, I wrote in my journal, "We can make our life as we want to." Only our maturity makes that adolescent optimism and hope possible. The model of maturity provides the map for that journey.

The fruits of growing into maturity can be happiness, mental and possibly physical health, marital and vocational success, sexual mutuality, parental fulfillment, mature children, constructive community involvement, and an ethical character. These outcomes are not certain but more probable than not. Growing into maturity leads to self-transcendence and the perspective that humor brings making suffering bearable and hope attainable.

That is the hope the study has discovered.

Appendix A

——————

GLOSSARY

ACL—Adjective Check List. 185 adjectives and brief phrases that participants checked about themselves at Times 2 and 3.

COG—Cognitive efficiency tests. Three created measures assessing cognitive efficiency and resiliency in analytic, conceptual, and judgmental tasks containing threatening and non-threatening information. Used only at Time 2.

DHQ—Developmental History Questionnaire. Seventy-two statements about childhood homes, parental personalities, and relationships with each parent. Fifty statements about maturity and other child-adolescent behaviors.

EST—An interactional sensitivity-type program, created by Warner Erhard, to enable participants to assume responsibility for their own decisions. Predecessor of current Landmark business.

IC—Interpersonal communication measuring degree of comfort talking about each of 20 different topics, e.g., insecurities, with partner, child, friend, and other. (See Appendix D-4 for the IC.)

INTD—Interview assessing effects of 50 determinants, e.g., home-atmosphere, selected by participants to have been one of four most decisive influences on change in each of principal personality sectors, i.e., mind, personal relationships, values, and self.

MMPI—Minnesota Multiphasic Personality Inventory. 566 statements measuring various personality indicators of maladjustment.

MSC—Marital Sexual Compatibility Scale. Seven rated attributes of marital sexual mutuality, such as enjoyment, consideration, and faithfulness. (See Appendix D-5 for five of the seven items of the original survey.)

PAS—Parental Adaptation Scale. 28 items about parental roles, degree of parental satisfaction about attributes of parenting, e.g., time demands, self-fulfillment, which participants rated on 5-point scales. (See Appendix D-3 for the survey.)

PSQ—Perceived Self Questionnaire. 50 items designed to measure dimensional maturity, e.g., integration, in five personality sectors, e.g., values, which participants rated on 8-point scales. (See Appendix D-1 for the questionnaire.)

PT—Phrase Association Test. 36 phrases containing aggressive, sexual, dependency and other themes to which participants associated which were scored for themes' anxiety thresholds. Test used to independently measure degree of threat of the same themes used in the measures of cognitive efficiency (COG).

PTS—Personality Trait Survey. 70 (80 for Times 5 and 6) traits selected from ACL and Bem's measure of masculinity and femininity which participants and three judges rated on 5-point scales as well as for amount of change since most recent assessment.

ROR—Rorschach ink blots. 10 blots to which participants reported their images.

SAT—Scholastic Aptitude Test scores. Verbal and Quantitative scores used by college admission departments to assist evaluating aptitude for college work. Highly correlated with TCM.

SCT—Sentence Completion Test. 30 incomplete sentences containing themes, e.g., about mothers, fathers, success, future, which participants completed. Modified form of Loevinger's measure of ego development.

SIQ—Self-Image Questionnaire. 30 personality traits, e.g. adventurous, 26 of which correlated with maturity but interpreted to measure self-esteem which participants and judges rated on bipolar 8-point scales.

Varied instructions for repetitions of SIQ measured the dimensional maturity of the self-sector of personality.

SV—Study of Values. Measures relative strength of six different value orientations, e.g., theoretical, economic.

SVIT—Strong Vocational Interest Test. 400 statements measuring temperamental and interest congruence with successful persons in numerous occupations.

TAT—Thematic Apperception Test. 4 pictures depicting male-female and male-male relations, and a man in a graveyard to which participants told stories, and a blank card to which participants first imagined a picture and then told a story about it.

TCM—Terman's Concept Mastery Test. Measures intellectual ability to deal with difficult abstract concept problems.

TMA—Terman's Marital Adjustment Questionnaire. Participants rated their actual marriage (27 items) and their ideal one (33 items).

VAL—Valuator Test. 15 created statements to measure dimensional maturity of values

VAS—Vocational Adaptation Survey. 28 items created to assess degree of satisfaction on 5-point scales with different vocational attributes, e.g., salary, self-fulfillment. (See Appendix D-2 for the survey.)

———⊳·o·⊲———

Questioning the Study:

Its Whys, Whos, Hows, and Whats

Why Begin Studying Healthily Growing Persons 50 Years Ago?

I was raised as a budding clinical psychologist on white rats, college sophomores, and schizophrenics, the most frequently studied animals in my post-World War Two days. My first clinical research was to discover if early childhood frustration produced more aggressive adults—in one semester! By depriving baby rats of their mothers, feeding them milk through an eye dropper, matching them as adolescents with pups who had suckled their mothers naturally, and recording every instance of initiated aggressiveness in a staged matched battle, I answered my problem with a resounding "Yes."

My Amherst senior research project explored if achievement on a reputed measure of intelligence affected expectations of performance on increasingly dissimilar abilities. .My answer was a comforting statistically reliable, "Yes." Success increased expectations of success in very different types of abilities, even perceptual motor ones. Failure decreased expecta- tions of success for every type of ability that I tested.

My Harvard Ph.D. study tracked down one reason for the thought disorganization typical of schizophrenics. Would they show more thought inefficiency when analyzing or judging problems that contained personally threatening information such as aggressive themes than the same problems with non-threatening information. I panicked when I discovered I could not analyze my high-stakes project. I sought the assistance of Harvard's fore- most statistician who had to create a new statistic that enabled me to answer "Yes"—a most anxiety-arousing and humbling experience that spurred me to later get post-doctoral work in statistics and experimental design at the University of Michigan.

I was minted as a clinical psychologist by the ideas of psychology's three legendary personality psychologists: Henry Murray, Gordon Allport, and Robert White. Their commitment to understand human motivation, personality organization, and their development shaped my orienting attitudes about the important attributes of persons to understand.

I found my specific niche, however, when I read Abraham Maslow's *Motivation and Personality* (1954), published my first teaching year, at Haverford College, on self-actualizing adults—not rats, not sophomores, not schizophrenics. I've since been called to understand how adults grow into their full potential. A central question for psychologists, educators, ministers, parents—in fact for any one interested in psychological or mental health, maturity, authenticity, effectiveness, optimal human functioning, human excellence, self-actualization, success, fulfillment, or salvation.

How Did You Find Such People to Study?

Since I knew of no adequate psychological tests available at the time to identify healthy, well-organized persons, I relied on the judgments of those who knew a large number of persons in different activities to identify the most all-around well- and least well-functioning persons they knew. Haverford College, a highly selective very small men's college at the time, provided an ideal population of 450 not only of potential participants but also of students, teachers, coaches, counselors, and deans to serve as judges. Using objective sorting and ranking procedures they collectively selected the men to study from the sophomore and junior years. A larger number of young men not selected for either extreme were randomly selected and also invited to participate—most of whom did.

Who Are the Participants in the Study?

The men are much more homogeneous than the women. All but two graduated from Haverford College during the late fifties and early sixties. They are predominantly liberal Protestants (41%), Jews (24%) no religious affiliation (16%), and Quakers (15%). With one exception, they are Caucasian. All but two had had some advanced graduate or professional education, i.e., 11 were physicians, including three psychiatrists, 12 lawyers, 17 principally college professors, deans, and scholars, 21 executives and entrepreneurs, and seven musicians, writers, and ministers. *Fulfilling Lives* (1991) and *Lives of Hope* (1994b) focus on the strengths needed to succeed in an adult's principal roles and the factors contributing to their strengths.

The participating wives are much more heterogeneous. Some never graduated from high school, but some, like Barbara, have advanced degrees. They come from diverse colleges, not only Bryn Mawr, Haverford's sister college at the time. They are ethnically and religiously more diverse. More are Catholic. They come from Eastern Europe, Sweden, Australia, and Japan. Their parental socioeconomic backgrounds vary from poor Eastern European farm families to a wealthy president of a Fortune 500 company.

I focus now not on success but on healthy growth and its causes. Since abstract statistically based generalizations obscure the great variety of differences between people, I cite some examples of the varied occupational achievements of the men and women on whom the book's statistical findings are based:

- President and owner of several engineering companies
- Past Chairman of two major university's history departments
- Vice president of a well-known liberal arts college
- One of country's foremost computer diagnosticians
- Founder of and former owner of three computer magazines and President of a *Fortune 500* software company
- Concert singer who debuted at Carnegie Hall
- Professor of physics who is world's foremost analyst of a famous composer
- Prominent labor lawyer
- Dean of prestigious School of Social Work
- World's foremost antiquarian bookseller
- Coordinator of public policy and societal projects for CEO of one of *Fortune's* largest 500 companies
- One state's chief appellate public legal defender
- Legendary Hollywood character actress
- Dean of medical school
- World's foremost expert on word usage
- Colonel, US air force
- Medical researcher nominated by colleagues for prestigious award for two original discoveries

- International executive awarded foreign country's most prestigious medal for service to the country
- Principal physician offering abortion services nation-wide
- One of gerontology's most influential experts
- Advisor to national and international politicians
- Deputy chief of one of National Health's Institutes
- A leader of women's movement
- World's foremost scholar of his history sub-specialty
- Popular night club singer

In 2002, the men's median net worth was 1.5 million dollars; 69 percent are millionaires. One lives on his wife's inherited wealth.

I make no pretense that the men and women are similar to any group other than bright, highly educated achievers. Appendix F compares the participants to those of the other principal longitudinal studies.

How Many Have Participated for Almost 50 Years?

I had no idea whatsoever of following the original 80 men throughout their lives when I began. Only one night 11 years later while teaching a course on child and adolescent development the spark of an idea flashed. I realized I had the makings of a comprehensive study about how men in their early 30s had grown healthily during their 20s—a blank page at the time in the research on the adult years. I was able to track down 68 of the originally selected men. I resisted my wife's urging that I also study the men's wives when the men were in their early 30s. I felt uncertain how the women might react to a stranger's invitation. I changed my mind when I discovered one wife standing outside the closed door of her living room listening to me interview her husband. She said how much she wished she could participate because she wanted to have a say about their marriage. I immediately invited the remaining wives or partners to participate in Time 3's section of the men's interview about their marriage and children.

When I decided to visit the men again in their early 40s, 40 women wished to participate. Sixty-five men participated; one had died and two declined my invitation. The study of the course of healthy growth from the early 30s into the early 40s proved to be too ambitious: too comprehensive; too exhausting for the participants (as well as for me). It was also too complex and wearying to report in the type of papers that I had published earlier about the results of the study about growth in the 20s and early 30s.

So instead I published the results in *Fulfilling Lives: Paths to Success and Maturity* in 1991. I revised and up-dated the study which I reported in *Lives of Hope: Women's and Men's Paths to Success and Fulfillment* in 1994.

I argued with myself for several years. Should I resume the study now that the men and women were approaching their mid 50s? The study's stresses and strains eventually receded in memory to the point that I yielded to a continuing study's own emotional momentum—and to my curiosity. That only 52 men and 29 women participated in their 50s taught me the perils of longitudinal research on busy achieving couples: marital strains and increased number of divorces and so loss of contact with the women, career absorption of time and energy, the repetition of the tests and procedures which led one man to say he felt he "wouldn't learn anything new about himself this time around," the resistance of some wives to be interviewed about very personal facets of their lives, especially sexual, who persuaded their husbands not to participate in their 50s, and illness or death of either partner.

The study of the men and women in their 40s is the weightier study to which I refer most frequently. It was the most comprehensive. The 40s were reputedly the most challenging decade of adult growth because of its alleged mid-life crisis. I have kept in touch with many who did not participate in their 50s.

What Has Happened to the Men and Women by Their 60s?

The men and women had lived through the Vietnam War, women's liberation movement, profound changes in their gender roles, and the dramatic changes in attitudes about divorce, sexuality, and drugs. Their distinguished achievements did not protect them from sorrow and tragedy. Three men never married; 55% of the participants have been divorced; several have been married three times. Twenty-four have remarried, most happily so. About 57% have sought some form of counseling, more often than not about their children and relationships with their partners. Eight have died: two men from AIDS, three women and one man from cancer; one man from an inoperable brain tumor and another from the effects of a massive stroke. Two children have apparently taken their own lives, and another died in a fall from a horse. One man has been in prison for falsifying his income tax; another for carrying undeveloped pornographic film into California—of all states! Five have been diagnosed or call themselves alcoholics but all are now free of their addiction, thanks primarily to Alcoholics Anonymous. Most are opposed to the use of drugs, even marijuana. One had been hospitalized for manic-depression, another for alcoholism.

Only a few couples have created a mutual marital companionship like that of chapter 1's Barbara and Jim. I sense the marriages of others are improving as their last child leaves home and they no longer have direct responsibility for one. When asked if they would like to have another child, if they could, only Barbara answered "Yes"—but not a teenager. Almost all reported that their children's early teenage years were their most challenging and frustrating years.

Why Did so Many Persist in Working with You for so Many Years?

They were curious about what they might learn about themselves, though as they aged and became more settled they became less and less strangers to themselves. My summary of their test results, especially of their strengths and the possible reasons why they had not fulfilled them, turned out to be provocative, even inspirational, to some—as for Barbara. Others wanted to learn about what they might face in the future. The procedures provoked much reflection about themselves and relationships; several women claimed they loved the entire day thinking about the questions. For busy people the questionnaires and interviews provided a moment of what psychologists call "stock-taking," stepping back to reflect about the past and what they might want for their futures. And then people do enjoy talking about themselves to a non-judgmental listener. Just how many people are genuinely interested in you and what you feel and think?

I also kept them informed by letters every several years about a few of the more intriguing statistical findings emerging from their most recent participation. I gave copies of my books about the study and their educational implications to each. Some feminists were disappointed in my analysis of the women or regretted they had not been selected as exemplars. I invited participants to dinner or paid their travel expenses to visit me. They knew they were invited to stay with my wife and me when visiting the college.

Important to some has been my willingness to be available in a counseling capacity if they felt I could assist them or their families with personal issues. I have been present when some were dying, such as Mary, or at the memorial service of their partner. I have traveled to Europe to mediate how a couple was to separate, to Australia to support a couple in a contentious

alcohol-related relationship, and visited others during momentous decisions, such as whether to adopt a Russian adolescent orphan.

As immediate personal issues have dimmed, the principal reason
expressed by some is their recognition of the rare nature and importance
of the study and their desire to assist me with its continuation. Some have
been so proud to be a part of this study they let others know. Because I
feel they should be publicly recognized if they so desire, I offered them the
opportunity to appear in this book undisguised and their recognizable lives
unaltered. They are my colleagues, the research is ours, and I hope they
know how much I respect and value them. They are my extended family.

How Can You Trust What They Said about Themselves?

I have not been too concerned about the reliability of the participants'
self-ratings and -descriptions. Use of multiple measures and judgments
from others provided the opportunity to track down inconsistencies. Since I
viewed the men and women as colleagues trying to understand themselves,
most became involved in our search. With only a few exceptions, they have
been extraordinarily open about sharing even very distressing moments
in their lives. They knew I was an up-front person and did not shade my
analyses or hide troubling results from them.

They have trusted me to protect their privacy. When writing about
them I guaranteed their anonymity by disguising their names, locations, or
idiosyncratic attributes that might identify them to their peers. They have
approved listing their distinctive achievements that might identify them
to their peers. I have refused to identify who others were in the study or
reveal what their partners, friends or colleagues said or rated about them.
I have not succumbed to one man's persistent urgings to invite all of the
participants for a "Heath reunion;" he has been trying to identify who they
may be a little too assiduously for my feeling of comfort. I have consistently
secured exemplars' written permissions to use their stories and given them
the opportunity to review what I may write about them. Most have felt
comfortable being very frank and honest about themselves.

What Steps Did You Take to Protect Your Findings from Your Biases?

I have monitored my biases by trying to be aware of how my values may
affect the selection of questions to include in the surveys, of why I have

selected the quotations and facts from the richly complex information each gave me, and how I may have skewed my interpretations of the results. I have tried to be faithful to my identity as a seeker of truth, even when I don't like some of the results, as is the case. I rely on the crosschecks that a richly comprehensive study can provide. And I have reminded myself more than once of one of the study's consistent findings: a mature person, as Freud told us, can maintain the fairness of his evaluations even when he must analyze or make judgments about personally troubling issues.

I am fond of all of the participants. I have tried to be non-judgmental. I respect each person for what he or she is. You may like some more than others. Some may incite your own biases. I hope you too will respect the men and women and not condemn them for their humanness and courage to invite you into their most personal lives. Moralistic judgments and condemnations will hurt them and me in whom they have placed such trust. Judge and condemn me if you must but not the men and women of my extended family.

Most importantly, I have sought to remain faithful to what I believe a science of healthy growth should be like. To protect its integrity from cultural and other biases it must test the generality of its findings in different socio-cultural and local settings as well as with both males and females and different age groups. That I have tried to do by using a model of healthy growth to organize the study. It had been originally created using American Protestant and Jewish young men (1965), cross-validated with northern Italian, Sicilian Catholics, and western and eastern Turkish Moslem male college students (1977a), also cross-validated with different Haverford students to assess their change from freshman to senior year. (1968) I have replicated the core methods on other students to explore the familial and childhood contributors to maturing (2003, unpublished), and identified the growth of several hundred high school students in Michigan's Bloomfield Hills public and alternative high schools. (1995) I have gratefully included women in the complete study since Time 4.

How Did I Select Barbara, Jim, and the Others as Models of Change?

When identifying whom to feature in this book, I kept bumping into my "biases," personal preferences, desires to do justice to and honor the men and women with whom I have journeyed for so many years. Whose story, whose real-life drama, would most readily capture and sustain your interest? Who would be most colorful, expressive, cooperative and receptive to an additional visit? Who would willingly and courageously share their names and not force me to disguise, distort, omit sensitive details to protect their anonymity and pride? I regretfully excluded from the book three completed chapters. One person who had consistently matured more than most was troubled by reading about his early life and objected to my analysis. Another thrice married man did not want me to seek permissions from his three former wives to quote them. Another man's story was omitted because of its length and unavoidable notoriety of his wife which compromised the privacy I had guaranteed the couple.

Engrossed in the full sweep of their adult lives one summer and fall was a moving emotional experience. I relived the sorrows of those who had lost their children or loved ones, of those dying of cancer and strokes, of those who suffered the pains of contentious divorces, of those entrepreneurs who wondered why they kept losing their businesses and wives.

Of course there were triumphs as well, like those of Barbara or of Frank's remarriage that resurrected his potency, of the joy of Susan who felt released from the oppression of an authoritarian husband. With few exceptions and for different reasons, almost everyone could be featured. If I were a talented novelist like Stephen King I had enough raw material to write at least three books, or like Tom Clancy I might be able to squeeze everyone into 1000 pages of a book. After spending months reading all of the files, my despair about whom to feature stymied me until I found my way back to the book's basic theme: Feature those who changed the most during their adult years, regardless of their successes and failures, and then discover why. Amount of change was objectively determined by the difference between two administrations of the Perceived Self Questionnaire (PSQ), the study's generated measure of the model of maturity presented in chapter 2 which you can complete in Appendix D-1 if you wish. I selected Barbara for two objective, bias-free, reasons: She was one of the three people who improved most in her vocational satisfaction (her husband, Jim, was also one of the three) and more generally she was one of the four men and women who continued to mature most on the Perceived Self Questionnaire from her early 40s to her mid 50s. Her impressive accomplishments had no effect on her selection; they were outcomes of her maturity, talent, and her fortuitous move out of Phoenix back to Washington. With only one exception, Mary, every exemplar of change was objectively selected.

How Rare is the Study?

Few longitudinal studies have continued longer, e.g., Terman's original study of intellectually gifted children (initiated in 1922), the Grant Study of "sound" Harvard sophomores. (initiated in 1939), and Gluecks study of juvenile delinquents (also initiated in 1939), I overview now some of the more general differences which Appendix F examines in detail. I have studied both partners as equal participants and continued with each even after they have divorced. I have been the participants' only investigator which can generate trust and confidence to relax one's defenses and reticence. Like some studies, I have relied on the judgments of partners, closest friends, and most knowledgeable colleagues for their perspective about each participant. Conservatively 750 judges, including also parents, siblings, and children, have provided information about the participants' competence about which they were most informed. To reliably compare change over time, measures were precisely re-administered if necessary. The research included several different measures of the same trait or outcome, e.g., marital competence could be indexed by combinations of different scores, including self- and partner-ratings, measures of intimacy, and sexual compatibility, similarity of values, interview questions, and so on. The variety of measures available has made possible the internal cross-validation of a number of key measures.

The study is also rare because of its comprehensiveness. Compared to other longitudinal studies, it has used a larger and more varied number of ways to secure information from and about each participant. It is unique because its basic core methods have been created to assess a theoretical model of healthy growth. Appendix A provides an overview of the study's methods and Appendix C describes the study's procedures.

Appendix C

————————

Understanding Maturity:
Methods and Procedures

Freshmen Year—Time 1

During Haverford College's freshman orientation period, a college counselor gave all entering students the Allport Vernon Study of Values (SV),
Strong Vocational Interest Test (SVIT), and the Minnesota Multiphasic
Personality Inventory (MMPI)—the infamous "I am afraid of losing my
mind" questionnaire, and 565 other items about personal habits, beliefs,
and character. As rebellious as Haverford students are wont to be, none
objected in the 50s to the MMPI's blatant violation of their privacy. (All
participants in my study were told not to answer any question in any of the
study's measures if they would be too uncomfortable doing so. Only a few
skipped questions about sex and income.) The original test forms have been
subsequently re-administered to provide reliable baselines for understanding change.

Junior-Senior Years—Time 2

In two days, the consensually selected 80 men were individually given the
Rorschach (the randomly selected men were given the group-administered
form). They next completed the Self Image Questionnaire (SIQ) by rating their private selves on 30 traits, 26 of which were found to measure
maturity. They also described their personality on an Adjective Check List

(ACL) and took the Terman Concept Mastery Test (TCM) that measured abstract conceptual intelligence.

A week later, the second session included two re-administrations of the SIQ; its instructions were designed to measure the dimensional maturity of the self-concept. Stability was measured by the difference between the first and subsequent second private ratings of themselves. The second day each person predicted how a close friend (or for subsequent times, partner, friend, and vocational colleague) would complete these SIQ social ratings for each about him. Each man's friend completed the SIQ about him. Accuracy of the self-concept was measured by comparing the private self and friend's (social) SIQ ratings—an index of accuracy of self-insight. An other-centered self-concept was measured by the difference between the predicted social rating and the friend's rating of him—an index of possible empathy. The integrated self-concept was measured by the difference between the mean of the men's two private self-ratings and their predicted social ratings—a possible index of acting with integrity or of being one's self in one's relationships. Autonomy of the self-concept was measured by the difference between the preceding first session's SIQ private self-ratings and a third re-administered private self-rated SIQ after a person's first ratings had been challenged by reported falsified ratings of other judges—a possible index of standing up for one's self in the face of personal challenges. The SIQ's 26 scales measuring maturity were summed to give a total self-esteem score. (Heath, 1965)

A lengthy experimental measure of cognitive stability or resilience was devised. (COG) Three cognitive processes—logical and conceptual thinking, analytical reasoning, and realistic judgment—were each measured by solving personally threatening (sexual, aggressive, and dependency themes) and non-threatening problems (work and recreational). Each individual's anxiety threshold for these contents was independently measured by signs of anxiety when associating to the problems' content in the Phrase Association Test (PT). (Heath, 1960, 1965)

A brief interview about their parental and their own achievements completed this session.

As for all subsequent studies, participants nominated judges, including their closest friend, to independently complete the SIQ and an Adjective Check List (ACL) about them.

Early 30s —Time 3

A much more extensive study built on and extended the prior themes of the first two times. Participants were mailed two packets of materials, the second sent upon the return of the first completed one. Sixty-eight men participated.

Packet # 1

Included were a summary Background and a Personal History that included Lowell Kelly's measures of health, religion, recreational activities, personal, marital, and sexual relationship, which he had used in his study of marriage. (1955) Terman's Marital adjustment (33) items and ideal marriage (27 items) were assessed. Spanier's 32-item questionnaire which included every major attribute which researchers had found predicted marital happiness was also included. (1976) Vocational satisfaction was measured by 28 items about job- and calling-related attributes with a Vocational Adaptation Scale (VAS). Other measures assessed financial decision-making, varied role competence and happiness. One of two counterbalanced Perceived Self Questionnaires (PSQ) (a retrospective PSQ rating as a graduating senior or a contemporary one), a private SIQ rating, the SVIT, and SV were included in the packet.

Packet # 2

A Valuator test (VAL) measuring the dimensional maturity of one's values, self-rated SIQ, the remaining counterbalanced PSQ rating, MMPI, Adjective Check List (ACL), and description of partner completed this phase.

When the machine-scored MMPI and SVIT returned, I prepared a partial report summarizing the test results before my visit. I completed it after the Rorschach and another test had been re-administered during the visit.

Time 3 Visit for Two Sessions

Session 1:   Within 20 minutes of arrival at my hotel or the participant's home, I re-administered the Rorschach following the earlier administration procedures exactly. The private self SIQ was re-administered.

A focused interview on the past, present, and future covered achievements, problems, worries, expectations, vocation, marriage, sexuality, and parenthood. I typed and also taped the interviews.

Session 2: The social SIQ asked a participant to predict how his partner, friend, and colleague would complete it about him.

A taped and typed Interview explored how he had changed since graduation generally and then in each of the four personality sectors of mind, relationships, values, and self, the sorting procedure described in chapter 1 about Barbara and Jim and their interview about the effects of the four most highly ranked principal determinants of change.

I had completed the analysis of the Rorschach (usually over night) and reported the full analysis to the man whose reactions I typed. I then answered any questions he or his partner had about the analysis or the study itself.

An interview of the man's partner completed the visit.

After I had completed about 30 participants, I acceded to the wishes of one wife and interviewed the remaining partners about their marriages and children.

Names and addresses of the men's closest friend and colleague most familiar with their work as well as their wives were secured. They subsequently rated the men on the VAS, SIQ, health and personal relationships questions. Wives and closest friend also rated the men's marital adjustment.

The tightly scheduled two sessions proved to be too tedious and tiring for some (and me by about the 40th participant!) but with few exceptions the men gave their full attention to the sessions. I am grateful for their dedication. The study's intensity and tedium may explain why two declined to participate later in their 40s.

Mid 40s—Time 4

I had not originally planned a longitudinal study. After a lapse of about ten years I began to wonder what was happening to the men and their wives during the popularized mid-life-crisis stage. As I said, the stresses of the travel and the intensity of the visits did not encourage me. However, my curiosity and fondness for the men and women, particularly those who had asked me to revisit them, got the better of me. I pruned out some measures which had not born much fruit, converted parts of the interviews into ratings, added some tests but made others like the Strong (SVIT) and MMPI optional, though all of the women took the SVIT and most of them and the men retook the MMPI. The participants were physically scattered even more widely; the stresses remained the same. As I approached the end of this time, I had three surgical operations and radiotherapy for cancer. But I pushed on and completed my visits within three years, only about half a year behind my hopes. Sixty-five men participated. (Of the 68, one had died and two were not interested.) Forty women participated.

Packet #1

An expanded 37 page Personal History questionnaire included most of Time 3's questions. I maintained constancy in measures and their order of presentation for comparison to the baselines I had secured. The men and women rated their well-being for every five-year period since graduation (a new question), health, 33 bodily symptoms and their change since my previous visit (a new question), religious, community, and recreational activities. They identified and then rated six attributes they believed defined optimal fulfillment of each adult role about their own role competence as a contributing citizen, competent professional in their occupation, close friendship with the same sex, happy fulfilling marital-partner relationship, sexually fulfilling relationship, and good parent (new). They also rated their partner on each of their attributes. They rated their vocational satisfaction (VAS), quality of relationships, competence in their adult roles, interpersonal communication as a measure of intimacy (IC) (new), and items (some revised) about marital and sexual relationships again. Parental responsibility for and agreement about discipline (new) and satisfactions with 28 attributes of parenting modeled on the VAS attributes (PAS) were included (new). Then entirely new surveys were added: ratings of strengths and conflicts about different needs, 70 personality traits and their change since my previous visit (PTS), and reactions to 30 likely future events, such as serious illness (also age when anticipated, feelings about, likely ability to cope with), importance of different roles and priority ranking of their fulfillment, and listing of their ten most important goals for their future and likelihood of fulfilling them.

A private SIQ and the optional MMPI and SVIT were also included.

Packet #2

Like Time 3, this packet was mailed after packet #1 had been completed and returned. It contained the PSQ, another self-rated SIQ, SV, Valuator test, and a modified Loevinger Sentence Completion Test (SCT) with stems appropriate to adults which a person completes.

The men completed ratings about the maturity of each of their children aged twelve or older. The ratings were the same as those included in a Developmental History Questionnaire (DHQ) sent by mail several years earlier about their own parents, home culture, and up-bringing as well as ratings of 50 attributes of their own adolescent maturity as defined by the model of maturity. The women received the DHQ in their packet.

Time 4 Visit for Two Sessions

Sessions 1 and 2 replicated Time 3's format except the interviews were more regularized and expanded to include data to confirm or disconfirm other researchers' hypotheses and findings about the 40s.

Session 1:   The Rorschach was re-administered in precisely the same way as in Time 3.

The private self-rated SIQ was then given.

Four Thematic Apperception Test pictures (TAT) were given tapping imaginative creativity about male and female relationships (Cards #4 and 7BM), death (#15), and a blank card (#16) to which a person imagined a picture and then told a story about it.

The typed and taped interview consisted of two parts. The first included questions about the past, present, and the future: accomplishments, qualities that contributed to them, worries and disappointments, and methods of coping with them, momentum of change, associations to different age periods, highest expectations and dreams, the outcome of Time 3's list of personal goals which they had predicted they would fulfill, importance of novelty, and feelings about and anticipation of death. The second part of the interview focused on vocational problems and anticipations; marital-partner relationships and their strengths, satisfactions, and problems; sexual changes and satisfaction; parenthood's problems, differences and similarities in child-rearing between partners and their own parents; and contemporary friendships. The participants rated the six qualities the other partner had earlier identified to be essential to be a contributing community participant, effective spouse, sexual partner, and parent.

Session 2:   The session began with the Social SIQ but was limited to predicting only the partner's and friend's ratings. A modified interview about change and its causes was repeated. To reduce its tedium the questions focused only on change in the sectors of mind, interpersonal relationships, values, and self.

Session 2 ended with fifteen interview questions and ratings about sex roles and attitudes.

I asked the participants for the names and addresses of the friend whose SIQ ratings they had predicted as well as of a colleague who knew their work or community activity most intimately. Each partner also served as judge of the other. The judges rated the participants' Personality Traits (PTS) and amount of change in each since the past decade, health, and their happiness and fulfillment of their potentials. The partner and colleague also rated their satisfaction with the participant's vocational adjustment (VAS). Partner and friend rated the participant's marital relations.

I then reported to each his or her test results, focusing on the personality changes that the tests suggested.

Mid 50s — Time 5

Longitudinal studies on couples are vulnerable not only to individual dissatisfaction and unwillingness to continue participating but reluctance by their partners to continue. At least four couples that did not participate at Time 5 had one partner, usually the husband, willing to continue but his partner was not desirous of participating; a few were also reluctant for their partner to continue. Susan's ex-husband had dropped out after Time 4. She had remarried several years after her initiated divorce. Though divorced, her first husband forbade her to participate at Time 5. She continued to participate.

The fifth wave resembled the fourth one, though it had been modified to reduce the amount of time asked of such busy people. Also the analyses of Times 3 and 4 suggested that the rate of change was slowing in some sectors of the personality. More of the participants felt they had not changed much. Fifty-two men and 31 women participated.

I made the Rorschach, MMPI, SV, and TAT optional; the SVIT was not offered since the participants were reaching their retirement years. The SIQ, Valuator (VAL), and the participants' identification of six attributes contributing to their role competence were abandoned. The long interview on change and sorting of its determinants was replaced by a simplified rating procedure; other changes in the Personal History and interview were also made that did not adversely affect the reliability of the earlier established baselines. The principal tests remained: PSQ, Personality Trait Survey (PTS)—expanded by ten items to include traits formerly used in the SIQ—IC, SCT, VAS, and PAS.

The report of the test results was now reduced in detail and presented in oral rather than written form. The visit now could be concluded in a manageable four to six hours.

The participants' partners or substitutes, friends, and colleagues completed the expanded Personality Traits (PTS) about the participant and rated his/her amount of change in the past decade for each trait; they also rated the participant's health, happiness, and fulfillment. The judges rated the competence he/she was most familiar with.

Early to Mid 60s—Time 6

The last assessment time took place about nine years later to enable me to complete *Growing More Mature* as the men and women approached retirement. The increasing numbers of deaths of my age group, seemingly never ending minor health nuisances, and increased signs of aging told me it was time to regretfully but thankfully bring the study to a close. Except for telephone calls and visits to some of the book's exemplars, I relied on a mailed 20 page questionnaire to bring closure to my work with the participants. Thirty-seven men and 14 women participated.

To measure change, the questionnaire repeated the core items of previous surveys and interviews. The Health section was expanded to include information about menopause, principal medical operations, and exercise regimes. The Vocational section was expanded to include items about retirement, net financial worth, and charitable contributions. Questions about Personal relationships, including friendships, marital and sexual relationships were left intact. The PAS (Parental satisfactions) was replaced by items about the participants' children's schooling and occupation, their greatest pleasures and concerns about, and quality of their relationship with each child. The rest of Time 5's questionnaire was left basically intact. The interview's associations to different periods of their lives and ratings about anticipated reactions to death were included.

Participants were invited to share their wisdom about healthy growth which they wished to pass on to others.

I sent summaries of Time 6 results, and later copies of *Growing More Mature,* as well as their own questionnaires and interviews, to every participating person who requested them.

Loose Ends

The raw test and interview quantitative data have been recorded on floppy computer disks and extensive statistical analyses have been completed. Time 3's results have been reported in technical articles, some of which are listed in the References. Time 4's results have been published in *Fulfilling Lives: Paths to Maturity and Success,* the Appendix of which describes in more detail the measures and procedures of the study's first four time periods. (1991) A revised and updated popularized version, *Lives of Hope: Women's and Men's Paths to Success and Fulfillment* (1994b) can be ordered from **www.conrowpub.com.** *Growing More Mature* reports the results of the adult assessments, including the most recent survey of the 60s and focuses on change, not on success.

The participants' complete files and computer disks and associated indices have been deposited with the Henry Murray Research Center, the Radcliffe Institute for Advanced Study, Harvard University, 10 Garden Street, Cambridge, MA, 02138. They are available only to qualified researchers who meet the Center's criteria and who are approved by me. Identifying names and other information about the participants have been omitted from the files.

More than 50 years ago I had sought the advice of Harvard's Harry Murray, the grandfather of personality studies, about my hopes. He said the project was not doable. "It would take a life-time." He was correct. It has turned out to be Harriet's and my adult life-time.

Appendix D-1

━━━➤◦◄═━

PERCEIVED SELF QUESTIONNAIRE (PSQ)

Procedure

Appendix D-1 has two parts.   1. Measures how you are NOW.

2. Measures how much you have changed since the PAST, such as TEN TO TWELVE YEARS AGO.

If you wish to complete number 2, Xerox a copy of the PSQ before completing number 1.

Complete the PSQ but do not score it now. Put it aside. Do not look at your answers for a week or so.

After a week or so complete your Xerox copy.

Score both by completing the Score Sheet at the end of Appendix D-1.

Answering the PSQ

Complete the questionnaire below by checking only *one of the eight boxes* for each scale that describes you NOW. For example, decide that nowadays the statement "I have a good memory" describes you more accurately than the statement "I have a poor memory" does. You also believe your memory is fairly good, so you mark one of the two middle boxes to indicate the degree to which the statement is true for you.

I have a good memory nowadays.   I have a poor memory nowadays.

❏   ❏   ☒   ❏   ❏   ❏   ❏   ❏

Very true   Slightly   Slightly   Very true

You will need to correct the gender in each scale's statement when so indicated:

Example (Males cross out man in both statements: females cross out woman in both.)
Statement now reads:

A. I prefer to go to a man/woman   I do not prefer to go to a man/woman
   for medical help.   for medical help.

❏   ❏   ❏   ❏   ❏   ❏   ❏   ❏

Very true   Slightly   Slightly   Very true

Statement now reads for males:

A. I prefer to go to a ~~man~~/woman   I do not prefer to go to a ~~man~~/woman
   for medical help.   for medical help.

☐   ☐   ☐   ☐   ☐   ☐   ☐   ☐
Very true   Slightly   Slightly   Very true

Statement now reads for females:

A. I prefer to go to a man/~~woman~~   I do not prefer to go to a man/~~woman~~
   for medical help.   for medical help.

☐   ☐   ☐   ☐   ☐   ☐   ☐   ☐
Very true   Slightly   Slightly   Very true

Read each question carefully but work as rapidly as possible. Don't try to recall how you answered a previous statement. If you feel either statement does not apply to you, answer it as if one does. Remember check only one of the eight boxes.

1. I can maintain a high level of   I cannot maintain a high level of
   intellectual efficiency for many   intellectual efficiency for more than
   days and weeks.   a few hours or days at a time.

☐   ☐   ☐   ☐   ☐   ☐   ☐   ☐
Very true   Slightly   Slightly   Very true

(Males cross out woman in both statements; females cross out man in both also.)

2. I am now unable to describe in detail   I could still describe in detail my
   my feelings and thoughts about a man/   feelings and thoughts about a man/
   woman friend I had four or five   woman friend I had four or five
   years ago.   years ago.

☐   ☐   ☐   ☐   ☐   ☐   ☐   ☐
Very true   Slightly   Slightly   Very true

3. I have not worked out a way of   I have worked out a way of life
   life that integrates most of my values that integrates most of my values and
   and desires and that gives me   desires and that gives me some direction.
   some direction.

☐   ☐   ☐   ☐   ☐   ☐   ☐   ☐
Very true   Slightly   Slightly   Very true

(Males cross out man in both statements; females cross out woman in both also.)

4. A man/woman who I love could not   A man/woman I love could easily
   persuade me to do things that go   persuade me to do things that go
   against my values.   against my values.

☐   ☐   ☐   ☐   ☐   ☐   ☐   ☐
Very true   Slightly   Slightly   Very true

5. Fundamentally, I am very different from most other persons.

☐   ☐   ☐   ☐

Very true   Slightly

Fundamentally, I am like most other persons.

☐   ☐   ☐   ☐

Slightly   Very true

6. My values and beliefs are centered more around the lives and needs of other people than around myself and my desires.

☐   ☐   ☐   ☐

Very true   Slightly

My values and beliefs are centered more around myself and my desires than they are around the lives and needs of other people.

☐   ☐   ☐   ☐

Slightly   Very true

(Males cross out man; females cross out woman)

7. I frequently am not able to figure out why I have misunderstandings with a man/woman I feel close to.

☐   ☐   ☐   ☐

Very true   Slightly

I usually can figure out why I have misunderstanding with a man/woman I feel close to.

☐   ☐   ☐   ☐

Slightly   Very true

8. My ideas about myself are quite changeable and differ considerably from what they were several months ago.

☐   ☐   ☐   ☐

Very true   Slightly

My ideas about myself are reasonably stable and don't differ too much from what they were several months ago.

☐   ☐   ☐   ☐

Slightly   Very true

(Males cross out female; females cross out male.)

9. I seldom am impulsively driven to act as if I were four or five years younger when with a male/female friend.

☐   ☐   ☐   ☐

Very true   Slightly

I frequently am impulsively driven to act as if I were four or five years younger when with a male/female friend.

☐   ☐   ☐   ☐

Slightly   Very true

10. My thinking is frequently inconsistent, vague, and tends to over simplify the complexities of a problem.

☐   ☐   ☐   ☐

Very true   Slightly

My thinking is usually consistent, detailed and takes into account the full complexity of a problem.

☐   ☐   ☐   ☐

Slightly   Very true

11. I usually remain reasonably certain about what I believe and value when someone directly challenges my convictions.

☐   ☐   ☐   ☐

Very true   Slightly

I frequently become very uncertain about what I believe and value when someone directly challenges my convictions.

☐   ☐   ☐   ☐

Slightly   Very true

(Males cross out man and him; females cross out woman and her.)

12. I am able to feel so fond of a man/ woman that I do things for him/her even at the expense of my own interests.

☐   ☐   ☐   ☐

Very true   Slightly

I am not able to feel so fond of a man/ woman that I do things for him/her at the expense of my own interests.

☐   ☐   ☐   ☐

Slightly   Very true

13. I can readily recall the facts necessary for analyzing and solving an intellectual problem.

☐   ☐   ☐   ☐

Very true   Slightly

I frequently am not able to recall the facts necessary for analyzing and solving an intellectual problem.

☐   ☐   ☐   ☐

Slightly   Very true

(Males cross out male; females cross out female.)

14. I develop new interests and become more sensitive to new feelings and thoughts as a result of a close male/female friendship.

☐   ☐   ☐   ☐

Very true   Slightly

I seldom develop new interests or become more sensitive to new feelings and thoughts as a result of a close male/female friendship.

☐   ☐   ☐   ☐

Slightly   Very true

15. What I think of myself is not easily influenced by what my friends and family tell me.

☐   ☐   ☐   ☐

Very true   Slightly

What I think of myself is easily influenced by what my friends and family tell me.

☐   ☐   ☐   ☐

Slightly   Very true

(Males cross out female and her; females cross out male and him.)

16. An argument with a close male/female friend usually changes my friendship with him/her.

☐   ☐   ☐   ☐

Very true   Slightly

An argument with a close male/female friend usually does not change my friendship with him/her.

☐   ☐   ☐   ☐

Slightly   Very true

(Males cross out female and she; females cross out male and he.)

17. I can not be myself with a close male/ female friend; there are parts of me he/she doesn't know.

☐   ☐   ☐   ☐

Very true   Slightly

I am very much myself with a close male/female friend; there is little he/she doesn't know about me.

☐   ☐   ☐   ☐

Slightly   Very true

18. My thoughts and judgments about intellectual problems are usually realistic and practical.

❏   ❏   ❏   ❏

Very true   Slightly

My thoughts and judgments about intellectual problems are often unrealistic and impractical.

❏   ❏   ❏   ❏

Slightly   Very true

19. I don't know myself very well and would not be able to describe myself very accurately if asked to do so.

❏   ❏   ❏   ❏

Very true   Slightly

I know myself reasonably well and could describe myself quite accurately if asked to do so.

❏   ❏   ❏   ❏

Slightly   Very true

20. My beliefs and values are still very closely related to experiences I had when younger.

❏   ❏   ❏   ❏

Very true   Slightly

My beliefs and values are now no longer influenced by experiences I had when younger.

❏   ❏   ❏   ❏

Slightly   Very true

21. I frequently feel I am a divided, inconsistent, and contradictory person; I am unsure of what I am or what my direction is.

❏   ❏   ❏   ❏

Very true   Slightly

I seldom feel I am a divided, inconsistent, and contradictory person. I am reasonably sure of what I am and what my direction is.

❏   ❏   ❏   ❏

Slightly   Very true

22. I still am able to describe in detail the motives and values that led me to make the major decisions I have made.

❏   ❏   ❏   ❏

Very true   Slightly

I no longer am able to describe in any detail the motives and values that influenced the major decisions I have made.

❏   ❏   ❏   ❏

Slightly   Very true

(Males cross out man; females cross out woman.)

23. When I am seriously fond of a man/ woman, my feelings persist for many months.

❏   ❏   ❏   ❏

Very true   Slightly

I have never been seriously fond of a man/woman or when I have been, my feelings don't last for more than a month or two.

❏   ❏   ❏   ❏

Slightly   Very true

(Males cross out female; females cross out male.)

24. The interests of a close male/female friend seldom become my interests.

The interests of a close male/female friend frequently become my interests.

☐ ☐ ☐ ☐   ☐ ☐ ☐ ☐

Very true   Slightly   Slightly   Very true

25. My evaluation of contemporary issues is often influenced more by the opinions of other persons than by my own judgment.

My evaluation of contemporary issues is usually influenced more by my own judgment than by the opinions of others.

☐ ☐ ☐ ☐   ☐ ☐ ☐ ☐

Very true   Slightly   Slightly   Very true

26. I find it difficult to reflect about my motives and values and to understand the reasons for much of my behavior.

I find it easy to reflect about my motives and values and to understand the reasons for most of my behavior.

☐ ☐ ☐ ☐   ☐ ☐ ☐ ☐

Very true   Slightly   Slightly   Very true

(Males cross out female and her; females cross out male and him.)

27. I am able to so like a male/female friend that I do things for him/her even at the expense of my own interests.

I am not able to so like a male/female friend that I do things for him/her at the expense of my own interests.

☐ ☐ ☐ ☐   ☐ ☐ ☐ ☐

Very true   Slightly   Slightly   Very true

(Males cross out man and him; females cross out woman and her.)

28. An argument with a man/woman I like usually changes my relationship with him/her.

An argument with a man/woman I like usually doesn't change my relationship with him/her.

☐ ☐ ☐ ☐   ☐ ☐ ☐ ☐

Very true   Slightly   Slightly   Very true

29. My desires and values rarely affect my judgments about the adequacy of an intellectual issue or theory.

My desires and values often affect my judgments about the adequacy of an intellectual issue or theory.

☐ ☐ ☐ ☐   ☐ ☐ ☐ ☐

Very true   Slightly   Slightly   Very true

30. I am not what I believe other people think me to be.

I actually am what I believe other people think me to be.

☐ ☐ ☐ ☐   ☐ ☐ ☐ ☐

Very true   Slightly   Slightly   Very true

31. My values are distinctively mine and are not easily influenced by what my friends and family believe.

❑ ❑ ❑ ❑
Very true   Slightly

My values are not really mine and are readily influenced by what my friends and family believe.

❑ ❑ ❑ ❑
Slightly   Very true

32 I am able to recall in detail the way I was and the feelings I had when I was much younger.

❑ ❑ ❑ ❑
Very true   Slightly

I am not able to recall in detail the way I was and the feelings I had when I was much younger.

❑ ❑ ❑ ❑
Slightly   Very true

33. In analyzing a problem, I seldom anticipate how other people also look at the problem.

❑ ❑ ❑ ❑
Very true   Slightly

In analyzing a problem, I frequently anticipate how other people also look at the problem.

❑ ❑ ❑ ❑
Slightly   Very true

(Males cross out man; females cross out woman.)

34. I develop new interests and become more sensitive to new feelings and thoughts as a result of a close relation with a man/woman.

❑ ❑ ❑ ❑
Very true   Slightly

I seldom develop new interests or become more sensitive to new feelings and thoughts as a result of a close relation with a man/woman.

❑ ❑ ❑ ❑
Slightly   Very true

(Males cross out women; females cross out men.)

35. My close friendships with men/women tend to last many months and years.

❑ ❑ ❑ ❑
Very true   Slightly

My close friendships with men/women tend not to last for more than a month or two.

❑ ❑ ❑ ❑
Slightly   Very true

36. My ideas about myself are still being shaped by experiences and feelings I had when I was much younger.

❑ ❑ ❑ ❑
Very true   Slightly

My ideas about myself are now no longer influenced by experiences and feelings I had when I was much younger.

❑ ❑ ❑ ❑
Slightly   Very true

(Males cross out female and her; females cross out male and him.)

37. I rarely feel I can be myself with a close male/female friend; there are parts of me I hold back.

☐   ☐   ☐   ☐   ☐   ☐   ☐   ☐

Very true   Slightly   Slightly   Very true

I am very much myself with a close male/female friend; there is little I hold back.

38. I would have difficulty accurately recalling the thoughts I had several years ago about various intellectual issues.

☐   ☐   ☐   ☐   ☐   ☐   ☐   ☐

Very true   Slightly   Slightly   Very true

I could accurately recall the thoughts I had several years ago about various intellectual issues.

(Males cross out man; females cross out woman.)

39. The interests of a man/woman whom I like seldom become my interests.

☐   ☐   ☐   ☐   ☐   ☐   ☐   ☐

Very true   Slightly   Slightly   Very true

The interests of a man/woman whom I like frequently become my interests.

40. My beliefs and values are quite changeable and differ considerably from what they were several months ago.

☐   ☐   ☐   ☐   ☐   ☐   ☐   ☐

Very true   Slightly   Slightly   Very true

My beliefs and values are reasonably stable and don't differ too much from what they were many months ago.

41. I constantly seek to relate and integrate intellectual ideas and facts into more comprehensive patterns.

☐   ☐   ☐   ☐   ☐   ☐   ☐   ☐

Very true   Slightly   Slightly   Very true

I have no great drive to relate and integrate intellectual ideas and facts into more comprehensive patterns.

(Males cross out female; females cross out males.)

42. My close male/female friends could persuade me to do things that go against my values.

☐   ☐   ☐   ☐   ☐   ☐   ☐   ☐

Very true   Slightly   Slightly   Very true

I can resist the influence of my close male/female friends if it goes against my values.

43. When a new experience challenges my opinion of myself, I remain reasonably certain of what I am fundamentally like.

☐   ☐   ☐   ☐   ☐   ☐   ☐   ☐

Very true   Slightly   Slightly   Very true

When a new experience challenges my opinion of myself, I become very uncertain of what I am really like.

(Males cross out man; females cross out woman.)

44. I could describe in detail my feelings and thoughts about a man/woman I was close to when I was younger.

☐   ☐   ☐   ☐

Very true   Slightly

I would be unable to describe in detail my feelings and thoughts about a man/woman I was close to when I was younger.

☐   ☐   ☐   ☐

Slightly   Very true

---

45. Most people who know me consider my convictions and values to be unrealistic and impractical.

☐   ☐   ☐   ☐

Very true   Slightly

Most people who know me consider my convictions and values to be realistic and practical.

☐   ☐   ☐   ☐

Slightly   Very true

---

46. I usually know what other people think of me.

☐   ☐   ☐   ☐

Very true   Slightly

I usually don't know what other people think of me.

☐   ☐   ☐   ☐

Slightly   Very true

(Males cross out male; females cross out female.)

47. I frequently am impulsively driven to act as if I were four or five years younger when with a male/female friend.

☐   ☐   ☐   ☐

Very true   Slightly

I seldom am impulsively driven to act as if I were four or five years younger when with a male/female friend.

☐   ☐   ☐   ☐

Slightly   Very true

---

48. I don't often feel torn and divided between several inconsistent and conflicting values, beliefs, and desires.
(Males cross out female; females cross out male.)

☐   ☐   ☐   ☐

Very true   Slightly

I frequently feel torn and divided between several inconsistent and conflicting values, beliefs, and desires.

☐   ☐   ☐   ☐

Slightly   Very true

---

49. I frequently can figure out why I have misunderstandings with my close male/female friends.

☐   ☐   ☐   ☐

Very true   Slightly

I frequently am not able to figure out why I have misunderstandings with my close male/female friends.

☐   ☐   ☐   ☐

Slightly   Very true

---

50. My thinking frequently becomes impaired and confused when I encounter intellectual ideas that are personally disturbing.

☐   ☐   ☐   ☐

Very true   Slightly

My thinking usually remains efficient and clear when I encounter intellectual ideas that are personally disturbing.

☐   ☐   ☐   ☐

Slightly   Very true

To Measure How You Are Now (Not How You Have Changed)

If you do not wish to measure how much you have changed, proceed to the next page of Appendix D-1 for the instructions about how to score your answers.

To Measure How Much You Have Changed

Do not look ahead. Wait for several days or a week before completing the Xerox copy of the PSQ questionnaire. Then think of a significant or memorable time ten to twelve years ago, like graduating from high school or college, or beginning your first job, or having your first baby. Next complete the Xerox copy of the PSQ by describing what you were like at that time. Work as rapidly as you can; do not try to recall how you answered the previous PSQ.

Scoring Your PSQs

Scoring Your Maturity for the PRESENT

1. The mature and immature poles of the PSQ scales have been randomly changed. To avoid making mistakes, label the mature pole for each scale to remind you which score to assign it.

The mature pole is on the **left** for scales: The mature pole is on the **right** for scales:

1	27	2	26
4	29	3	28
6	31	5	30
9	32	7	33
11	34	8	36
12	35	10	37
13	41	16	38
14	43	17	39
15	44	19	40
18	46	20	42
22	48	21	45
23	49	24	47
		25	50

For each scale, score 8 for the extreme Very True *mature* end, 7 for the next, 6 for the next and 5 for the Slightly True, 4 for the Slightly True for the *immature* end, 3 for the next, 2 for the next and 1 if you checked Very True for the extreme *immature* end. For example, scale #1's score below is 3.

1. I can maintain a high level of intellectual efficiency for many days and weeks. I cannot maintain a high level of intellectual efficiency for more than a few hours or days at a time.

☐   ☐   ☐   ☐   ☐   ☒   ☐   ☐

Very true   Slightly   Slightly   Very true

2. Enter your score for each scale in the Summary Score Sheet for the PSQ answers for your personality ratings NOW. In the example above, you would enter 3 in the Mind Stability box for the #1 statement.

3. Add up the scores for each column for each of the five dimensions of maturity and enter them in the box labeled Total for the columns.

4. Add the scores for each row for each of the five sectors of your personality and enter the total in the right hand box labeled Total for the rows.

5. Add the five column totals to get a grand total and enter in its box. Do the same for the five row totals. The column total should be the same as for the row total.

Scoring Your Maturity for the PAST

1. Follow the same scoring procedure.

2. Enter the scores in the correct position for each scale.

3. Add the five column totals and enter the grand column total on the score sheet.

4. Do the same for the five row totals.

Comparing Your Past Maturity with Your Present Maturity and with the Persons of the Study

Subtract the grand total for PAST from the grand total for NOW.

A positive difference indicates the amount you have matured; a negative difference indicates the amount you have regressed in the past ten or so years.

You may now compare your scores with those of the men and women of the study found at the end of Appendix D-1.

Summary Score Sheet for PSQ

Dimensions		Awareness		Other-Centered		Integration		Stability		Autonomy		Total
Mind	Scale	13	38	18	33	10	41	1	50	25	29	
	Now Score											
	Past Score											
Values	Scale	22	26	6	45	3	48	11	40	20	31	
	Now											
	Past											
Self	Scale	19	32	5	46	21	30	8	43	15	36	
	Now											
	Past											
Same sex	Scale	2	49	24	27	17	37	16	35	9	42	
	Now											
	Past											
Opposite sex	Scale	7	44	12	39	14	34	23	28	4	47	
	Now											
	Past											
Grand Totals	Now											
	Past											

Scoring Your Maturity for the PAST

1. Follow the same scoring procedure.
2. Enter the scores in the correct position for each scale.
3. Add the five column totals and enter the grand column total on the score sheet.
4. Do the same for the five row totals.

Compare Your Past Maturity with Your Present Maturity
and with Those of the Study

Subtract the grand total for PAST from the grand total for NOW.

A positive difference indicates the amount you have matured; a negative difference indicates the amount you have regressed in the past ten or so years.

You may now compare your scores with those of the men and women of the study.

PSQ Scores from the Study

PSQ Scores for Different Ages

Dimensions	Men's Age				Women's Age	
	20s*	30s	40s	50s	40s	50s
Awareness	56	63	63	63	64	66
Other-center	49	54	44	43	57	58
Integration	49	60	59	60	59	61
Stability	56	64	64	66	64	56
Autonomy	48	55	53	54	56	57
Sectors						
Mind	54	62	62	64	59	62
Values	50	59	59	60	61	64
Self	48	55	56	58	56	59
Interpersonal same sex	56	58	58	57	62	62
Interpersonal opposite sex	51	61	59	59	63	62

*Men retrospectively completed PSQ as they were like upon graduation from college. (See Notes, chapter 10, #3)

Mean and Score Range of Total Scores

	Men		Women	
	Score		Score	
Age	Mean	Range	Mean	Range
20s	258	192-334	N/A	
30s	298	211-360	N/A	
40s	295	218-345	299	215-359
50s	298	233-352	308	219-362

====>•-•-<=====

Vocational Adaptation Survey (VAS)

Rate your degree of satisfaction with your occupation

	Very Satis- fied	Quite Satis- fied	Satis- fied	Dissat- isfied	Very Dissat- isfied
1. My type of occupation					
2 Working conditions					
3 Quality of work I accomplish					
4 My competence for the type of work I am doing					
5 Quality of personal relations with those with whom I work					
6 The social value of my work					
7 Meets most of my strongest needs					
8 Amount of freedom and independence available					
9 Degree of responsibility I want					
10 Amount of recognition of my work from others					
11 Salary or income I receive for my work					
12 Opportunity for innovation and creativity					
13 Way of life of my work					
14 Ethical standards and practice of my work					
15 Temperamental-personality suitability for my work					

	Very Satis- fied	Quite Satis- fied	Satis- fied	Dissat- isfied	Very Dissat- isfied
16 Degree of my personal involvement in and devotion to work					
17 Amount of personal growth I have experienced in my work					
18 Status and prestige of my work					
19 Effects of job on other areas of my life, e.g., marriage					
20 Job utilizes my best potentials					
21 Degree of self-fulfillment I secure from my work					
22 Provides opportunity to achieve eventually at the level of my potential capability					
23 Amount of time I spend on my job					
24 Amount of energy my work demands					
25 The job serves as the central organizing focus of my life and identity					
26 My work is a source of new friends and interests					
27 Provides opportunity for continued personal growth and satisfaction for my working life					
28 My relations with my boss or those who have some authority or power over my work					

1. Assign the following weights to each of the five degrees of satisfaction for the items answered:

Very Satisfied	5
Quite Satisfied	4
Satisfied	3
Somewhat Dissatisfied	2
Very Dissatisfied	1

2. Add the weights for the 28 items for a total VAS score
3. Assign the average of the items answered to the items left unanswered. If more than four or five sources of satisfaction are left unanswered, a Total VAS score is

probably not reliable. If a person answered by marking a line between two sources
of satisfaction, assign the lower score for the indecision.

4. Recalculate total score including the adjusted weights for unanswered items

Comparing Total Score to Mean Total Scores
for the Study's Participants*

For Males

Age	Mean Self-rate	Score Range	Mean Colleague	Score Range
30s	102.3	42–130	103.9	56–137
40s	100.2	46–140	104.6	62–135
50s	113.6	54–140	103.4	47–139
60s	112.0	70–140	N/A#	N/A#

* Greatest satisfaction = 28 items x 5 points = 140
# Data not secured from colleagues

For Females

Age	Mean Self-rate	Score Range	Mean Colleague	Score Range
40s	94.4	54–134	109.3	71–139
50s	100.1	36–133	100.6	49–136

Appendix D-3

———⊲•⊳———

Parental Adaptation Survey (PAS)

Rate your degree of satisfaction about being a parent.

	Very Satis-fied	Quite Satis-fied	Satis-fied	Dissat-isfied	Very Dissat-isfied
1. My role/occupation as a parent					
2. Living conditions and location where raising children					
3. How good a job I do as a parent					
4. My overall skills for and knowledge about raising children					
5. Quality of my relations with my children					
6. The social value of being a parent					
7. Being a parent meets most of my strongest needs					
8. Amount freedom and independence that being a parent gives me					
9. Degree of responsibility that I want as a parent					
10. Amount recognition I receive from others for being a parent					
11. Not receiving a salary or income for being a parent					
12. Opportunity to be creative and try new ideas as a parent					
13. Way of life of being a parent					

	Very Satis-fied	Quite Satis-fied	Satis-fied	Dissat-isfied	Very Dissat-isfied
14. Current social-ethical standards and practices associated with parenting					
15. My temperamental-personality suitability for being a parent					
16. Degree of my personal involvement and devotion to being a parent					
17. Amount personal growth I have experienced from raising children					
18. Status and prestige of being a parent					
19. Effects of being a parent on other areas of my life, like marriage, job					
20. Being a parent uses my best potentials					
21. Degree self-fulfillment I feel from being a parent					
22. Being a parent provides opportunity to achieve at the level of my potential .					
23. Amount of time I spend being a parent.					
24. Amount of energy being a parent demands					
25. Being a parent serves as a central organizing focus of my life and feelings about my self					
26. Being a parent is source of new friends and interests					
27. Being a parent will provide the opportunity for continued growth and satisfaction most of my adult life					
28. Amount agreement with my partner about our child-rearing methods .					

Scoring the PAS and Means of Study's Men and Women

1. Assign the following weights to each of the five degrees of satisfaction

Very Satisfied	5
Quite Satisfied	4
Satisfied	3
Somewhat Dissatisfied	2
Very Dissatisfied	1

2. Add the weights for the 28 items for a total PAS score.

3. Assign the average of the items answered to the items left unanswered.

If more than four or five sources of satisfaction left unanswered, a Total PAS score is probably not reliable. If a person answered by marking a line between two sources of satisfaction, assign the lowest score for the indecision.

Means of Total Score for Study's Men and Women*

Age#	Men Scores		Women Scores	
	Mean	Range	Mean	Range
40s	99.2	53–135	98.4	58–135
50s	98.9	40–140	98.3	37–137

* Optimal satisfaction about parent role 28 items x 5 for weights = 140
# Age of women more variable and younger than men by several years.

Appendix D-4

———=▶●◀=———

INTERPERSONAL COMMUNICATION

OR INTIMACY (IC)

Rate how comfortable you are or would be discussing each topic below with your partner and your closest same sex friend.

>5 very comfortable
>
>4 comfortable
>
>3 occasional discomfort
>
>2 considerable discomfort; seldom discuss
>
>1 great discomfort; never discuss

	Spouse/Partner	Same Sex Close Friend
Sample: Events of day	4	5
1. My successes		
2. Problems with my children		
3. Strongest unfulfilled needs		
4. Angry feelings		
5. Conflicts-frustrations at work		
6. My dreams		
7. My sexual desires and activities		
8. Hopes for the future		
9. Feelings about my partner and marriage		
10. Joyful, happy times		
11. My socially unacceptable wishes, dreams, and acts		

	Spouse/Partner	Same Sex Close Friend
12. Feelings about death		
13. Feelings of sadness and discouragement		
14. My financial situation		
15. My greatest insecurities		
16. Feelings about my parents		
17. Any bodily illness		
18. My failures		
19. Feeling about my closest same sex friend		
20. Accomplishments of my partner and children		
Total Scores		

To get Partner and Friend total scores add each of their columns*

Mean Total Score and Score Range for Participants' Intimacy with

	Partner				Same Sex Friend			
Age	Men		Women		Men		Women	
Decade	Mean	Range	Mean	Range	Mean	Range	Mean	Range
40s	81.3	38–100	83.4	53–100	75.9	35–100	76.4	34–100
50s	82.3	42–100	77.7	30–100	69.9	53–100	72.7	32–98
60s	81.1	41–100	N/A	N/A	66.9	29–100	N/A	N/A

* Maximum score for optimal intimacy = 100
N/A Not available. Too few respondents.

Appendix D-5

══➤•●•◄══

MARITAL SEXUAL COMPATIBILITY

Survey questions reduced in number and weights altered to be comparable across the decades. No similar questions given at Time 3. Please circle each one of your answers.

1. How well-mated sexually (similar level and type of desires) would you rate you and your partner?

1. Very	2. Quite	3. Somewhat	4. Not very	5. Not at all

2. Which best describes your feelings about sexual relations with your partner during the last three years?

1.	2.	3.	4.	5.
Great enjoyment	Mild pleasure	Indifference	Mild displeasure	Disgust or aversion

3. Which best describes the feelings of your partner about sexual relations with you during the last three years?

1.	2.	3.	4.	5.
Great enjoyment	Mild pleasure	Indifference	Mild displeasure	Disgust or aversion

4. How considerate do you feel your partner is of your feelings about sexual relations?

1. Extremely	2. Quite	3. Somewhat	4. Not too	5. Not at all

5. Rate the degree to which the following is true for you: Sexually unfaithful since my partner relationship began.

1. Very	2. Quite	3. Somewhat	4. Not very	5. Not at all

Scoring

For item # 1: Very = 5; Quite = 4; Somewhat = 3; Not very = 2; Not at all = 1

For items # 2, 3, 4:

        Great enjoyment and Extremely considerate score = 5

        Mild pleasure and Quite considerate score   = 4

        Indifference and Somewhat score   = 3

Mild displeasure and Not too considerate score   = 2

Disgust and Not at all considerate score   = 1

For item # 5: Not at all = 5; Somewhat = 4; Moderately = 3; Quite = 2; Very = 1

Total Scores for Study's Men and Women

Age Decade	Men Mean	Range Low Hi	Women Mean	Range Low Hi
40s	19.4	12–25	20.9	14–25
50s	20.1	11–25	18.7	6–22
60s	20.1	8–25	N/A	N/A	*

* Too few women responded to give reliable results.

Appendix E

———»–•–«———

QUALIFYING THE STATISTICAL ANALYSES

Because of the number of factors, e.g., temporary moods, misinterpreted instructions, that can affect the stability of specific personality scores, I preferred to use several different measures of the same or similar traits. I define a trend by exact repetitions of measures over at least three decades. Because it took two to four years to complete securing the information for one assessment time, I refer to a trend as occurring in the 30s, 40s, 50s, and 60s rather than report the participants' mean ages and their standard deviations. All reported results are based on statistically significant two-tailed .05 probability correlations or *t* levels unless stated otherwise. I frequently use "reliability" to refer to the more precise but formalistic phrase "statistically significant."

The data collected when the men were in their 40s (Time 4) are the most useful and trustworthy. Ninety-three percent of the men who had participated at Time 3 continued with the study at Time 4. Because of the attrition of Time 5's men and women and occasional incomplete data, I used matched samples, i.e., included only men for whom I had the same data from both time periods. However, the results using matched and unmatched samples did not vary enough to merit consistent matching. I chose to use as large samples as possible rather than precision in matching. To make the book as widely accessible as the type of data make possible, I limit inclusion of technical and precise numerical results to means and percentages.

Cross-validation of all the study's principal measures, especially those created for the study, have been done to establish the measures' meanings, e.g., 11 of Holt's Rorschach scores have been correlated with each other at each of their four administrations and with all of the trait and competence measures. Sample results for Time 4 are available from the National Auxiliary Publications Service, information about which can be secured from the Preface of *Fulfilling Lives* which provides details for ordering. Those preferring factor analytic methods for digesting thousands of correlations may find the data illuminate other relationships that have escaped me.

Appendix F

———⟫•◦•◦⟪———

COMPARING STUDY TO IDENTIFIED
PRINCIPAL LONGITUDINAL ONES

To answer the query, "What is so novel about your work?" I contrast it with longitudinal research initiated prior to 1970. Fifty years ago when I first began to create measures of maturity, only a handful of researchers were interested in empirically exploring longitudinally the idea of psychological health or what has expanded to be now called positive psychology. As my research grew into a longitudinal study it joined an even smaller number of studies. Each had its own biases, types of participants, foci, and methods. While numerous longitudinal studies have been initiated in the past several decades, they are limited in the amount of time elapsed and comprehensiveness of information secured. The early longitudinal studies were initiated to study child and adolescent development. I briefly identify those and others that studied change during the comparable adult years that I studied.

Lewis Terman initiated in 1922 the study of one thousand of California's most gifted children with IQs of 140 or higher to discover what high intelligence predicted. As adults they completed questionnaires every five years and later some adults were periodically interviewed. Changing teams of researchers had followed them for more than seventy-five years. Personal histories of marriage, vocation, achievements were supplemented by personality measures. (1959)

George Vaillant's book, *Aging Well,* summarizes his study of adult development that combined three longitudinal studies: Harvard's Grant study, Gluecks' study of Boston's nondelinquent and delinquent boys, and a sample of Terman's women. (2002)

1. The Grant study was initiated in 1939 studying 268 sophomores, selected by Harvard deans for their "soundness," and continued until the men were in their 80s. Its focus was on healthy youth. The men have been periodically studied by changing teams of professionals, including psychiatrists, psychologists, and family workers using various medical and psychological tests, interviews, and biennial questionnaires. The Grant study, Vaillant wrote, is "the longest prospective study of physical and mental health in the world." (2002, p.16) His series of papers and books reported in the References reveal how comprehensive his work has been. It is the gold standard of longitudinal studies and most likely will never be repeated. He continues to follow his men into their late 80s and 90s.

2. The Gluecks' study was also initiated in 1939 studying 500 boys in reform school and 500 matched controls and continued until the men were in their late 60s and early 70s. Teams of social scientists and psychiatrists studied them until they were 32 after which Vaillant "inherited" the study. Like the Grant study, Vaillant used periodic questionnaires and five-year physical examinations with 456 men until their late 60s and early 70s. He also writes that this study is "the longest prospective study of 'blue collar' adult development in the world." (2002, p. 16-17)

3. The Terman sample of forty women was interviewed at the average age of 78. Again, Vaillant claims it is "the longest prospective study of women's development in the world." (2002, p.17)

For readers who wish a humanely wise and thoughtful evaluation of the contributions and limitations of longitudinal studies *Aging Well* is without a peer.

Maas and Kuypers' study (1974) combined the parents of two samples of children studied in California in 1928: Nancy Bayley's study of children's mental, physical, and motor development, called Berkeley Growth study, and Jean Macfarland's study of children's personality development, called the Guidance study. The 142 parents had been interviewed in their 30s as parents of Bayley's and Macfarland's studies. In their 70s they were given a specially designed focused interview.

Jack Block reanalyzed the archival files of the Harold and Mary Jones' Oakland Growth Study and Jean Macfarland and Marjorie Honzik's Guidance Study, deposited with Berkeley's Institute of Human Development. Both had followed children into their 30s. Block's sophisticated analysis of the methodological problems of longitudinal studies is without peer. I include his work because it sets a high bar for subsequent studies to reach. (1971)

The Mills College study, initiated by Ravenna Helson in 1958, studied 107 female college seniors at five varying intervals until they were 61 using existing personality tests and securing background information. The follow-up studies expanded the tests and interviews. (1967)

Emmy Werner and Ruth Smith's Kauai longitudinal study of Hawaiian ethnic groups from birth to the age of 40 identified low and high risk children and studied their resilience over the years. They originally studied 698 babies at ages 1, 2, 10, and reassessed them when 17–18, 31–32 and 40; an impressive 70% of the children participated in the adult follow-ups. They have focused on adaptation and coping using a variety of methods. (2001)

Two other studies, while not strictly longitudinal but frequently cited in the adult development literature as such:

1. In late 1960s and early 1970s, Marjorie Lowenthal and associates compared four cohorts spaced along an age continuum preparatory to initiating a longitudinal study: high school seniors, newly wed couples, middle age parents, and pre-retirees. The 216 participants were interviewed and compared with respect to gender and age about significant transitional events throughout the life span. They used focused interviews and several psychological tests. (1976)

2. In 1969, Daniel Levinson and associates studied forty men between the ages of 35 and 45, ten of whom were hourly factory workers, ten executives, ten novelists, and ten academic biologists. Five to ten one- to two-hour interviews were given over a period of two to three months and an exit interview two years later. Wives were interviewed once. Levinson interpreted his results as providing a model of development that predated and extended beyond the ages of the men studied. (1978)

Similarities and Dissimilarities of My Study
to Principal Longitudinal Ones

Funding: Almost invisible when compared to all of the studies.

Size of research population: The study is like a minnow swimming with whales like Terman's and Vaillant's. It is most similar to Levinson's and Helson's. It is too small to identify reliably different courses of maturing for different personality types, which Block had pioneered and advocated.

Researchers: I have been the only researcher for fifty years, therefore maintaining constancy in interviews and testing relationships over the years.

All other studies used teams, frequently multi-disciplinary professionals and graduate students.

Examiner-participant relationship: My more intense and personal relationships with participants over a long period of time may have had unknown or unassessable positive effects, e.g., increased openness and trust, and negative ones, e.g., unknown biasing effects on participant's responses. My attitude was that our study was a collaborative one.

Selection of participants: Most similar to the Grant study, though I relied on a variety of judges to select each person using objective sorting procedures scanning the entire Haverford College, excluding freshmen, of about 300 students. Degree of acquaintance with the students was assessed and the most knowledgeable judges were asked to participate as selection judges. The Grant study's Harvard deans had a much more limited basis for identifying "soundness" of students from several sophomore classes of 300. It eliminated immature students from consideration. Block argues longitudinal studies should use such selective criteria rather than random samples to reduce heterogeneity and control for confounding effects, such as social-class, intellectual level and range, and educational experiences.

Participants' characteristics: They were similar to the Grant study's participants: white, highly intelligent, upper middle and upper class socioeconomic and independent and public school backgrounds, primarily suburban. The Grant study's impressive retention rate matched mine until my men were in their mid 50s when a marked fall-off in participation occurred. My women are more heterogeneous than Helson's.

Length of time studied: Most similar to Helson's Mill's College study of women from college graduation to mid 60s.

Focus: Block recommended that longitudinal studies be more systematic and theoretically organized which I have done. Much of my basic instrumentation has been designed to measure the guiding model of maturing. Different foci and methods of other studies limit comparisons of their results. The Werner and Smith study's focus on adaptation and its relation to participants' maturity (though not directly measured as such) is similar in some of its findings. Vaillant's use of the Grant Study material to explore in considerable depth the correlates of psychological health most closely parallels my work; I view my work as a modest replication of his findings as well as an extension to female psychological health which he did not study.

Method of study: While all studies used interviews, I, like Lowenthal and Maas and Kuypers, used focused interviews to facilitate comparisons between participants; my extensive questionnaires and psychological tests are similar to the Grant study's. Exact replication of basic assessment methods for three adult assessment times to measure change from baselines is, I believe, along with Helson's, singular.

Timing of reassessments: Retesting and interviewing about every twelve years was most similar to Helson's test schedule and to Werner and Smith's adult phases, except for my inclusion of the early 30s.

Novelty of measures: My study probably created the most novel methods for testing the model of maturity and interviewing for causes of change; others also designed their own questionnaires and interview protocols. My test measures required intra-study validation but made specific comparisons to other researchers' methods ambiguous. Reliance on projective tests such as TAT cards was similar to most other studies but no other study used repeated Rorschach assessments. My emphasis on identifying life events and their maturing and regressive effects begin to meet Block's call for measures of environmental effects.

Reliance on others' evaluations: My reliance on three types of judges and interviews to evaluate effectiveness was similar to the early Grant study which used a social worker's interviews of parents and teachers. I did not use other professionals and psychologists to collect data but I did for scoring Rorschachs and Loevinger's Sentence Completion Test. Vaillant used psychiatrists for independent evaluations of the participants' mental health. I used trained judges to score interviews for maturing effects of environmental events.

Couple interactions: Inclusion of partners as full participants made complementary analyses of personality, marital, sexual, and parental relationships possible that were not done in other studies.

NOTES

<hr>

Preface

1. A comprehensive longitudinal study has two potential limitations in exploratory studies. First, to identify the important attributes of growing persons, I had to cast a wide net of existing measures and create new methods and ask searching questions. Second, when I subsequently followed the participants into adulthood, I had to continue using earlier measures to establish baselines even though other measures, like Gough's CPI and social maturity scales, had become available in the meantime. (1966, 1971) The CPI has since spawned a large amount of longitudinal research providing a different approach to understanding growth as recently seen in Helson's work on women. (2003) For a review of positive psychology's topics such as optimism, well-being, happiness, and emotional states and physical health see Seligman and Csikszentmihalyi. (2000)

Chapter 2

1. Jane Loevinger (1976) created the Sentence Completion Test to measure her model of different stages of ego development beginning with an impulse-ridden one leading to the final integrated or most mature stage. PSQ-defined mature in contrast to immature men scored higher in integration.

Chapter 4

1. Loevinger (1976), and her colleague, Browning who scored our SCTs, agreed in describing likely traits of men and women of high ego development which I then compared with the study's judge-ratings of the men's

and women's personality (PTS). Male's increasing ego development, or maturity, was directly related to 13% of the traits judged, including ethical sense, integrity, and commitment to ideals. Females of high ego development were only judged to be loyal. (As an aside, male ego development was not related to measures of familial and parental attributes; females of high ego development consistently had negative views of and relationships with their mothers. My studies found that SCT scores did not predict competence. According to Holt, however, her scores do predict a wide variety of real-world achievements as well as independent test measures of personality. (e mail letter, May 29, 2005)

Chapter 6

1. Schuster (1990) compared four cohorts of gifted middle aged women's life satisfaction and competence. She discovered that women born in the 1940s, like Mary, who had lived through the women's liberation movement were reliably more fulfilled, satisfied with their lives, and competent than those older women of their mothers' age.

Chapter 8

1. Josh's comment, ""Just to sleep with someone in the same bed is as satisfying as having sex with somebody" expresses one of the core values of the gay culture, according to W. Mann, the gay writer of *Where the Boys Are.* (2003) He poignantly describes twenty and thirty-year old "boys" desperate to avoid growing old without a gay friendly family and an enduring loving relation with another male. Sex, drugs, dance, and parties are only means for creating an intimate friendship and gay friendly family.

Chapter 10

1. Block and Haan (1971) analyzing the Berkeley studies express reservations about the continuity of psychological adjustment given its variability in the late adolescent years, a view the study does not support.
2. Helson's longitudinal study of female graduates of Mills College offers an alternative and thoughtful view of development through the same middle age years. (2003)

3. Though retrospective ratings have been found by others to be valid, their high correlation between Time 3's PSQ and Time 2's SIQ scores secured when seniors in college supports the retrospective PSQ ratings as well.

4. The Total MMPI score for maladjustment is the mean of the eight MMPI clinical scales. Similar results for the four re-administrations of the MMPI were obtained with its raw and normed scores with and without the K corrections. Total maladjustment validly predicts the principal measures of health used in the study. It is inversely correlated with combined self- and judge-ratings of health, the PSQ measure of maturity, SIQ judged maturity, Loevinger's measure of ego development, self- and judge-rated vocational adaptation, and self-rated marital sexual compatibility. Total maladjustment is directly correlated with Holt's Rorschach measure of primary process and other of his scores.

5. Because Helson *et al* (2003) has already summarized evidence documenting continued change in the middle years, therefore not supporting McCrae & Costa's critique (1990), I do not review her summary.

6. Some argue that concepts like masculinity and femininity are cultural stereotypes. However when the participants were rated by three judges on Bem's 20 identified traits of masculinity and 20 of femininity (Bem, 1974) men reliably differed from women in masculinity and women from men in femininity; neither reliably differed on the opposite sex's specific traits. Reliable differentiating masculine traits were self-reliant, independent, analytic, self-sufficient, dominant, aggressive, and individualistic; reliable femininity traits were sensitive to others' needs, sympathetic, warm, and tender. Each person may be judged to have both masculine and feminine traits in different degrees. (Heath, 1991, Note 10) An item analysis showed that femininity items like shy, flatterable, gullible, and child-like did not predict the total femininity score. This tells us that not all 20 items of a scale contribute equally to its total score, thus meriting further analysis of change in individual traits.

Chapter 11

1. Osherson's (1980) study of men in their middle years also found regressive as well as maturing periods. He accepts Levinson's idea that mid life is a stressful regressive period during which the self needs to be reorganized.

Chapter 12

1. I am partial to Neugarten's (1968, p. 143) comment that "in all societies an age-status system exists, a system of implicit and explicit rules and expectations that govern the relations between persons of different ages. Certain behaviors come to be regarded as appropriate or inappropriate for each age group." My transcultural study of the American, Italian, and Turkish cultures (1977a) illustrates her observation by an intensive comparative study of each country's differing rules for expressing nine different needs in 96 different age-status relationships.

2. Vaillant has studied the relation of defenses and health. (1976) I do not refer to his book *Adaptation to Life* which reports in detail his work on the hierarchy of defenses. I did not have the resources to hire, train, and score my extensive interviews for his defenses and so independently validate their findings, relation to, and contribution to maturing. The interviews can be secured from the Murray Research Center for those who have such resources.

3. Davitz, J. & Davitz, L. (1976) also assign sub-stages to mid life. Helson, (2003), proposes that middle age, defined as beginning in the mid 30s and ending by 65, can be divided into three successive phases: ascendant ending in the early 40s, executive ending in the mid to late 50s, and acceptant ending around the mid 60s. She marshals empirical data and theoretical ideas to justify these sequential phases. I find her argument intuitively persuasive; but I do not have the kind of data to support it. Her analysis and organization of the existing research deserves reading and replication.

Chapter 14

1. The Developmental History Questionnaire (DHQ), completed in the participants' 40s, included 72 attributes about how healthy their childhood families, parental relationships and personalities, and their own relationships with their mothers and fathers had been. The attributes had been drawn from other researchers' studies of healthy family backgrounds and personalities. They also rated their own maturity on the 50 items of the adolescent form of the PSQ.

2. Heath (1999b) *Morale, Culture, and Character.* reports the personality traits of students involved in high school activities, traits of tolerant and intolerant students, and traits of students educable for moral education.

3. One of Freud's more perceptive observations about an adaptive ego was that "Thinking must concern itself with the connecting paths between ideas, without being led astray by the intensities of those ideas." (1900, p. 602)

4. The total maladjustment score was defined as the average of the weighted MMPI's eight clinical scales, i.e., HS, D, HY, PD, PA, PT, SC, and MA. Conversion of raw scores into comparable normed t scores enables their combination.

5. Werner & Smith (2001) also report that the effects of early infant and child events diminish over time. About a third of their high-risk children successfully adapted when adults.

REFERENCES

Bem, S. L. (1974) The measurement of psychological androgyny. *Journal of Consulting and Clinical Psychology,* 42, 155–162.

Bergquist, W. H., Greenberg, E. M., & Klaum, G. A. (1993) *In Our Fifties. Voices of Men and Women Reinventing Their Lives.* San Francisco: Jossey Bass.

Block, J. & Haan, N. (1971) *Lives Through Time.* Berkeley: Bancroft Books.

Block, J. D. (1980) *Friendship. How to Give It, How to Get It.* NY: Macmillan.

Browning, D. (1986) Psychiatric ward-behavior and length of stay in adolescent and young adult inpatients: A developmental approach to prediction. *Journal of Consulting and Clinical Psychology,* 54, 227–230.

Bruner, J. (1966) *Toward a Theory of Instruction.* Cambridge, MA: Harvard University Press, p. 89.

Davitz, J. & Daviz, L. (1976) *Making It from 40 to 50.* NY: Random House.

Dewey, J. (1897) Ethical principles underlying education. In R. D. Archambault (1964) (Ed.), *John Dewey on Education.* NY: Random House, p. 109.

Dewey, J. (1923) *Human Nature and Conduct.* Troy, MO: Holt, Rinehart & Winston.

Erikson, E. (1950) *Childhood and Society.* NY: W. W. Norton.

Freud, S. (1900) *The Interpretation of Dreams.* NY: Basic Books, 1956.

Glueck, S. & Glueck, E. (1950) *Unraveling Juvenile Delinquency.* NY: Commonwealth Fund.

Gough, H. G. (1966) Appraisal of social maturity by means of the CPI. *Journal of Abnormal Psychology,* 71, 189–195.

Gough, H. G. (1971) Scoring high on an index of social maturity. *Journal of Abnormal Psychology,* 77, 236–241.

Gutmann, D. I. (1987) *Reclaimed powers. Toward a new psychology of men and women in later life.* NY: Basic Books.

Harrison, J. (2003) Impaired lawyers, judges helped by statewide assistance program. *Bangor Daily News,* July 14, p. B1.

Heath, D. H. (1960) The Phrase Association Test: A research measure of anxiety thresholds and defense type. *J. General Psychology,* 62, 165–176.

Heath, D. H. (1965) With the assistance of Harriet E. Heath. *Exploration of Maturity. Studies of Mature and Immature College Men.* NY: Appleton, Century, Crofts.

Heath, D. H. (1968) *Growing Up in College. Liberal Education and Maturity.* San Francisco: Jossey-Bass.

Heath, D. H. (1976) Adolescent and adult predictors of vocational adaptation. *Journal of Vocational Behavior,* 9, 1–19.

Heath, D. H. (1977a) *Maturity and Competence. A Transcultural View.* NY: Gardner Press.

Heath, D. H. (1977b) Some possible effects of occupation on the maturing of professional men. *Journal Vocational Behavior,* 11, 263–281.

Heath, D. H. (1978a) Personality correlates of the marital sexual compatibility of professional men. *Journal of Sex and Marital Therapy,* 4, 67–81, p. 81.

Heath, D. H. (1978b) What meaning and effects does fatherhood have for the maturing of professional men? *Merrill-Palmer Quarterly,* 24, 265–278.

Heath, D. H. (1980) Wanted: A comprehensive model of healthy development. *The Personnel and Guidance Journal,* 58, 391–399.

Heath, D. H. with the Assistance of Harriet E. Heath. (1991) *Fulfilling Lives. Paths to Maturity and Success.* San Francisco: Jossey-Bass.

Heath, D. H. (1994a) *Schools of Hope. Developing Mind and Character in Today's Youth.* San Francisco: Jossey-Bass.

Heath, D. H. with the Assistance of Harriet E. Heath. (1994b) *Lives of Hope. Women's and Men's Paths to Success and Fulfillment,* Haverford, PA: Conrow Publishing House.

Heath, D. H. (1995) Assessment of Effects of Model High School. *Report to Superintendent and School Board.* Bloomfield Hills, MI.

Heath, D. H. (1999a) *Assessing Schools of Hope. Methods, Norms, and Case Studies.* Haverford, PA: Conrow Publishing House.

Heath, D. H. (1999b) *Morale, Culture, and Character. Assessing Schools of Hope.* Haverford, PA: Conrow Publishing House.

Heath, D. H. (2003) Unpublished replicate study of *Fulfilling Lives* and of familial and early childhood determinants of maturing. Data deposited in Henry Murray Research Center, Cambridge, MA.

Helson, R. (1967) Personality characteristics and developmental history of creative college women. *Genetic Psychology Monographs,* 76, 205–256.

Helson, R. & Kwan, V. S. Y. (2000) Personality development in adulthood: the broad picture and processes in one longitudinal sample. In S. E. Hampton (Ed.) *Advances in Personality Psychology,* Vol 1, Hove, England: Psychology Press, pp 77–106.

Hoare, C. H. (2002) *Erikson on Development in Adulthood.* NY: Oxford University Press.

Holt, R. R. (2005) *Primary process thinking: theory, measurement, and research.* (2 vol.) Guilford, CT: International Universities Press. Also in *Psychological Issues,* Monographs No. 65/66.

Kelly, E. L. (1955) Consistency of the adult personality. *The American Psychologist,* November 659–681.

Kitto, H. D. (1951) *The Greeks.* Baltimore, MD: Penguin Books.

Kohlberg, L., LaCrosse, J., & Ricks, D. (1972) The predictability of adult mental health from childhood. behavior. In Wolman, B. B. (Ed) *Manual of Child Psychopathology,* N.Y: McGraw Hill, Ch. 42.

Lederer, R. (1987) *Anguished English.* Charleston, SC: Wyrick.

Lederer, R. (2003) *A Man of My Words.* NY: St. Martin's Press.

Levinson, D. J., Darrow, C. N., Klein, E. B., Levinson, M. H., & McKee, B. (1978) *The Seasons of a Man's Life.* NY: Ballantine Books.

Loevinger, J. (1966) The meaning and measurement of ego development. *American Psychologist,* 21, 195–206.

Loevinger, J. (1976) *Ego Development: Conceptions and Theories.* San Francisco: Jossey–Bass.

Lowenthal, M. F., Thurnher, M., & Chiriboga, D. (1976) *Four Stages of Life.* San Francisco: Jossey-Bass.

Lowry, D. (1967) Frustration reactions in twenty-two six-year-old boys. Unpubl. thesis, Haverford College.

Maas, H. S. & Kuypers, J. A. (1974) *From Thirty to Seventy*. San Francisco: Jossey-Bass.

Mann, W. J. (2003) *Where the Boys Are*. NY: Kensington Publishing Co.

Maslow, A. H. (1954) *Motivation and Personality*. NY: Harper & Row.

McCrae, R. R. & Costa, P. T., Jr. (1990) *Personality in Adulthood*. NY: Guilford.

McGrath, E. J. (1959) *The Graduate School and the Decline of Liberal Education*. NY: Bureau of Publications, Teachers College, Columbia University, p. 6.

Neugarten, B. L.(1968) Adult personality: toward a psychology of the life cycle. In B. L. Neugarten, (Ed), *Middle age and aging: A reader in social psychology*. Chicago: University of Chicago Press, 1968, Ch. 14.

Neugarten, B. L. & Kraines, R. J. (1965) Menopausal symptoms in women of various ages. *Psychosomatic Medicine,* 27, 266–273.

Neugarten, B. L.(1968) Adult personality: toward a psychology of the life cycle. In B. L. Neugarten, (Ed), *Middle age and aging: A reader in social psychology*. Chicago: University of Chicago Press, 1968, Ch. 14.

Nicholson, A., Laumann, E. O., Glasser, D. B., Moreira, E. D., Paik, A., & Gingell, C. (2004) Sexual behavior and sexual dysfunctions after age 40: The global study of sexual attitudes and behavior. *Urology,* 64, #5, 991–997.

Osherson, S. D. (1980) *Holding on or Letting Go*. NY: The Free Press.

Piaget, J. (1947) *The Psychology of Intelligence*. NY: Harcourt, Brace, and World, 1950.

Schorr, M. (2001) Sexual decline in women due to aging, menopause. Reuters Health, Sept, 16 2001, Summary of Dennerstein, L. in *Fertility and Sterility,* 2001, 79, 456–460.

Schuster, D. T. (1990) Fulfillment of potential, life satisfaction, and competence: comparing four cohorts of gifted women at mid life. *Journal of Educational Psychology,* 82, 471–478.

Seligman, M. E. P. & Csikszentmihalyi, M. (2000) (Eds.), Special Issue on Happiness, Excellence, and Optimal Human Functioning. *American Psychologist,* 55, #1, January.

Sheehy, G. (1976) *Passages*. NY: Bantam Books.

Sheehy, G. (1982) *Pathfinders*. NY: Bantam Books.

Spanier, G. B. (1976) Measuring dyadic adjustment: New scales for assessing the quality of marriage and similar dyads. *Journal of Marriage and the Family,* 38, 15–28.

Terman, L. M. & Oden, M. H. (1959) The gifted group at mid life, thirty-five years follow-up of the superior child. *Genetic Studies of Genuis,* v.5. Stanford, CA: Stanford University Press.

Tomlinson-Keasey, C. & Little, T. D. (1990) Predicting educational attainment, occupational achievement, intellectual skill, and personal adjustment among gifted men and women. *Journal of Educational Psychology,* 82, 442–455.

Vaillant G. E. (1974) Natural history of male psychological health. II. Some antecedents of healthy adult adjustment. *Archives of General Psychiatry,* 31, 15–22.

Vaillant, G. E. (1975) Natural history of male psychological health. III. Empirical dimensions of mental health. *Archives of General Psychiatry,* 32, 420– 426.

Vaillant, G. E. (1976) Natural history of male psychological health. V.The relation of choice of ego mechanisms of defense to adult adjustment. *Archives of General Psychiatry,* 33, 535–545.

Vaillant, G. E. (1977) *Adaptation to Life.* Boston: Little, Brown & Company.

Vaillant, G. E. (1978) Natural history of male psychological health: VI. Correlates of successful marriage and fatherhood. *American Journal of Psychiatry,* 135: 6, 653–659.

Vaillant, G. E. (1979) Natural history of male psychological health. Effects of mental health on physical health. *New England Journal of Medicine,* 301, 1249–1254.

Vaillant, G. E. (1980) Natural history of male psychological health: IX. Empirical evidence for Erikson's model of the life cycle. *American Journal Psychiatry,* 137: 11, 1348–1359.

Vaillant, G. E. (1981) Natural history of male psychological health, X: Work as a predictor of positive mental health. *American Journal of Psychiatry,* 138: 11, 1433–1440.

Vaillant, G. E. (1993) *The Wisdom of the Ego.* Boston: Harvard University Press.

Vaillant, G. E. (1995) Adaptive mental mechanisms: Their role in positive psychology. In Seligman, M. E.P. & Csikszentmihalyi, M. (Eds.), Happiness, Excellence, and Optimal Human Functioning, *American Psychologist,* 55, #1, 89–98.

Vaillant, G. E. (2002) *Aging Well.* Boston: Little, Brown, & Company.

Van Doren, M. (1943) *Liberal Education.* Troy, MO: Holt, Rinehart & Winston, p. 57.

Werner, E. E. & Smith, R. S.(2001) *Journeys from Childhood to Mid-life: Risk, Resilience, and Recovery.* Ithaca, NY: Cornell University Press.

White, R. W. (1952) *Lives in Progress.* NY: The Dryden Press.

Whitehead, A. N. (1916) The aims of education. In *A. N. Whitehead, The Aims of Education and Other Essays.* NY: Macmillan, 1929.

Whitehead, A. N. (1917) Technical education and its relation to science and literature. In *A. N. Whitehead, The Aims of Education and Other Essays.* NY: Macmillan, 1929.

Whitehead, A. N. (1923) The rhythmic claims of freedom and discipline In *A. N. Whitehead, The Aims of Education and Other Essays.* NY: Macmillan, 1929.

Willis, S. L. & Reid, J.D. (1999) *Life in the Middle: Psychological and Social Development in Middle Age.* San Diego, CA: Academic Press.

Yeh, E-K & Chu, H.-M. (1974) The images of Chinese and American Character. Cross-cultural adaptation by Chinese students. In W. P. Lebra (Ed.), *Youth, Socialization, and Mental Health.* Honolulu: University Press of Hawaii, Ch. 15.

INDEX

―――∞∞∞――――

A

Achievement: academic grade predictors, 229–230; and maturity, 248–250; mental health of professionals, 136–138; occupational, 262–264; types of 248 (*See* Exemplars, Scholastic Aptitude Test)

Adaptation: sequential dimensional process, 215 *(See* Dewey, healthy growth, maturity model, Piaget)

Adjective Check List (ACL), 193, 257, 258, 271, 272

Allport, Gordon, 261

Androgyny, 141, 155, 184, 247: of Barbara, 35–36; definition of, 123; of Elise, 173; and friendship, 157; and maturity, 194; and well-being, 118 (*See* Ethical character, masculinity, femininity)

Associative word reactions, 127, 129, 215–216, 217, 219–221

Autonomy: adult growth in, 120, 152, 255; assessment of Barbara, 33; causes of, 33, 58, 67, 91; and creativity, 33; examples of, 111, 131, 152; and maturity, 32, 90, 118, 119; of mind, 32, 54, 111; of relationships, 32, 53, 67, 120; of self, 53, 58, 59; 76, 90, 94, 95; SIQ measure of, 32, 186; students' descriptions of, 32, 33;

tabular description of 27; of values, 32, 132, 174; Whitehead's view of, 32; of women's changing roles, 91, 117 (*See* Maturity measure of)

Awareness, 31, 58, 78: adolescent contribution to maturation, 251–252; of Barbara, 26, 28–29; Bruner description of, 26; causes of, 29, 53; fatherhood effects upon, 58–59; and maturity, 2, 31, 80, 193; measurement of, 26, 28–29; of mind, 53, 54, 94; motherhood effects upon, 94; of relationships, 53, 67, 76, 77, 94; of self, 53, 58, 59, 76, 90, 94, 95, 101, 132, 133; SIQ measure of, 185; students' description of, 26, 28; tabular description of, 27; of values, 94 (*See* Maturity measure of)

B

Barbara: xii; 1–37; achievements, 3, 6–7; complaints about Jim, 9–10; causes of growth, 14–17, 33; creativity of, 33; dimensional maturity of, 29, 30, 31 32, 33; history of, 2–3, 6; insights about maturing, 18, 244; Jim's effects upon, 15–16; marital fulfillment of, 9–12, 15; maturity of, 26, 29: parental effect upon, 17; parental satisfaction of, 10, 12–14; personality traits of, 15,

320

C

D

H

Happiness, 59, 118, 186, 194, 233,
247–248: character associated with,
19, 20; marital, 159; and maturity,
227, 232, 248, 256; over life-span,
232–233; predicts, 233; sex, 178; and
virtue, 79

Haverford College, 1, 238, 261, 307, 316

Health, mental and physical, 111

Healthy growth: 23–24; and
achievement, 248–250; ambiguity of
meaning, ix, 23; assumptions about,
24–25; causes of, 13–17, 20–23,
53–54, 90–91, 110–111, 131–132,
202, 208, 262, 278; developmental
sequence of, 24, 25, 263; generic
conditions to increase, 255–256;
generic conditions to retard, 256;
and happiness, 248; insights about,
18, 55, 78–79, 93, 114, 134–135,
155; and maturity, 29–33, 232, 248;
measures of, ix, 14–15; myths about,
xi, 207–213; principles for furthering,
234–241; scientific study of, xi, 14,
26, 267; strengths contributing to,
10, 27; of women, 114–119 (*See*
Maturity)

Holt, Robert, Rorschach scoring system,
37, 159, 191, 302, 310, 311 (*See*
Rorschach)

Homosexual: and friendship, 140–157,
310 (*See* Gay)

I

Identity: causes of stabilization of
Jewish, 152

Incomplete sentences, 35 (*See* Sentence
Completion Test—SCT)

Integration: assessment of: Barbara, 31;
Buck, 78; barriers to, 254; causes: of
mind's, 27, 30, 54, 67, 132, 151, 172,
174, 220, 225; of relationship's, 77,
91, 152, 220, 254; of self's, 31, 59,
67, 90, 113, 152, 175, 177, 225; of
values', 30, 90, 104, 131, 220, 254;

fatherhood effects of, 59; measure of,
185; students' description of, 30–31;
tabular description of, 27; van Doren's
description of, 30 (*See* Maturity
measure of sectors)

Interpersonal communication (IC), of
Barbara and Jim, 10–11; measure of
10, 257 (*See* Intimacy)

Interpersonal relations 28: cultural
differences in, 156–157

Interview (INTD): description of, 51, 66,
120, 154, 224, 273, 275; identifying
causes of maturing, 29, 273, 277;
about life events' effects, 276

Intimacy (IC), measure of, 10 (*See*
Interpersonal communication,
marital happiness, marital sexual
compatibility)

J

Jewish heritage of: Charlie, 121; Dave,
152; of Rich, 40–41, 48–49

Jim: achievements of, 7–9;
administrative temperament, 7–8;
causes of growth, 14–17; complaints
about Barbara, 11, 16; conflict
with daughter, 13–14; described in
Lives of Hope, 8 ; history of, 2, 7–9;
insights about maturing, 18, 243–244;
interests of, 7; intimacy with Barbara,
10–11; marital fulfillment, 11–12,
15; maturity of, 32, 34; parental
satisfaction, 12–14; personality traits
of, 15–16; vocational history, 7–8 and
satisfaction, 8

Josh, 140–157: academic achievement
of, 141, 146; alcohol and drug use,
145, 146, 152; assessment of, 147,
154–155; causes of growth, 151–153;
death from AIDS, 154; emotionality
of, 146–147; EST effects of, 141,
148–149, 151–152; family history,
141, 144; friendships of, 143–147;
friendship's cultural differences,
156–157; growth from mid 30s to

OTHER BOOKS ON MATURING

BY DOUGLAS HEATH

————————

Fulfilling Lives: Paths to Maturity and Success

(1991) Jossey-Bass. (Currently out of print)

An intensive longitudinal study spanning more than 30 years answers questions such as: What are the keys to finding fulfillment in life? What personality traits do successful individuals have in common? What factors determine whether a child will grow up to be a successful adult?

> "This is a remarkable book, unique in the resources of humanistic psychology. . . . Heath's project joins the small elite company of life-span longitudinal studies, with an explicit focus on illuminating the nature of optimal development. . . . What he has to say is informed and humanely wise. . . . This is a book that I hope crosses the barrier bounding academia to become a best seller . . . the wisdom of Heath's book has more general implications. Readers of it should emerge with enriched conceptions of both maturity and success"
>
> —M. Brewster Smith, former president of the American Psychological Association. From review in *The Humanistic Psychologist,* 1991, pp. 217–219.

> "A fascinating book to read, and one I would recommend to anyone who wishes to go beyond endless predictions of school performance to understanding what kind of attributes matter in life after schooling."
>
> —Robert Sternberg, former president of the American Psychological Association

"Douglas Heath's book is a sustained labor of love. For more than a quarter of a century he has followed his cohort of college students with curiosity, care, and scientific rigor. His data and longitudinal strategy document that, in spite of our fears, nice guys do win pennants."

—George Vaillant, M.D., director,
Harvard Study of Adult Development

The books described below are designed, along with *Growing More Mature,* to create a complete set of books on maturity and the types of schools that could further it.

Lives of Hope: Women's and Men's Paths to Success and Fulfillment
1994, Conrow Publishing House (Soft cover only)

To make *Fulfilling Lives* available and more accessible in paper back, it was revised and updated with follow-up interviews and the inclusion of several other exemplars of success.

"*Lives of Hope* is a moving and appealing gift to a potentially huge audience of thoughtful adults who want to take a close look at their own lives. It has extraordinary richness for people helping others grow, whether as parents, partners, teachers, friends, or colleagues at work. It is the ultimate how-to book."

—David Mallery, Director of Professional Development,
National Association of Independent Schools

Schools of Hope: Developing Mind and Character in Today's Youth
1994, Originally published by Jossey-Bass; reprinted by Conrow Publishing House. (Soft and Hard cover)

What must we do to turn around the failure of our schools, the apathy and despair of so many of our youth, and the continuing disparagement of caring and dedicated teachers?

"*Schools of Hope* speaks directly to our great unease about what is happening to our children in and out of schools. Clearly the product of years and years of reflective teaching, research, and investigation of the teaching-learning act, this book offers Americans a coherent, attractive vision of what their schools can be."

> —Kevin Ryan, director, Center for the Advancement
> of Ethics and Character, Boston University

"Provocative and insightful. A practical blueprint for action. It will be of enormous interest and benefit to anyone who cares about the future of education."

> —Ernest Boyer, former president Carnegie
> Foundation for the Advancement of Teaching

The American Educational Studies Association gave *Schools of Hope* its 1994 Critics' Choice award for its "outstanding contributions to an area related to Educational Studies."

Morale, Culture, and Character: Assessing Schools of Hope

1999, Conrow Publishing House. (Soft and Hard cover)

Above all else, schools are social systems. Their morale and culture are core attributes essential to the maturing of character on which mind's growth depends. *Morale, Culture and Character* illustrates how they can be measured with simple but novel methods that have assisted hundreds of schools and colleges to better understand and so improve themselves.

"America's best school diagnostician takes us to another level beyond only . . . testing to share his brilliant insights for assessing the most important elements of a quality education. His analysis will provoke and disturb you and fundamentally change the way you look at improving schools. I wish I could buy a copy for every politician involved with educational policy."

> —Gary Doyle, former superintendent,
> Bloomfield Hills School District, MI

"Heath argues passionately and persuasively that schools can make a difference . . . by honestly assessing their culture and morale . . . and by holding themselves truly accountable. The ultimate message of this lucid, tough-minded book is one of hope and challenge: a message no educator could choose to ignore."
—Steve Clem, former executive director of
Association of Independent Schools in New England

Assessing Schools of Hope: Methods, Norms, and Case Studies

1999, Conrow Publishing House. (Soft cover only)

This technical manual supplements and is keyed to chapters of *Morale, Culture, and Character.* It describes how to take the first steps to understand and evaluate organizations as social systems. To hold schools meaningfully accountable for their students' healthy growth, we must assess the healthiness of their learning environments as revealed by their members' morale, culture, and effectiveness in achieving their mission goals—typically interpersonal, ethical, and academic ones.

"Doug Heath's message for education leaders at all levels is that there are extremely useful and revealing tools available for documenting the powerful influence organizational culture has. Use them or risk operating in an information vacuum about the interpersonal health of your organization. What you don't acknowledge about your organization can be dangerous to both your and its health."
—William Spady, Senior Partner,
Change Leaders, Dillon, Colorado

"Doug Heath's methods for diagnosing organizations have broad applicability...I am impressed in particular with his ability to capture organizational culture, and do it with straight forward and efficient measures."
—Robert E. Kaplan, co-president of a managerial
consulting firm and author of *Beyond Ambition*

Information and Ordering

Please see Conrow Publishing House's web site, www.conrowpub.com, for additional information and ordering procedures. Any purchaser of *Growing More Mature* may select a complimentary copy of one of the above books (*Morale, Culture, and Character* includes its technical manual for this invitation), providing copies are still available.